International Acclaim for *Infinite Variet*
Legend of the Marchesa Casati

This is a book about an extravagant, ...ginal phenomenon, my grandmother. Scot D. ...ando Yaccarino have researched their subject with ...ghness, without which this book could easily have been th... ...e fiction. They have brought to life a true feeling of the Belle Ép...que and the extraordinary, exotic, outlandish character of La Casati. It is a bizarre story, and this telling of it shows a love and affection for the subject that she would certainly have recognized.

    —LADY MOOREA BLACK, SPECTATOR

Ryersson and Yaccarino are judicious historians of frivolity who capture the tone of a life that was obscenely profligate yet strangely pure.

    —JUDITH THURMAN, THE NEW YORKER

A meticulously researched biography, *Infinite Variety* is as much art history as chronicle of personal obsession.

    —LESLIE CHESS FELLER, NEW YORK TIMES

A beautifully written biography . . . Prepare to be astonished by this little-known story of a genuine legend.

    —ELLE

Casati set about transforming herself into the world's most amazing woman. She succeeded brilliantly. Weird and wonderful . . . both scary and hypnotic.

    —COLIN MCDOWELL, SUNDAY TIMES (London)

The Marchesa Casati was one of the great exhibitionists of the twentieth century . . . a spectacularly crafted piece of self-invention. Riffle through the pages of *Infinite Variety* . . . it is quite simply engrossing.

    —NICK FOULKES, EVENING STANDARD

The fabled Marchesa Casati was the "dark lady" of her day. The gap on the shelf where her biography always should have been is now magnificently filled by Ryersson and Yaccarino with one of the most amazing stories of our time.

—SHERIDAN MORLEY, *INTERNATIONAL HERALD TRIBUNE*

It was Casati's life that was the real work of art. As described by Ryersson and Yaccarino, Casati comes to life—a breathtaking nova, burning at fever pitch until imploding. *Infinite Variety* is a rare and heady flower of a book.

—OLIVER ROBINSON, "PAPERBACK OF THE WEEK" IN *TIME OUT LONDON*

The drifting shadow of the former legendary prowler of St. Mark's Square, the Marchesa Casati, is back to haunt the end of the century. *Infinite Variety* re-creates a life which seemed fantastic even as it was being lived. This book will satisfy any lover of the decadent and avant-garde.

—PHILIP HOARE, "BOOKS OF THE YEAR" IN *GAY TIMES*

Infinite Variety tells the story of a dreamer, a fantasist, a grand eccentric. . . . An amazing portrait of an amazing woman.

—JUDY STOFFMAN, *TORONTO STAR*

Casati plunged into extravagant exhibitionism–aestheticism–narcissism, living a life of striking surrealism . . . *Infinite Variety* is a fascinating biography . . . With or without her cheetahs, Casati's circus of the self makes her a natural for the new millennium.

—LAURA JACOBS, *VANITY FAIR*

Luisa Casati was a Belle Époque eccentric, big time. . . . Remarkable . . . bizarre . . . a superstar bio.

—KIRKUS REVIEWS

Infinite Variety

The Marchesa Luisa Casati, by Adolph de Meyer, 1912

Infinite Variety

THE LIFE AND LEGEND OF THE MARCHESA CASATI

Scot D. Ryersson and Michael Orlando Yaccarino

Foreword by Quentin Crisp

The Definitive Edition

University of Minnesota Press
Minneapolis
London

The poem "74th Chorus," by Jack Kerouac, is reprinted by permission of Sterling Lord Literistic, Inc. Copyright by Jack Kerouac.

Unless otherwise noted, all illustrations are reprinted courtesy of Ryersson and Yaccarino/The Casati Archives.

First published in the United States by Viridian Books, New York, 1999

First published in Great Britain by Pimlico, an imprint of the Random House Group UK, 2000

First University of Minnesota Press edition, 2004

Published by the University of Minnesota Press
111 Third Avenue South, Suite 290
Minneapolis, MN 55401-2520
http://www.upress.umn.edu

Printed in the United States of America on acid-free paper

Library of Congress Cataloging-in-Publication Data
Ryersson, Scot D.
    Infinite variety : the life and legend of the Marchesa Casati /
Scot D. Ryersson and Michael Orlando Yaccarino ; foreword by
Quentin Crisp.—The definitive ed., 1st University of Minnesota Press ed.
        p. cm.
    Includes bibliographical references and index.
    ISBN 0-8166-4520-5 (pbk. : acid-free paper)
    1. Casati, Luisa, marchesa, 1881–1957. 2. Eccentrics and eccentricities—
Italy—Milan—Biography. 3. Celebrities—Italy—Milan—Biography.
4. Milan (Italy)—Biography. 5. London (England)—Biography.
I. Yaccarino, Michael Orlando. II. Title.
    CT9991.C36R94 2004
    945′.21091′092—dc22
                                        2004006301

The University of Minnesota is an equal-opportunity educator and employer.

12 11 10 09 08 07 06 05 04   10 9 8 7 6 5 4 3 2 1

DEDICATED TO THE MEMORY OF
CHRISTOPHER MICHAEL HUGHES

Contents

Foreword

QUENTIN CRISP

Quentin Crisp wrote this contribution to the original edition of this book published in November 1999, the month of his death.

Quite suddenly and simply by chance, I once met a bizarre lady while taking tea with some friends in London. She arrived wearing black velvet from head to foot, her mouth painted blood red, and carrying a very tall umbrella with a decorated handle. And, you must understand, this ensemble was being worn in the middle of the day. This picturesque ruin of a woman was very tall and thin, and gave the impression of formidable strength. It was then I was introduced to the Marchesa Luisa Casati for the first and last time. She had made her entrance into that room looking wonderful and saying very little. She wasn't beautiful—she was spectacular. Here was a woman possessing a presence one would never forget. A few days later, an artist for whom I was posing started back in surprise upon seeing me. He asked if I had ever met the Marchesa Casati and I answered, "Yes, I did, just two days ago." He then asked what she had said to me on that occasion. When I replied, "Nothing," he said he didn't wonder because I was so *exactly* like her! Presumably, he was joking.

Without question, the Marchesa Casati was an exhibitionist. But exhibitionism is a potent drug: after a short time, a dose strong enough to kill a novice no longer works. Many have criticized the extreme aspects of the Marchesa's life. But I believe she had a specific purpose. She wanted to fulfill an ideal, a vision of how she should look and exist—to become a being of her own invention, not one of any particular sex, or time, or size, or shape. And the Marchesa had total self-confidence, never doubting herself for one single moment. She knew never to be too predictable. If the public can predict you, it starts to like you. But the Marchesa didn't want to be liked. She wanted to incite. This shrewd lady had a knowing scorn of the world and presented those who adored her with an image of something they could never hope to be—a being somehow beyond criticism and convention.

The Marchesa Casati was part of a world that was as fragile as it was beautiful, one that has disappeared altogether from the face of the earth. It was a time of fabulous parties at which people wore the most extraordinary costumes designed for just a single evening. Never a day went by without these antics being mentioned in the press—they fascinated everybody. Looking back, it all seems quite unbelievable now and possibly just a little bit absurd. But fun was both very extravagant and very serious then. In today's age, everyone must be useful, independent, practical. To that I say, "What a tremendous bore!" I do believe the Marchesa would agree.

INTRODUCTION
Siren of the Century

> I want to be a living work of art.
> —*The Marchesa Luisa Casati*

"I want to be a living work of art." These are among the only words spoken by the Marchesa Luisa Casati that have been documented. No detail-filled diary or series of revealing letters survive directly from the lady herself to uncover, in her own words, the mind, heart, and spirit of this elusive subject. But we are fortunate in that a wealth of portraits of her—in oil, ink, wax, clay, and bronze as well as in words—do remain. Left by the many she astonished, patronized, and befriended, each gives testament to the unforgettable power of this extraordinary woman.

For the first three decades of the twentieth century, the Marchesa Casati was the brightest star of the European haut monde. Artists painted and sculpted her, poets praised her strange beauty, and couturiers fought for her patronage. She had even become the notorious fictional heroine of more than one author's risqué roman à clef.[1] She journeyed wherever her fancy took her—Venice, Rome, Paris, Capri—collecting palaces and a menagerie of exotic animals, and she spent fortunes on lavish parties. She astonished Gabriele D'Annunzio, fascinated Serge Diaghilev, frightened Arthur Rubinstein, and intimidated T. E. Lawrence. Léon Bakst, Paul Poiret, Mariano Fortuny, and Erté dressed her. She hosted parties where Vaslav Nijinsky invited Isadora Duncan to dance, became the Italian futurists' muse, and helped conjure up an elaborate marionette show with music by Maurice Ravel. Everywhere she went she set trends, inspired genius, and astounded even the most jaded members of the aristocracy.

The public eagerly devoured every report they could uncover about this café society siren. They relished the stories of her marriage to a titled Milanese huntsman; her brazen romantic affair with Italy's most vainglorious, poetical war hero; and her subsequent divorce in Budapest. They shook their heads at the tales of the outlandish bacchanals that took place in her roofless ruin of a palazzo on the Grand Canal and at her palace of red marble outside Paris. They blanched at the rumors that she had obtained wax images of her past lovers, which were said to contain their ashes. They gasped as they read of her gilded servants, her nocturnal promenades with cheetahs on leashes, and her overt fondness for snakes. Yet they would have been disappointed had she not lived up to their expectations and their illusions. It seemed that the more extravagant and scandalous the Marchesa Casati became, the more allure she possessed. She was, in the words of author Philippe Jullian, a "woman whose life never for one moment belied her legend."[2]

Luisa Casati's egocentrism is both undeniable and linked inextricably to her historical significance. It was specifically the Marchesa's mania for continual transformation that propelled her quest for geniuses to document this lifelong process. The by-product of this journey was the discovery of numerous artists at the inception of what would prove to be considerable careers. Unlike the typical society patron, Casati was fearless in becoming an eager accomplice to the talent she supported. For them, she became a tangible and effective promotion of their radical artistic experiments.

As possibly the most artistically represented woman in history after the Virgin Mary and Cleopatra, Luisa was the subject of portraits, sculptures, and photographs that would fill a gallery. She was painted by Giovanni Boldini, Augustus John, Kees van Dongen, Romaine Brooks, and Ignacio Zuloaga; sketched by Drian, Alberto Martini, and Alastair; sculpted by Giacomo Balla, Catherine Barjansky, Prince Paul Troubetzkoy, and Jacob Epstein; and photographed by Man Ray, Cecil Beaton, and Adolph de Meyer. Casati's intriguing persona also influenced writers as diverse as Tennessee Williams and Jack Kerouac, as well as filmmakers both during and after her lifetime. Theda Bara, Tallulah Bankhead, Vivien Leigh, Valentina Cortese, and Ingrid Bergman have each portrayed theatrical and cinematic characters based on her.

It seems a curious injustice, then, that one of the most portrayed women in history should be so little known. Even though numerous references to Casati appear in many art, history, and fashion books, only one romanticized account of her life has been published before this book—and that nearly two decades ago and solely in Italian.[3] Therefore we hope the present volume will correct this omission and introduce the reader of the current fin de siècle to the divine Marchesa of the last.

Dream Child

1881-1903

Luxury stains everyone it touches.
  —*Charles Ritz*

Fashion without style is meaningless.
  —*Coco Chanel*

1

Legend would have us believe that the Marchesa Luisa Casati sprang fully formed from the head of Gabriele D'Annunzio. Perhaps even she herself eventually believed this myth and, until the day she died, perpetuated it through a persona both eccentric and extravagant. With a face powdered dead white, massive eyes ringed with kohl, and a tangle of hair ignited into a henna inferno, no one could deny that she was the living incarnation of one of the decadent Italian author's notoriously flamboyant heroines.

The most potent photograph of Casati, taken in 1912 at the height of her unconventionality by Baron Adolph de Meyer, depicts her as a modern-day Medusa. From a shadowy background, the disconcerting image of a woman emerges to stare hypnotically at the viewer. Her deliberate pose, incandescent countenance, and long, pale arms and hands—fingertips caressing almost skeletal cheekbones—all conspire to bring attention to one point: those extraordinary eyes, with their defiant and bewitching aura. During its first gallery showing, the picture made a pronounced impression on a reviewer from *International Studio Magazine*:

> Among the portraits of individuals, that of the Marchesa Casati, while it was the most remarkable photograph in this particular exhibit, is perhaps the most remarkable photograph in existence. This somber, almost weird, portrayal of a very intense personality is vibrant with life and character, fully as much, if not more, of a human "document" than the greatest canvas of Sargent, for the camera has seen things beyond the perception of the human eye and has set them down with a surety which even a master brush must fail of attaining. There seems to be a mass of black hair, from which two dark, mysterious eyes fix themselves upon the beholder—and that is all, yet of such salient character that there remains, after seeing the picture, the distinct impression of a personal encounter.[1]

But this critic, as well as most of Casati's associates, never had the opportunity to compare this photograph, taken by one of the world's leading fashion portraitists, to those private family snapshots of her earlier, much less exhibitionistic life.

A photograph from the December 1901 wedding of Francesca Amman to Giulio Padulli, Conte di Vighignolo, shows the well-dressed wedding party posed on the steps of the Villa Amalia, the Amman family's residence outside Milan in the town of Erba. Garbed in a high-collared white gown, adorned with a floral corsage, the bride is joined by her spouse in full cavalry uniform. A representative cast of the wealthy bourgeois society of which they were a part surrounds the couple. Silken top hats of mustachioed elder statesmen reflect the bright winter sunlight. Rotund dowagers beam contentedly in plumage and dark lace. Doll-like beneath the frills of an enormous bonnet, a small girl sits on the villa's mountainous steps, her hands folded neatly in her lap. Nearby, a helmeted officer is caught nattily brushing the sleeve of his gold-buttoned livery.

Also pictured in the photograph is the bride's sister, Luisa, half hidden by the shadows of her own hat and those cast by another guest. She appears lost beneath the estate's towering columns and draped Palladian windows. Here she is as the wife of the Marchese Camillo Casati Stampa di Soncino, a descendant of one of the country's most eminently titled houses. Their daughter, Cristina, had been born just several months earlier. Surely, anyone on those steps would agree that the privileged young marchesa had already attained all the happiness to be gained by a woman of the Gilded Age. Luisa Casati was twenty years old.

At the time of Luisa's birth in 1881, the city of Milan was enjoying a cultural and economic renaissance unlike that known by any previous generation. Less than twenty-five years before, her birthplace had won its independence from foreign control and triumphantly joined the newly united kingdom of Italy. But the city still retained an international ambience after centuries of domination by the French, Spanish, and Austrian empires. Fin de siècle Milan was noted for its frenetic pace and shrewd business acumen while still continuing to maintain its reputation as one of the world's most refined cities. Its modern cobblestoned streets, lined with a proliferation of newly erected banks, theaters, business offices, and galleries, were symbols of the city's ever-increasing prosperity. Such an ingenious marriage of commerce and culture secured Milan's position as the vibrant epicenter of the country.

Milan had always been known foremost for the business of cotton. Advances in engineering and technology would make the city the world's premier exporter of textile goods. In very quick succession, this led to the development of related enterprises, including dye and chemical production, cloth making, and a fashion trade to rival that of Paris. The city's links with the efficient banking systems of Switzerland and Germany and a booming stock exchange of its own enhanced prospects for merchant, craftsman, and financier alike.

Struggling in Milan's cloth trade, Alberto Amman, Luisa's father, was among the ambitious new breed known as the *cotonieri*. Alberto was born in 1847 to the Austrians Franz Xaver Amman and Rosa Weinzierl. Relocating to northern Italy from the family's hometown of Göfils, his father developed a lucrative commercial relationship with the Habsburg Empire as a textile and yarn merchant. Franz Severin changed his citizenship and Italianized his name to Francesco Saverio. He later established profitable cotton spinneries in Legnano, a city close to the expanding metropolis of Milan, and in Chiavenna, a small town at the base of the Swiss Alps. Young Alberto learned every aspect of the industry under his father's instruction before seeking a prosperous future of his own in Milan.

In the early 1870s, Alberto Amman met and forged a partnership with Emilio Wepfer to create a new and more modernized cotton mill.[2] Besides a firm background in company management, refined in France and England, the older Italian businessman also offered Amman a keen understanding of advanced machine technologies. Adequate financial support for building the plant was made possible through fiscal advantages awarded by the government to those companies willing to invest in the recently annexed zones of the Italian kingdom.

Almost equal in distance between the adjoining Austrian border and the affluent harbor city of Venice, the town of Pordenone was a perfect location for the envisioned plant. The area boasted enough of an active year-round water supply to power the largest generators and a humid climate ideal for spinning cotton. Nearby, the trains of the Veneto-Illiria Railroad offered direct links to the vital markets of Milan, Vienna, and Rome. No less important was a readily available and inexpensive work force previously trained for several generations in the processes of spinning and dyeing cotton. The Amman–Wepfer cotton mill officially began operations in September 1875.

The alliance between Alberto Amman and Emilio Wepfer proved to be auspicious, as seen by the immediate success of their mill. One of the strengths of their organization was the exceptionally high standard of living enjoyed by the workers. Employees were given lodging in specially built dormitories and provided with high-quality day care for their infants. Insurance funds and pension plans, among the very first of their kind in the industry, were implemented. Schooling was offered for the hired children, and the factory's products were made available to all staff at reasonable prices. The mill was even equipped with its own firefighting corps, as a fire could quickly devastate any cotton operation. This support and generosity both satisfied the workers and guaranteed the owners an abundant return in image and capital.

Amman himself visited Pordenone only when absolutely necessary because he could rarely abandon his duties at the plant's administrative offices in Milan. There he founded the powerful guild, the Associazione Cotoniera Italiana, which oversaw the entire cotton trade in the country. Amman was soon regarded as an important magnate in the financial world of the Lombardy region. In recognition of his entrepreneurship and increased revenue for the country, King Umberto I bestowed upon him the title of Conte.

In 1879, Alberto Amman married Lucia Bressi. Lucia had been born in Vienna in 1857 to the Italian Gedeone Bressi and Johanna Fäut, an Austrian. Enjoying the benefits of their growing fortune, the Ammans maintained several residences. A house on the grounds of the cotton mill was inhabited during prolonged stays to oversee operations. Very near the royal family's Villa Reale in Monza, the Ammans kept a home of their own, where King Umberto was a frequent guest. But these houses were diminutive in comparison to the Villa Amalia. Set in the hills of Erba, a town north of Milan near the shores of Lake Como, this vast Grecian-styled house was joined to a prior monastery, graced with ceiling paintings by Luini. Around the villa stretched landscaped gardens perfumed by azaleas and camellias, magnolia trees, and rosebushes. Tiny silver bells, ringing ethereally in the breeze, decorated the branches of mimosa trees. There was an amphitheater, a temple of love, terraces paved with mosaic patterns, and a marble fountain in which sculpted swans sprayed the figures of Leda and the Nymphs. The Ammans also owned apartments in the center of Milan on the via Brera, not far from the administrative offices of the Cotonificio Amman on the via Monte di Pieta.

At the Ammans' city dwelling, on January 22, 1880, Lucia gave birth to their first child, a daughter named Francesca. The following year was an exceptional one as well: not only did the Amman–Wepfer cotton mill win the gold medal for textiles at the Esposizione Nazionale in Milan but also, on the twenty-third day of January 1881, a second daughter was born. Conte and Contessa Amman christened the baby Luisa Adele Rosa Maria, and the family sometimes affectionately called her Ginetta.[3]

The Amman sisters' upbringing was typical for those of their affluence. There was the traditional succession of governesses to look after them. Early on, Luisa distinguished herself by an avid interest in the visual arts, and frequent visits to the neighboring Palazzo di Brera were arranged. Home to the Academy of Fine Arts and Sciences, the numerous galleries of this seventeenth-century Milanese palace contained works by the Italian masters and other revered artists. Subsequent outings included the convent of Santa Maria della Grazie to view the crumbling splendor of da Vinci's *The Last Supper* and the Bergognone frescoes of San Simpliciano.

Luisa devoted herself to daily, self-taught drawing practice. She would spend hours copying the images in her mother's favorite magazines, most notably the Parisian periodical *L'Illustration*. Ensemble portraits of contemporary personalities filled the pages of this popular review. Luisa applied an identical technique to sketches of her own family. Groups of uncles, aunts, cousins, and their acquaintances were pictured in formal poses or shown casually playing croquet on the lawns of the Villa Amalia. Although often absent on business affairs, her father, Alberto, was commonly represented as the most dominant figure. While Luisa's work was greeted with some jealousy by her elder sister, their proud mother and her female friends delighted in attempting to guess which of the Amman relatives had been immortalized on paper that day by the young artist.

Such attention did little to embolden a child who, according to family reports, tended naturally toward shyness.[4] This trait was only exacerbated by the generally isolated existence of well-to-do children of the era. Except for familial gatherings, Luisa had little contact with other girls her age. Private tutors provided all necessary schooling. Then there was the question of her physical attributes. By the age of thirteen, Luisa had become aware of her sister's more traditional attractiveness. The almost boyish appearance of her own jutting cheekbones, full lips, and thin, wide-nostriled nose, along with a mass of unruly, dull, chestnut-colored hair, made any comparison between the two sisters seem unfair. Yet the first feature one would note was the unnatural size and intensity of Luisa's eyes. Large, almond-shaped, and vividly green, they seemed to dominate her entire face. Although she was also endowed with the slender height and graceful figure of a dancer, Luisa soon matured into a painfully withdrawn adolescent.

The Ammans entertained frequently and lavishly in their homes, but Luisa much preferred to spend quiet afternoons with Francesca and their mother. Together, the trio explored the fabulous world celebrated in the pages of the latest French fashion magazines. Years later, Luisa recalled a sensual memory of her mother as she leaned over her bed for a goodnight kiss before departing for a gala: "Her laces, jewels, and pearls brushed my face, mingling with the scent of her perfume."[5] With a flair for the theatrical, the Contessa would also enthrall her daughters with romantic tales of her Viennese homeland. Documenting this imparted love for make-believe, a childhood photograph shows Luisa and Francesca in elaborate costume, the latter hidden behind an artificial beard. Sometimes, alone in the privacy of her mother's wardrobe, Luisa would model an array of Parisian gowns by Doucet and Worth. In such adult finery, the girl could imagine herself to be the fantastic heroines of these legends and of her favorite storybooks or those from the opera matinees the family attended at La Scala.

Contessa Amman had little need to draw from the rich heritage of Austrian fables to amuse her girls. There were enough real-life figures, most notably of royal lineage, whose exploits rivaled the most outrageous fiction. Luisa was five years old when King Ludwig II of Bavaria drowned under mysterious circumstances. Known as the "Dream King," this insane monarch was less concerned about the management and political stability of his country than with the creation of neo-Gothic fairy-tale castles. He would wander through their majestic filigreed halls in solitude, lost in a utopia of his own creation. Although hardly as unstable as her younger cousin Ludwig, Empress Elisabeth of Austria did not always behave in the manner expected of a respectable ruler. It was the habit of the famously beautiful wife of Emperor Franz Joseph to traverse the globe under an assumed name, Countess von Hohenembs. But Elisabeth's adventurous spirit was crushed after the tragic events surrounding her son's death: in January 1889 the Crown Prince Rudolf shot his teenage mistress, Mary Vetsera, and then himself in the notorious murder-suicide at Mayerling. The empress would later meet her own untimely fate at the point of an assassin's stiletto.

Most crowned heads govern no more than a single kingdom. Sarah Bernhardt, though, reigned triumphant throughout the world as the unquestioned sovereign of the theatrical stage for almost five decades, bridging both the nineteenth and twentieth centuries. "La Magnifique" acted, sculpted, painted, wrote, and designed her costumes and homes with a flair for the ostentatious, adding a touch of the morbid so admired by the symbolist and decadence movements.

The transformative power of the imagination could be well learned from these extraordinary individuals, and the details of their glamorous and often catastrophic lives impressed the young Luisa Amman. Years later, she would call upon these childhood idols to give them a second life.

When Emilio Wepfer died in March 1890, complete control of the Pordenonese cotton plant was transferred to Alberto Amman as director. Amman's younger brother, Edoardo, was brought in for consultation and management assistance.

In the spring of 1894, Alberto planned a holiday for his entire family in Turin, but this much anticipated vacation was unfortunately postponed when he and his wife were called to Florence on business. Shortly thereafter, the Contessa was stricken by a sudden undisclosed illness. Still in Milan, the sisters received word that their mother had died unexpectedly before they could be at her bedside. Lucia Amman was only thirty-seven years old at her death on the evening of April 11.

Neither this devastating event nor the continual insistence of his brother to lessen his involvement persuaded Conte Amman to delegate the supervision of his complex industry. Now the more personal issue of the upbringing of his motherless daughters was added to these professional obligations. Oversight of the thriving cotton mills and persistent meetings with the Associazione Cotoniera Italiana kept Amman separated from the girls. Tragically, Alberto too would die just two years later, on July 11, 1896, at the age of forty-nine, most likely a casualty of his maddening, hands-on approach to the never-ending demands of the Amman–Wepfer cotton mill.

Edoardo Amman and his wife Fanny accepted the responsibilities of their orphaned nieces and the whole of the family business in 1896.[6] Francesca and Luisa surely needed their uncle's guidance since they had just become the wealthiest heiresses in the country. Their inheritance included the Amman cotton factories; the villas at Erba and Monza; the apartments in Milan; and a fortune in stocks, bonds, and funds. After a respectable mourning period, the Villa Amalia was decided upon as the most satisfactory residence for the girls.

Although their uncle looked after them with practical sense and affection, the teenaged Francesca and Luisa soon felt restless. The suffocating lifestyle expected of proper young ladies of wealth was lightened by visits with their cousins Bice and Mario, and Edoardo's other children, at the Villa Amman at Ello. Even so, Francesca and Luisa would find a variety of reasons to escape family life at the villas. Milan was close enough for outings to art museums and libraries, and for shopping trips as well. Fashions were changing dramatically during this era as the American "Gibson Girl" captured the international popular conscience. With her sporty figure, light apparel, and playfully domineering demeanor, the pen-and-ink vixen was as tired of traditional values as her admirers. Following suit, the Amman sisters took up tennis and horseback riding as further diversions, although such extroverted activities did little to diminish Luisa's shyness.

The younger of the Amman sisters would reach her seventeenth birthday in 1898 and was soon preparing for her unavoidable debut into Italian society. Meanwhile, the world around her had ignited in a cultural and technological explosion as the next century rapidly approached. In a small but unexpected way, Luisa Amman devised a fin de siècle innovation of her own: she cut her hair. All of the brownish wisps forever swirling their way across her forehead and brows were gone with a snip of the scissors. The newly formed fringe softened her features and revealed the hidden brightness and color of her remarkable eyes. Although she would frequently and sometimes drastically alter its tint, this self-created hairstyle never changed for the rest of Luisa's life.

2

While she was a debutante, Luisa reluctantly attended countless cotillions, theatrical productions, and parties. At one such event the timid eighteen-year-old heiress captured the attention of Camillo Casati Stampa di Soncino. Born on August 12, 1877, Camillo was the first son of Gian Alfonso Casati, a knight of honor and devotion of the Order of Malta, and his wife, Luigia

Negroni Pratti. The mustachioed young man had just reached his twenty-first birthday and, as a dashing lieutenant in the second cavalry reserve, was doing his best to live up to the family's motto of "Liberty and Independence." Years of military service had already honed his skills as a proficient horseman and hunter. More important, Camillo was a marchese from one of Milan's oldest and most distinguished aristocratic families. Italy's register of national nobility contained many dukes, marcheses, and counts, as well as a more colorful assortment of bishops, senators, ambassadors, and adventurers, all bearing the Casati name. This potential match was desirable to both families, for although the name of the nouveau riche Ammans lacked an impressive ancestry, the Casati coffers were not as grand as their lineage.

Soon the couple began a traditional courtship. Camillo was introduced to Edoardo Amman and Francesca at the Villa Amalia, and Luisa visited the sixteenth-century Casati estate in the town of Cinisello Balsamo. Once officially engaged, Luisa's trousseau was prepared without any concern for expense. The first few months of the new century were spent in a flurry of society events and dress fittings, all in anticipation of the coming wedding.

It was considered essential by the European beau monde for a soon-to-be bride—especially one about to attain the title of marchesa—to be immortalized on canvas. Luisa submitted to this tradition with considerable reticence. Vitellini, a Milanese society portraitist, was selected for what descended rapidly into an unenviable task. Luisa found the required posing so tiresome she could sit still only for a half-hour at a time. The unfinished portrait reveals her almost total lack of cooperation with the painter—the artist never had the opportunity to complete his model's arms and hands, which were later only sketched in. What remains is a staid rendering of a wide-eyed, mannequin-like young woman in a floral dress set against a banal landscape.

Finally, after months of parties and intricate preparations, the Marchese Camillo Casati and the Contessa Luisa Amman were married on June 22, 1900. Their honeymoon in Paris took place during the Exposition Universelle de 1900, as well as during an oppressive heat wave that continued for the entire length of their stay. But even the scorching summer sun could not keep millions away from this tremendous world's fair, which lasted from April through November of that milestone year. Exhibitions of art nouveau masterpieces and elaborate pavilions from every point on the globe dazzled the international visitors. An unparalleled gala in every respect, this titanic amusement attracted many celebrated revelers into its arched gateway in the place de la Concorde. Claude Debussy frequented the Oriental theaters along the Seine, contemplating their exotic harmonies; Auguste Rodin strolled with the French ex-Empress Eugénie in the halls of the exhibition that honored his sculptures; and even the then infamous Oscar Wilde, with only weeks to live, was seen sipping drinks at the Café d'Égypte.[7]

Parisian artist and master of the drypoint technique of engraving, Paul-César Helleu was responsible for the first known portrait of Luisa after her marriage to Camillo Casati. Completed during the summer of her honeymoon, the sepia-tinted, black and white image shows a sophisticated Belle Époque woman whose upswept coiffure is crowned by a circular hat of black plumes. The portrait is particularly memorable for the knowing look in its subject's eyes.[8] Luisa also sat that same year for the famed academic classicist Vittorio Matteo Corcos at his studio in Rome. Although the result of this initial association was an unfinished bust portrait, Corcos would later execute an oil of his subject as an Amazon.

After returning from Paris, the newlyweds began their domestic life together at the Villa Casati in Cinisello Balsamo. As most moneyed couples, the Casatis were not bound to a single residence. A German chauffeur was hired to transport them between properties in a newly purchased Mercedes. They spent the spring and winter months at Cinisello Balsamo or their pied-à-terre in the center of Milan on the via Soncino near the Duomo. They escaped the summer's heat by excursions to the Swiss Alps. Camillo also valued winter activities at his family's hunting château in Cusago, an affluent suburb in the Milanese countryside, and his prized stables at the Villa San Martino in Arcore.

Through Camillo, Luisa was introduced to similar young aristocrats and industrialists, including members of the powerfully wealthy Sforza and Visconti di Modrone families. Besides local gossip and business concerns, the occult was often a topic of conversation and, at times, even incorporated into parlor games like séances and fortune-telling. At the fin de siècle, interest in the macabre and magical had a definite vogue, especially among the upper classes. One of the most bizarre, and therefore repeatedly discussed, real-life figures that embodied these elements was Cristina Trivulzio.[9]

Known as the Principessa di Belgiojoso, Trivulzio was a renowned Italian political revolutionary and the living ideal of the early nineteenth-century Italian romantics. A deathly white face framed by ebony hair and a tall figure of extreme emaciation were the strange charms that enticed a multitude of lovers, including Frédéric Chopin, Honoré de Balzac, Eugène Delacroix, and the French poet Alfred de Musset. The most provocative incident connected with Trivulzio was the discovery of a partially embalmed male corpse in her boudoir wardrobe. The deceased, a twenty-seven-year-old consumptive named Gaetano Stelzi, was said to have been one of the

Principessa's numerous paramours. His disinterred coffin contained nothing more than a wooden log. The truth behind this gruesome episode has never been properly explained, as Trivulzio was able to avoid any legal action.

Most startling to Camillo and his friends was Luisa's partial resemblance to this legendary woman, who had supposedly preserved the hearts of some of her many suitors in golden reliquaries. Musset once described Trivulzio's bewitching eyes as "les yeux terribles de sphinx." Luisa was complimented on possessing the same inescapable stare, which led her to be cast as the Principessa in their drawing-room theatricals. These involved reenactments of the discovery of the mysterious corpse (with Camillo's younger brother, Alessandro,[10] in the role of the deceased) and séances summoning Trivulzio's spirit. The Principessa di Belgiojoso made such a deep impression on Luisa that Camillo agreed to name their baby Cristina in her honor if they ever had a daughter. The couple kept their pact when Luisa gave birth to their only child on July 15, 1901.

Another Italian beauty worthy of Luisa's fascination was Virginia Oldoini, the Comtesse de Castiglione and mistress to Napoleon III.[11] The emperor's blonde-haired, green-eyed lover had a fondness for dressing in revealing fashions at the costumed balls she attended seemingly without cease. In one of the greatest feats of artistic self-absorption, Castiglione commissioned a series of more than four hundred photographs of herself. The surviving set of pictures traces almost the entire career of this remarkable *grande courtisane*—from her time as a court jewel at the Tuileries until her final years, when she had become obese, toothless, and nearly bald.[12]

At this point in the Marchesa's life her enduring obsession with the mystical fully emerged. Always sensitive to the otherworldly, she expanded her knowledge by seeking out books on magical practices, telepathy, and spells. Her husband, family, and friends were amused by these then acceptable pastimes, although Luisa was enticed by them far more than most. Yet she did not omit other, more popular activities from her recreational regimen, and she was on horseback during a hunting expedition with her husband when she caught the admiring attention of the one man most destined to change her life. Although not possessing genuine supernatural powers, he was undeniably a magician—a conjurer of words, war, and passion.

A Slow Awakening
1903-1910

She was the D'Annunzian Muse incarnate.
—*Sir Harold Acton*

The Casati–D'Annunzio conjugation was the final and most perfect achievement of the Decadence.
—*Philippe Jullian*

1

Gallarate is a small town in the northwestern section of Italy near Lake Maggiore. Simply by chance, Gabriele D'Annunzio happened to be observing an aristocratic party of foxhunters when he caught sight of the striking figure of an attractive noblewoman. Silhouetted tall in her saddle, she handled her restive mount with an élan that intrigued the jaded writer. Later, D'Annunzio recalled this unknown person as "a young, slender Amazon."[1] The lady of his admiring scrutiny was, in fact, the Marchesa Luisa Casati. This decisive moment in 1903 would mark the beginning of an intense and bizarre union that would be broken only by death several decades later.

Although their meeting may have been fortuitous, fate had very little to do with D'Annunzio's attendance at such an event. Even as a bystander, the mercenary lover would be assured of meeting at least several well-to-do women at these society functions. D'Annunzio's liaisons traditionally involved bored, wealthy wives who were seeking clandestine diversions away from the miasma of polite luncheons and inattentive spouses. By the time of this particular foxhunt, he had already plundered numerous hearts and purses, including those of renowned tragedienne Eleonora Duse. But his greater fame was as Italy's—and perhaps Europe's—most notorious and popular poet, playwright, and novelist.

At twenty-two, Luisa was beginning to sense the restrictions required by being the demure Catholic wife of the Marchese Casati. Camillo expected her to be dutiful and as exquisitely maintained as their homes while he lavished most of his attentions on hounds and hunting. Luisa also achieved her husband's financial goals by providing her own personal fortune to their combined worth. This was essential to Camillo, who often needed to borrow funds from his relatives to maintain a certain lifestyle. It was rumored that despite his title and lineage, the Marchese had brought only seventy thousand lire into the marriage and that his esteemed family allotted him a subsidy of thirty thousand lire in a lean year or, possibly, three hundred thousand in an affluent one.[2] These sums were nothing in comparison to the personal wealth of his wife.

Soon, Luisa came to understand the stifling role demanded of her. At first she began to rebel with what would be dismissed as tolerable feminine pastimes. Camillo passively indulged his wife's growing instinct for novel decorating schemes and her continuing fascination with the occult. But even this nodding encouragement was rare since he often deserted their home for the hunting field. As her shyness slowly fell away, because of Camillo's inattention and her own boredom, Luisa's dissatisfaction with the marriage became more apparent. Her frustration now took the form of an uncharacteristic and growing boldness. During those times when she did join Camillo's hunting parties, she spurred her horses at blinding speeds through the most dangerous jumps. And even the torrential rains that plagued a particular meet did not hinder Luisa from being the only woman in attendance. In fashionable top hat, she pursued her quarry through the treacherous fields keeping pace alongside counts and captains. At other times, she had her private carriage drawn by a quartet of racehorses, a penchant that soon developed into an avid interest in the fastest automobiles.

Gabriele D'Annunzio became a familiar figure at the hunting expeditions attended by the Casatis. Soon, he was devising plans to achieve an even greater intimacy with his latest female obsession: "One evening . . . she was standing near me . . . she had on a gray dress, a gray of black pearl. I was sitting. Her thigh was at the level of my eyes . . . I was troubled down to the root of my being, but my schemes to get close to her were well thought out."[3]

D'Annunzio first lavished his attentions on the Marchesa's recently married sister, Francesca. This dalliance went unconsummated, but Luisa now became aware of the puckish writer who had an equally boundless imagination and tendency toward self-absorption. She was also taken by the total freedom of his character. That D'Annunzio was not trapped by restrictive concerns of highborn etiquette or notions of feminine behavior was more than simply refreshing to her—this was a revelation. But what won her admiration was his inimitable appearance and zest for new experiences, even though, being forty years old, D'Annunzio was nearly twice her age at the time of their first contact. Luisa would soon meet her seducer's aesthetic and amorous challenge by unfettering her own originality. The two began an intensely romantic sexual affair.

Throughout his life, the poet was searching eternally for the perfect "D'Annunzian" woman, as well as additional income, and he had learned that the road to solvency could be attained through the boudoir. He achieved victories in that particular arena in spite of "total baldness and a dandified turkey-cock stockiness that made him look like a hard-boiled egg inside a Fabergé eggcup."[4] These inadequacies were overlooked by the appreciative recipients of D'Annunzio's considerable amatory, intellectual, and artistic prowess—a priceless commodity in an era and class in which women were rarely considered more than costly ornaments. Many of his mistresses, especially if the coupling had been sensually—and financially—fruitful, would be immortalized in prose or verse. Discarding her mundane given name, he would then choose a new one that best suited her personality. In this way, D'Annunzio believed he was creating his own breed of fantastic deities. Past lovers had included "Nike," "Barbarella," and "Bassilissa."

The Grecian name for the goddess Persephone was Kore. According to legend, after her abduction by Hades, this former incorrupt maiden was transformed into the dreaded Queen of Hell. Considering D'Annunzio's knowledge of mythology and his lover's continuing metamorphosis, it is not surprising that he selected this symbolic appellation for Luisa. Undoubtedly, it took D'Annunzio little effort to envision himself as master of the underworld. Additionally, a kore is a classical Grecian statue characterized by an androgynous image and enigmatically alluring smile. By deciding on this name, D'Annunzio proclaimed he had found the modern-day embodiment of both myth and ancient artwork combined in Luisa:

> [Luisa Casati was] a very beautiful woman, when I asked what emotion she must experience in bearing that sublime mask on her neck, she answered me that as she walked it sometimes seemed to her that she was joyously imprinting her image on the very air, as if on a retentive material, and leaving behind her a succession of impressions that would perpetuate her in the places she had passed through. She was expressing, surely unconsciously, the will to dominate that beauty possesses when it is manifested in an infinite element. Not with each step only but with her slightest movement, Kore imprinted her face in my immortal substance.[5]

Although delighted by her D'Annunzian baptism, Luisa accomplished what not one of the poet's previous lovers had been bold enough to hazard. Feeling the "K" too harsh in appearance, she altered it to a more pleasing "C," then frenchified this sobriquet by the addition of an accent mark. So "Kore" became "Coré." Dazzled by her audaciousness, D'Annunzio approved and declared himself her "Ariel," after the mischievous spirit from Shakespeare's *The Tempest*. Luisa's action, although seemingly insignificant, set the tone for the relationship to follow. It was her consistent ability to exceed D'Annunzio's most outrageous feminine ideal that both astounded him and encouraged her behavior.

Infidelity was far from uncommon among the elite. Whereas adultery was hardly acceptable for women, the maintenance of an enviable mistress was a laudatory pursuit for most established men. But for either sex, the determination and blatancy with which Luisa pursued her affair with D'Annunzio was exceptional. She had been married for only three years when she first met him, although the evolution into brazen adulteress was not as sudden as it might seem. Here was a formerly unassuming, not particularly attractive wife and mother, similar to so many others in Milanese high society. But unlike them, Luisa had been more than weaned on her mother's tales of extravagant personages; she had taken them seriously to heart. Far more significant than simple sexual gratification, the liaison with D'Annunzio ignited within her a life-altering realization. She would now gain confidence by exploring the same innate artistic sensibilities that linked her to these childhood inspirations. Equally important, her own wealth could provide the means to build a world dictated by her whims and personal style alone.

Not surprisingly, the author and his new muse quickly became a target of gossip for the smart set. Much of their time was spent together at numerous foxhunts, races, and parties during the next few years. They even became a society news item when the May 4, 1905, edition of *Ruy-Blas* noted D'Annunzio's plan to enjoy a relaxing idyll with a stylish but unnamed lady. This particular marchesa was described as "a sports fanatic who is very famous among the Milanese aristocracy, of which she is one of the most elegant ornaments." To satirically commemorate the scandal, a painting was reported to have appeared depicting the couple embracing while standing on the Casati marital bed—the Marchesa wearing a nightgown and D'Annunzio in military costume, including riding boots, while cherubs circled overhead.[6] Luisa must have delighted in this newfound limelight, regardless of its negative implications.

If Camillo's still unknown opinion of the affair did not hinder them, the rural location of his houses was spoiling the lovers' access to each other and to any real cultural center. This was especially true of the Villa Casati at Cinisello Balsamo. The stately house was located at the edge of a vast park dotted with tangles of rosebushes and centuries-old trees. Fronted by fortress-like gates, with pillars crowned by stone lions, the villa was a considerable distance from any proper city. The married couple resided here most of the year with their young daughter, Cristina, and the child's strict German governess. Isolated from art museums and boutiques, Luisa was also separated from her sister. Francesca had moved to a villa on the via Goito in Rome with her own titled husband, the Conte Padulli, a captain in the Italian cavalry.

In her solitude, Luisa directed her imagination toward the decoration of the Casati houses, as well as the organization of or attendance at an occasional costume ball. These elaborate affairs were often arranged by Italy's wealthy as charity benefits. Some of the galas became almost legendary. Most notable were the Ballo Giapponese, set in a décor of temples and cherry blossoms inspired by Puccini's *Madama Butterfly,* and the Dantesque New Year's Eve celebration of 1903 at Milan's Teatro Eden, where the building's floors were decorated as the different levels of the poet's *Commedia*. The

Inferno was in the theater's basement, Purgatory took over the stage and wings, and Paradise was re-created in the upper rooms and reserved only for the city's elite.

Such parties further excited Luisa's passion for fancy dress and flamboyant impersonation. In the course of four consecutive nights in March 1905, she appeared in just as many different guises in Rome. At the Pro Infantia charity ball at the Grand Hotel she wore a precise reproduction of Sarah Bernhardt's costume for a stage role as the Byzantine Empress Theodora, including jewelry and a crown designed by René Lalique. The following evening, she attended a cotillion fashionably garbed in white lace and a black silk cloak trimmed with ermine. The next night, she joined revelers at the "Baby Ball." While members of international society wore frilled bonnets, played with toys, and drank champagne from baby bottles, Luisa chose a close-fitting lace cap and frock inspired by the work of British children's book illustrator Kate Greenaway. On the fourth evening, she was seen in a garment thickly embroidered in gold at the court ball held at the Quirinal Palace in the presence of the king and queen of Italy.

An account of this period is found in *Italian Castles and Country Seats*, written by Tryphosa Bates Batcheller, an acquaintance of Luisa. An evocative portrait of the Marchesa is offered, along with a description of the interior of the Villa Casati:

> I have written you before much of the artistic grace and what I call "Byzantine" fascination of the Marchesa. She must feel a keen sympathy with the soft colourings and strange contrasts of the East, for she never was more brilliant in her life than on the evening when she wore at a fancy dress ball in Rome the marvellous costume of the Empress Theodora; indeed her lustrous eyes recalled the famous mosaics at Ravenna. . . . The artistic hand of the Marchesa Casati is evident on every side [of the Villa Casati]. The dining-room is the finest I have yet seen in Italy, enormously high, with ancient beams beautifully decorated in colour; and a few large fine portraits of former Lords of this noble house hang on the walls. The dinner table is beautiful tonight, with rare pink orchids. Indeed, I always refer to the Marchesa as "my lady of the orchid"; for she seems the living emblem of that exotic plant . . . tonight she wore one of her rare Venetian lace gowns, artistically combined with cloth-of-silver. . . . The Marchesa is considered by many one of the best-dressed women in Europe, and she has a definite, characteristic "cachet" quite her own.[7]

During the first few years of her relationship with D'Annunzio, Luisa's physical appearance began a slow but deliberate metamorphosis. Her once dull brown hair was gradually tinted to a more tawny hue, and her out-fits became increasingly venturesome as well. Gossip circulated about these changes in image and behavior, some of it connected to D'Annunzio's known experience with the occult. It was speculated that the previously reserved wife had been caught in an erotic spell cast by the "Prince of Decadence." Rumormongers even suggested that Luisa was a sorceress her-self. But at this phase, she was discovering the powerful tool of a brazenly outlandish persona. With it, Luisa could simultaneously seize her recent freedom while still masking her shyness.

The sympathies of the Casati friends were mainly with husband and child. Indeed, the once dutiful Luisa chose to conduct not only an openly extramarital affair, but also one with a man who was notorious through-out Europe. Camillo may not have been just a cuckold, however, since his tolerance earned him a variety of benefits. Luisa had already provided a healthy child, artfully designed their residences into envied showplaces, and planned parties that were widely admired; moreover, she had greatly sub-sidized their bank accounts. It is not known whether her husband was carrying on affairs of his own, but more important, Camillo exchanged his "blind eye" for the freedom to indulge in his own passion for horses, dogs, and hunting. This obsession led to extended absences in England to revel in the quintessential foxhunt with high-ranking British lords and ladies. Years later, Camillo was invited to represent Italy as one of the judges at England's prestigious International Horse Show.

D'Annunzio, though, expressed hypocritical contempt for the neglectful husband by attempting to deny his existence altogether. The poet avoided all but chance contact with Camillo, whom he referred to only as "le mari" to Luisa—although he would attend a dinner given by the couple at the Hotel Excelsior in Rome, specifically as a guest of the Marchesa. The silent tension between the men is best illustrated by D'Annunzio's account of one uncomfortable moment:

> [Luisa] was supposed to leave for St. Moritz. I was having breakfast alone with her. It seems she was all ready to go. In any case, as always, I wanted her. I had brought her a long brush, for her bath. A way to touch her from afar, with magic fingers. The husband walked in. The brush, wrapped in paper, was on the mantel of the chimney. He took it in his hands. I don't know what sort of redness filled my face.[8]

Unlike any of D'Annunzio's former mistresses, Luisa was developing a distinct narcissism that prevented him from conquering her wholly. It was this inaccessibility, coupled with complete aesthetic compatibility, that thrilled the stunned seducer. He proclaimed, "She possessed a gift, an omnipotent knowledge of the masculine heart: she knew how to be or appear, incredible. She was, in fact, the only woman who ever astonished me!"[9] He compared her pure uniqueness to that of the legendary unicorn. Here was no double-edged mistress, offering temporary financial solvency while demanding endless attention in return. For her part, Luisa did not require either stability or monogamy from D'Annunzio. Instead, they would share exotic ideas, grandiose tastes, and even occultist joys without the censure each had been accustomed to from supposed loved ones and society.

Luisa Casati's defiance expressed itself through the continued alteration of her appearance into the epitome of the decadent ideal. Besides her ever-brightening tresses, she now accentuated her unusual height and androgynous thinness. The Belle Époque style, exemplified by the Parisian fashion houses of Worth and Doucet, remained the childhood fantasy garments from her mother's boudoir. Those confections did not appeal to Luisa's more outré aspirations. Instead, she draped herself in gowns of intricately woven Venetian lace with balloon sleeves and lengthy trains. Jeweled and brocaded belts tightly cinched her narrow waist. She gave prior paleness an almost cadaverous pallor by increasing the use of what D'Annunzio referred to as "a sort of burning powder that is like pollen on her dry skin."[10] This facial whitening further dramatized her most striking attribute: by ringing her already large eyes with kohl, Luisa made them even more unnaturally immense and startling.

Curiously enough, individual elements of Luisa's emerging personal style seem to have been carefully selected from the women who had most influenced her. Sarah Bernhardt's flashing red hair and the macabre cosmetics of the Principessa di Belgiojoso became her own. Through such artifice, Luisa discovered a newfound confidence, fueled by her obvious visible distinction from most other women. With increasing frequency, she abandoned her earlier timidity and dealt with others in a more spontaneous but often imperious manner. Yet, her true personality and private thoughts remained a mystery, as later noted by writer Sir Harold Acton: "Wisely, she seldom uttered: ordinary sentiments from the lips of so chimerical a creature were inconceivable: they would have struck a discord."[11]

The extent of Casati's transfiguration not only elated D'Annunzio, but also never ceased to mystify him:

> What was the real essence of this creature? Was she aware of her
> continuous metamorphosis, or was she impenetrable to herself,
> excluded from her own mystery? In her expressions how much was
> artifice and how much was spontaneity?[12]

As she was transformed by the alchemy of her affair with D'Annunzio, Luisa came to view the customary role of wife and mother as a stagnant trap. Lonely stretches of time at the villa at Cinisello Balsamo were now insufferable, but the Marchesa was equally discontented with her Milanese residence on the narrow, twisted street of the via Soncino. Dwarfed by its own inordinately immense pillared portico and the much grander mansions of the neighborhood, the house was a constant eyesore to Luisa, who was becoming increasingly determined to redesign it on a more palatial scale.

One of the major precipitating factors in Luisa's growing restlessness and dissatisfaction with her houses was D'Annunzio's continuous praise of the glories of that foremost D'Annunzian city, Venice. The poet passionately proclaimed, "Venice or the creation of happiness . . . the most wonderful union of art and life. The whole city at my eyes was burning with desire."[13] This floating kingdom of luxurious decay on the Adriatic was a source of enchantment for him.

Luisa was soon no longer content with just listening to D'Annunzio extol its pleasures; she wanted to experience them herself. But even his grandiloquent descriptions did not prepare her for the reality of Venice, where such expatriates as Lord Byron, Henry James, Robert Browning, James McNeill Whistler, and so many other artists, writers, and intellectuals had fled. D'Annunzio's aria of praise had been a truthful one. In such a place, Luisa imagined, anything could be possible.

During her journeys to Venice, Luisa noticed that pairs of enigmatic blackamoors, sculpted from painted wood or plaster and uniformed in gilt turbans and velvet jackets, guarded the entrances of the palazzi lining the city's waterways. She quickly purchased a set of her own and placed them in the vestibule of the apartments in Milan. Yet her enthusiasm for renovating the house on the via Soncino rapidly dwindled. Any interest in spending more time in Milan had been obliterated by an obsession for all things Venetian. Even so, an additional house, this one in Rome, was being considered. As frequent visitors to the Italian capital for shopping, cultural excursions, and familial gatherings with Luisa's sister and her children, the Casatis kept suites at the Grand Hotel. But a more permanent Roman address was becoming a necessity since Camillo had been appointed to the presidency of the prestigious Jockey Club there. The Marchese soon received further honors. When the Marquis de Roccagiovine died, Camillo succeeded him to the title of Master of the Foxhounds and he became joint Master of the Staghounds with Prince Odescalchi, with many of the stag hunts being held on the fields of the prince's fifteenth-century Castello Odescalchi on the shores of Lake Bracciano.

By 1906, Camillo commissioned royal architect the Marchese Achille Mainoni di Intignano and the engineer Carlo Pincherle to design a villino, a term given to the type of elegant town house that became popular among Italy's elite at the start of the twentieth century.[14] This latest residence would have to be one befitting the Casati pedigree, complete with garages and stables. Construction began near the center of the city at 51 via Piemonte, an area known as "high" Rome because of its concentration of wealthy inhabitants. Obviously, by this time what was left of the couple's relationship must have been minimal. Although Camillo had wanted a son to carry on the family name, their daughter, Cristina, would remain an only child. Besides its practicality, perhaps building a new house would continue the illusion of a secure marriage.

The Casatis' modern, three-floor residence became not only one of the most imposing in the district but because of Camillo's decision to place Luisa in charge of its decoration, a symbol of unnerving incongruity as well. Visitors venturing beyond its front iron gates would find none of the red brocaded velvet or heavily gilded furniture traditional in the homes of their conservative Catholic neighbors. Through the oversized portal on the via Piemonte, one would first come directly upon an ornate, column-flanked fountain in the center of an atrium within a small, well-manicured garden. Growing there were rare and exotic plants and trees. But the entrance to the successive inner courtyard could only be reached by safely bypassing Angelina, a howling mastiff that obeyed no one except its mistress. Luisa was often required to appear at the gates to personally escort the gargantuan hound to its doghouse so that arriving guests could enter unscathed. Once inside the villa, callers would be admitted into an oval antechamber, the floor of which was set with tiles of black and white marble that formed an intricate basket-weave design. From there one would pass into a gallery with walls of white marble decorated with terra-cotta medallions and bas-reliefs of sculpted alabaster. Luisa often entertained visitors in a small drawing room nearby, its ceiling frescoed with peacocks and parrots. In the outer hall, a curvilinear staircase of marble swept impressively upward, bound on one side by a burnished iron and gold-plated railing. On the next level were further chambers enriched with marble and wooden inlay.

Guests were struck by Luisa's overwhelming and uncommon use of white throughout much of the interior: white walls adorned with Venetian mirrors, white ceilings, and white velvet drapes and upholstery. Polar bear pelts were strewn about on the ebony floors. A fine view of this opulent setting could be obtained from an upper landing, its ceiling painted a bright peacock blue. Ascending the stairway, visitors were serenaded by the unexpected chirping of a choir of clockwork goldfinches housed in a gilt cage suspended from above. Casati also amazed them by equipping one salon with an alabaster floor capable of being lit from beneath. The cumulative effect of the villa was so incredible that when the Princesse Maria Ruspoli visited it, she immediately dubbed it "le bijoux Casati."[15]

"All was refined and aspired to the perfect success of every effect. . . . One was induced to speaking in whispers or walking on tiptoes, just like in church."[16] That was how Camilla Sella Padulli, Francesca's daughter, would remember her aunt's Roman home. Camilla often reminisced about the villa and the demanding requests Luisa made on her staff. More than once, servants were given very specific and protracted instructions on just precisely how the spray of a small fountain located in the entrance hall was to fall in order to create a musically rhythmical pattern.

Luisa's taste for the increasingly exotic was reflected in a passion for unusual pets. Besides the mastiff that guarded the front gates, the Casati household also contained a bevy of lounging Persian, Siamese, and Syrian cats. The house was further adorned by a pair of greyhounds, chosen to harmonize with the color scheme of its interior. Whereas one greyhound was entirely white and the other black, both slender necks were encircled by collars set with jewels similar to those of hounds in Renaissance paintings. Guests were also greeted at the main entryway by a pair of statues of golden gazelles, placed there whenever the Marchesa was in residence—but these mascots were not often seen. Even though the house was extremely costly and painstakingly designed, its charms were insufficient to entertain a mistress who always wished to be elsewhere.

To the wealthy community along the via Piemonte, Luisa Casati the woman was as equally unsettling as her house. A wardrobe now almost exclusively black and white offset her chalky features and vermilion hair. Although she owned a magnificent collection of emeralds, Luisa's preference was for impressive strings of pearls stretching nearly to the floor. Since she mingled infrequently with them, her neighbors responded to her with a cool reserve. They also considered her to be nouveau riche; unlike their own affluence and position, the Marchesa's personal fortune was founded in the too recent past. Moreover, besides being a reputed adulteress, she was known to be consorting freely with artists.

Ever since she was a child, Luisa had developed a fondness for the visual arts. As a potential patroness in the capital, she encountered a wealth of both famous and undiscovered artists eager to make their studios accessible to someone with such a discerning eye and open pocketbook. Shortly after her move to Rome in 1906, the Marchesa met Alberto Martini. The Trevian-born painter, sculptor, and illustrator was five years her senior and already well established in Italian artistic circles with a reputation for erotically macabre pen-and-ink drawings. The two quickly discovered a shared fascination for Venice, which was displayed by Martini's earliest known rendering of Casati. Depicting its subject in full-length profile against a nocturnal lagoon, this sedate image gives little indication of the phantasmagoria soon to follow.[17]

At about the same time, the Marchesa had also become friends with Filippo Tommaso Marinetti. This advocate of the then developing futurism movement was born and raised in Alexandria, Egypt, and he and his family had just recently relocated to Milan. High-spirited and polemical by nature, Marinetti had abandoned law studies for literature and verse. He was soon inaugurating the publication *Poesia* as a forum for his and his associates' ideas. Luisa, delighted by her acceptance into this subculture of tumultuous creativity, showed her appreciation by bringing many of these varied men together for the first time. At a ball given by the Casatis, Marinetti commissioned Martini to create the premiere cover for his new magazine. This collaboration between two of her new friends pleased Luisa immeasurably.[18]

Finding herself frequently in the company of such talented individuals and wishing to further her involvement with them as a patron, Luisa undertook regular visits to the National Gallery in London and the Louvre in Paris to expand her already impressive knowledge of the fine arts. But it was during yet another stay in Venice that the Marchesa would meet an artist capable of transferring her unique essence onto canvas. It was now 1908, and Luisa Casati had begun a serious search for a new residence with the assistance of her friend the Baroness Ernesta Stern, society doyenne and author.[19] A Venetian palazzo, to rent several seasons each year, would be an ideal setting for the costume balls envisioned by the Marchesa. Here guests would include not only the international "smart set," but also those artistic Bohemians possessing freer spirits more akin to her own than the arrogant neighbors in Rome.

During this latest visit to Venice, Gabriele D'Annunzio invited Luisa to breakfast at the Hotel Danieli. She dressed from head to toe in black, adorned with one of her by now customary lengthy strands of pearls. As the Marchesa neared the table, she noticed her lover was not alone. Next to him was a man in his midsixties, as exceptionally short as he was rotund, with a thick gray mustache and a pair of pince-nez clipped to the end of his bulbous nose. Just then, the necklace snapped from around Luisa's throat, and its pearls bounced on the dining room floor. The stranger fell onto his hands and knees to offer his assistance.

"We all hurried under the tables to retrieve the pearls and it was under one table that I found myself face to face with her and saw for the first time, close up, her immense eyes."[20] This savior happened to be the premier society portraitist, Giovanni Boldini. By the time of this fortunate mishap, his brush had already recorded the images of many of the era's most flamboyant notables, among them the artistic dandies Comte Robert de Montesquiou and James McNeill Whistler and operatic sensation Lina Cavalieri. Boldini's immediately recognizable style captured the subject's head and face with photographic exactitude, whereas the remainder of the body was completed in a less defined, more fluid manner. His actual slashing, broad brushstrokes earned him fame as the "swordsman" of the canvas.

The Marchesa's unusual demeanor instantly captivated the painter. At the age of sixty-five, he was content with a platonic but passionate infatuation, and Luisa willingly accepted his personal as well as artistic appreciation of her remarkable tastes and appearance. Boldini would never tire of recounting his involvement in the affair of the falling pearls. He immediately made preliminary studies of Casati's face and extraordinary eyes and approached her to begin a portrait at his studio in Paris. Upon her return to Rome, Luisa announced her intention to undertake an extended stay in the French capital. She would not allow domestic duties of any kind to forfeit this opportunity to be immortalized.

2

At the farthest end of the rue de la Paix, near the rue de Castiglione and the Faubourg Saint-Honoré, is one of the true glories of Paris, the enclave of the place Vendôme. Built during the reign of the Sun King, Louis XIV, the series of twenty-eight town houses that line the square—with their refined façades embellished by Corinthian pillars and crowned by sloping mansard roofs—soon became the city's most exclusive addresses. Throughout its history, the place Vendôme had been home to the notable and infamous alike. At number 16, Dr. Franz Mesmer founded his controversial clinic for the treatment of nervous disorders through hypnotism; Frédéric Chopin died at number 12; and one of Luisa's idols, the Comtesse de Castiglione, transformed number 26 into a morbid home. Known as "the madwoman of the place Vendôme," the Comtesse veiled the windows of the house in black and covered every mirror to avoid seeing how age had ravaged her once exquisite reflection. The recluse ventured out to wander the square only after dark, using a hidden side entrance.

The town houses of the place Vendôme retained their private grandeur for one hundred years, surviving even the chaos of the French Revolution. Then, beginning in the late nineteenth century, a number of these buildings were converted into luxury hotels. The Paris Ritz is the best known and is still operating to this day. The Ritz opened its gilded doors on June 1, 1898, and its 210 rooms and apartments were patronized immediately by the world's most distinguished guests—the Rothschilds, the Vanderbilts, and such famed *grandes horizontales* as Liane de Pougy and la belle Otéro all made the hotel their second home. Marcel Proust, one of the Ritz's most frequent visitors, observed, "The Ritz is a quiet place; great ladies whose fortunes would enable several generations to live comfortably sip their tea there like elegant ghosts."[21] When the Marchesa Luisa Casati entered the Ritz during the autumn of 1908, she arrived alone, a fact that did not go unnoticed by the other guests. Not only did she leave behind a husband and child in Rome, but rumors about her affair with D'Annunzio had already reached the French capital, and even the *enfant de volupté* of the pen and boudoir had not accompanied her. He was in Rome as well, basking in the sold-out triumph of his new play, *La Nave*.

Idle whisperings at the Ritz that season about Luisa Casati were not solely connected with D'Annunzio. Most spoke of her increasingly strange behavior. The stylish but slightly alarming figure that hurried through the hotel's hushed lobby in an ebony blur was visible proof enough. It was confided in murmured tones at the bar in the Ritz Club or beside the fires of the salons that Luisa's infidelity and high-priced tastes had resulted in an unusual agreement with her husband. By this mutual accord, she was free to flit about the world to explore her egocentric artistic ambitions while the Marchese was at liberty to pursue his preoccupation with horses and hounds. Their abandoned daughter was left in the care of her governess or, when she was fortunate, her more doting aunt Francesca. But such gossip was of little interest to Luisa—she had journeyed to Paris on a mission of greater importance.

Giovanni Boldini exuberantly welcomed Luisa to his studio, the Villetta Rossa, as she had agreed to pay the princely fee of twenty thousand francs for a finished portrait. While her beauty was certainly motivation enough, Boldini's imagination was further inspired by his sitter's unexpected ensemble. Most of the painter's patrons chose sensibly refined dresses of white, beige, or pastel shades for their portraits, but Luisa arrived as if from some flamboyant funeral. Her tall figure was snugly fitted into a floor-length gown of black satin, designed by couturier Paul Poiret, further adorned by a sable muff and an oversized hat trimmed with black ribbons and feathers. Offsetting this black excess, Casati wore a bouquet of silk violets at her waist. A similarly colored sash snaked down to her black shoes from two slender arms sheathed in white evening gloves. To complete this arresting image, her black greyhound was present, wearing a silver mesh collar. Luisa selected this combination of black and violet deliberately: not only was it undeniably chic but the occult meaning of this color scheme still symbolizes triumph over death in many cultures.

Casati soon found Boldini a disconcerting craftsman. With the canvas placed at a distance from its subject, the artist would be in constant motion, dashing between his easel and model. Boldini was also a fervent aficionado of grand opera and took pride and pleasure in serenading his sitters. The situation was not improved by the elderly man's hearing loss; these arias were never sung in less than full voice. More entertaining was the painter's obsession with the latest gossip, always accompanied by acidic commentary on the foibles of the aristocracy.

While posing, Luisa could not help noticing a recently completed portrait, awaiting a final glazing, in one corner of the studio. The oil, known as *La Passeggiata al Bois,* showed an elegantly attired couple promenading through an autumnal landscape. Casati recognized them as Captain Philip Lydig and his New York–born Spanish wife, Rita de Acosta, the elite of the American leisure class. Fearing potential competition, Luisa was distressed to hear Boldini's plan of exhibiting the portrait of the Lydigs along with her own at the upcoming Paris Salon. This annual art show was not focused just on aesthetic judgment; it had become an event fashionably important to attend, but the showing of a portrait was also the equivalent of a society introduction for the sitter. Unlike the already internationally famous Rita Lydig, Casati's fame was still bound mainly by the borders of her own country. The Marchesa longed for a similar reputation, so she would have to concede, however unhappily, to Boldini's plan.

Sittings for the portrait, for which she was chronically late, alternated with frenetic shopping sprees. During her weeks in Paris, Luisa had met and become friends with the French actress Cécile Sorel. Sorel's many years with the Comédie Française and the Casino de Paris made her almost as adulated a performer as Sarah Bernhardt. In Sorel's honor, Casati arranged a luncheon at Larue, one of the best restaurants in the city, located at the tip of the rue Royale near the place de la Concorde. Since these Parisian streets were lined with renowned boutiques, Luisa decided to shop for a few early Christmas purchases before the scheduled afternoon engagement. A corsage of lilies was also ordered for her special guest.[22]

Luisa was very much affected by Cécile Sorel, whose tendency toward incessant talk was as famous as her stage work. Sorel was fond of her own outspoken persona and also of being recognized by her many admirers. Since the restaurant's white and gold paneled walls were hung with mirrors, it proved an ideal place for the actress to keep a discreetly watchful eye on the venerating glances of her fellow diners. In spite of such conceit, Casati came to esteem Sorel's sense of style so much that she described her years later to the famed fashion designer and photographer Cecil Beaton as the best-dressed woman she had ever known.[23] In return, the actress was taken by Luisa's originality and natural flair for the theatrical. The luncheon was a success and the women would remain friends for the following two decades.

Many more weeks would pass before Boldini was satisfied enough with his work on the portrait to dismiss the sitter. Luisa, however, did not travel back to Rome until she had exhausted a small fortune on further shopping extravaganzas and numerous social events. Boldini arranged a meeting for Casati with another of his patrons, the popular actress Ève Lavallière.[24] The length of Luisa's Parisian stay, which extended beyond Christmas, confirmed the disintegrating state of her relationship with Camillo and her inattention toward their daughter. It was not until just after the New Year's celebrations of 1909 that she returned to the villa on the via Piemonte.

Once there, she learned of D'Annunzio's latest woes, which included a disastrous theatrical production of *Fedra* and the equally unfortunate launch of Acqua Nunzia, a perfume of his own concoction. These financial failures would lead to D'Annunzio's self-imposed exile to France, lasting for the next five years. But even separated by international borders, his love affair with Luisa continued through frequent correspondence and excursions.

Coinciding with the *Fedra* debacle, the Ballets Russes was preparing its first production in the French capital at the Théâtre du Chatelet. The avant-garde dance company astounded audiences with the premiere of *Cléopâtre* on March 16, 1909, under the direction of Serge Diaghilev. This ambitious impresario from St. Petersburg was immediately recognizable by his imposing, dandily attired figure, topped off by a thick black mane, which was streaked by a single lightning bolt of white hair. With an instinct for detecting artistic genius, he would introduce the world to such future luminaries as the dancers Nijinsky, Pavolva, and Karsavina and the designers Bakst and Benois. Diaghilev's never-ending demands drove his troupe to dizzying heights of creativity. These Russian invaders created such a commotion among their Parisian admirers and affluent art patrons that it aroused Luisa's attention in Rome and Milan.

Less than a month later, on April 14, the Paris Salon held its grand opening. Hundreds of paintings, ranging from traditional landscapes, still lifes, and mediocre society portraits to the more controversial decadent nudes and a few revolutionary experiments in abstract art, were on view. As Boldini had envisioned, Luisa's portrait was exhibited alongside that of the Lydigs.

Confined to a sickbed at home, the artist was unfortunately not present to witness the reaction his work stirred in critic and public alike. Luisa's fear of being overshadowed by the illustrious Rita Lydig proved unnecessary. For although Lydig's image was well received, it was thought standard Boldini fare in comparison to the incredible *La jeune femme au lévrier*. Considered frightening and enthralling, some even claimed that the portrait possessed certain satanic overtones, as evidenced by the model's disreputable black and violet gown and aggressive stare. Of course, in very little time everyone was curious about who exactly was this young woman with the greyhound.

Although some denounced both its subject's demeanor and its artistic worth, others praised the portrait as a masterpiece, accepting its diabolical associations as part of its provocative power. Art critic Arsène Alexandre did so in his review from *Le Figaro*:

> Today, [Boldini's] talent has reached its climax. I am almost afraid to write that his portrait of Mme La Marquise Casati is the most beautiful piece of pure painting in the whole Salon. By paradox, he attains with true greatness, by what seems in Art justly the enemy of greatness: the boldest negation of lines. . . . It reminds me of the Old Masters' technique. . . . The harmony of black and violet is of extraordinary power. . . . [Tintoretto] never painted such beautiful black eyes as these; Goya never captured in a more attractive way the enigma of a lovely face. This Marquise's face is unusual. It presents an almost "witches sabbat" mein in its big-eyed appearance . . . in its anti-Gioconda countenance that crowns the long question mark of a body wrapped in black satin.[25]

The portrait induced that "pontiff of aestheticism," the perennial dandy and sometime poet Comte Robert de Montesquiou, to dedicate a few lines to Boldini's seemingly hellborn temptress:

> Madame Casati devant elle a sa grâce
> Son mystère, ses chiens, son énorme chapeau
> Et son bouquet de fleurs qu'un seul coup d'oeil embrasse
> Lorsque le temps est clair et que le jour est beau

Luisa was ecstatic with the portrait's tumultuous reception. The twenty thousand francs had been well spent. Regardless of the middling quality of Montesquiou's verse, his homage reminded her of the sonnets composed by Renaissance suitors for the maidens they courted. But her thrilling episode of public attention was shortly, and temporarily, tarnished.

With the single exception of the French fashion magazine *Femina*, not one periodical carried a reproduction of her portrait.[26] Luisa soon learned that many reviews of the exhibition, and especially *L'Illustration*'s pivotal Salon edition, featured the Lydigs' image alone. A series of angry letters arrived at the Villetta Rossa studio. Boldini responded with a calm explanation to Casati's correspondence: "I always detest reproductions because, generally, they are horrible, and, moreover, I have the impression I am prostituting my work."[27] The artist then worsened matters by attempting to appease his patron with a little trickery. Feigning innocence, he implied that it was Luisa herself who had denied the duplication of the portrait. Several more furious letters were issued from Italy before Boldini recanted: "Dear Marchesa, with one stroke of my pen I authorize all French and foreign journals to reproduce my paintings and the *Marchesa* in particular! You may be amused by seeing the horrible reproductions that will now follow!"[28]

Luisa's growing exhibitionistic mania was satisfied by the small victory, and she and Boldini soon rekindled their mutual admiration. But Casati now confronted an additional obstacle on her quest to conquer the international set—another non-Parisian with similar aims. This threat took the unappealing shape of the American-born socialite the Princesse Edmond de Polignac, a woman more commonly known as Winnaretta Singer in the United States. Heiress to the immense Singer sewing machine fortune and sister of dancer Isadora Duncan's current lover, Paris Singer, she was a talented musician and patron of the arts. But her hatchet-like exterior, heavy nasal voice, and lesbian tendencies were as equally commented on as her beneficence.

Singer had achieved her high standing by cultivating relationships with some of the most outstanding artists of the day, especially those who showed musical genius. Her Parisian salon in the avenue Henri-Martin attracted many titled nobles who were hoping for acceptance into the latest arts scene. Singer withstood their vacuous companionship with a hypocritical smile in order to achieve her goal, but it required Robert de Montesquiou to see through the velvets and frills to the ironclad shrew beneath.

Montesquiou was a trained society assassin. When he decided to point both barrels of his devastating wit directly at Singer, he did so with gleeful sarcasm in the pages of *Le Figaro*. His prey was portrayed as "a Nero, a thousand times more cruel than the original, who dreams of seeing his victims pricked to death by sewing machines."[29] Montesquiou's deliberately calculated and continuous offensive succeeded in ruining Singer's advancement. Although she retained some influence, she would never attain the coveted crown of doyenne of the grand monde.

As a witness to this ominous attack, Luisa chose not to play such games with Montesquiou and the Princesse. Instead, she accelerated her plan to conquer Venice. Costume parties were currently the rage among the French and Italian elite. Casati was certain her masquerades would leave the city, and possibly all of Europe, astounded, but she needed the correct venue in which to hold them. Known as Italy's wealthiest woman at this time, Luisa's own fortune could finance any extravagance. Such personal wealth and independence made her husband's consent, in a word, unnecessary.

News soon came from the Baroness Ernesta Stern that a palazzo on the Grand Canal was coming up for lease. Casati was assured of the structure's many unusual assets—and it was available immediately. Relying on the Baroness's description alone, Luisa took possession of what was considered the most unique palace in all of Venice, the fabulous Palazzo Venier dei Leoni.

1001 Nights on the Grand Canal

1910-1914

The fabled Luisa Casati lived in her half-built Palazzo. . . .
I saw her drifting down the Grand Canal under a parasol
of peacock's feathers, but this surprise was nothing to the
succession of glorious shocks that were to come.
   —*Lady Diana Cooper*

The Marchesa Casati, at sunset, reclining in her gondola,
wrapped in tiger skins and fondling her favorite leopard, is
a sight to be seen only in Venice.
   —*Baron Adolph de Meyer*

1

In 1749, the Venier family decided to destroy its residence. Since their ennoblement almost two centuries earlier, this ancient Venetian dynasty had produced three doges, eighteen procurators of San Marco, and numerous military captains and generals in service to the Republic. Located on the Grand Canal, their ancestral manse, a fifteenth-century Gothic palace known as the Venier delle Torselle, held an enviable position just adjacent to the Palazzo Dario and directly opposite the Prefettura. The house of the Veniers was to be pulled down and the site cleared to make way for the construction of a new, even more grandiose dwelling.

The finished palace, designed by architect Lorenzo Boschetti, was to have the widest façade of any palazzo on the Grand Canal and was to consist of a ground floor, a mezzanine level, a pair of *piani nobili*, and an attic. Also laid out was an immense garden, a feature rare in a Venetian home even of this grandeur. In fact, the proposed Venier palace would boast the single largest private garden in the city, filled with tangles of vines, gnarled trees, and tall cypresses. But during the lengthy period in which the house was being erected, the riches of the Venier family were depleted. The structure, unfinished and abandoned, became known by the local people as the Palazzo Non Finito.[1]

Even with only its first level and garden completed, enough of the palace existed to suggest the impressive scale of what might have been. The façade of the ground floor was fronted with smooth, white Istrian stone, broken along its length by a pair of giant columns that flanked the main entryway. A row of arched windows faced the lagoons. A low wall of similar white stone, embellished by eight roaring lion heads, was constructed just above the water level of the Grand Canal. In time, these imposing felines would grow cowls of lichen and moss.

At the time of its design, the curious building was to be known as the Palazzo Venier dei Leoni. A theory claims that this name arose from the Veniers' supposed habit of keeping a chained lion in the front garden, but more likely the palace's carved lion heads inspired it. Its newest occupant, though, had no need to hearken back to previous owners of any kind. After the elimination of the Venier family name from its title, the palace, now redubbed the Palazzo dei Leoni, would belong to Luisa alone.

Luisa Casati took occupancy of the palace in 1910 from its proprietor, the Comtesse de la Baume-Pluvinel, who resided at the neighboring Palazzo Dario. Most recently, after its ownership had passed through numerous hands, the Venier home was being used as a modest boarding house. The resultant neglect gave the building the appearance of nothing more than a mound of uninhabited, overgrown rubble. Upon acquisition of the property,

Luisa arranged for and personally financed a team of the country's best designers, carpenters, and painters to restore the sprawling wreck. She ordered them to mend its structural soundness while retaining its decaying ambience. They succeeded admirably, for within those deteriorating walls all was magnificence.

Chandeliers from the workshops of renowned local glass artisans cast a golden luster throughout halls of white marble. Further illumination came from alabaster vases crowned by ivory roses and chunks of amber and rock crystal, all of which were lit from within. A staircase of verdigris metal connected the main floor to the lower level. Curtains of gold lace adorned the many windows, glinting brightly in the sunlit reflections of the surrounding canals. Again, much like Casati's Roman villa, the palazzo's interior color scheme was black and white, with the exception of one salon that was decorated entirely in antiqued gold leaf. Luisa also transported a black and white marble floor in its entirety from the villa in Rome to Venice each season. Landscapers tamed back the palace's rambling jungle of a garden. Flocks of white peacocks and albino blackbirds strutted about a dense confusion of ivy and liana or flew between the branches of the cypress trees, their screeches echoing across the lagoons.

Not unexpectedly, inquisitive talk began to circulate among the area's affluent neighbors. They wondered who this woman was to repair so expensively what was considered an eyesore, one that should have been leveled completely years ago. To further the confusion, the workmen's constant activity appeared to entail no noticeable exterior remodeling at all. In the midst of her own physical and aesthetic transformation, it was ironic that Luisa chose an incomplete piece of architecture in which to reinvent herself.

Once Casati settled into her refurbished ruin, certain essentials needed immediate attention. A reliable gondolier was on call at all times. He and all future boatmen were clothed in elaborate eighteenth-century fashion. Their unique uniforms included velvet suits, embroidered waistcoats, and powdered wigs topped by panther-skin skullcaps. Expanding this conceit even further, the Marchesa had the boat itself decorated with black damask, silk scarves, and tiger and leopard pelts. Luisa once enraged the Commune of Venice by having her gondola painted white in direct opposition to the sumptuary law curtailing such expressions of extravagance. [2]

The black and white greyhounds had been transported safely from Rome. They were probably more pleased with the freedom of the palazzo's garden than with having to share it with Casati's newest acquisition—a pair of cheetahs. Although most reminiscences identify them as leopards, they were instead these more docile African cats. In an audacious realization of the myth of the Venier family's pet lion, Luisa would often be seen leading her own felines about the terrace on a jeweled leash. The cats were even allowed to accompany their mistress on excursions in her gondola. Casati also acquired the assistance of a singular attendant, a towering black man named Garbi. This living embodiment of her favored Moorish ornaments soon became indispensable in her forthcoming masquerades and public "performances."

Luisa's fabrication of a mythical persona was nearly complete upon her arrival in Venice in 1910. As did the actresses and royal eccentrics she admired in her youth, she achieved this most successfully through theatrical costuming and effects. By applying powders of consistently paler color, her face now glowed with a dead-white hue. Immense circles of kohl ringed her already enormous green eyes. These sooty wreaths were wide enough to reach from just beneath her eyebrows to the top of her prominent cheekbones. Luisa also stained her eyelids with India ink or glued on thin strips of black velvet to achieve the desired intensity. She used false eyelashes of increasing lengths, and her vermilion lips vied for brightness with the henna inferno that now crowned her strange countenance. Never a disciple of the fashions of the day, Luisa ironically tired of her Venetian lace gowns once the city of their origin had been finally reached. Her quest for continual exoticism soon led to the sanctum of Mariano Fortuny y Madrazo.

The son of an esteemed Spanish painter, Fortuny had spent his early years studying painting and photography before turning to chemistry and its application to dyeing fabric. Bolts of silk, satin, and linen were bathed in gargantuan steaming vats of vegetable coloring in his Venetian palace's private laboratories. Through such experimentation Fortuny would discover the seemingly mystical techniques and formulas that would earn him unparalleled fame. His deceptively simplistic but completely modern fashions incorporated and reinterpreted Egyptian, Grecian, Renaissance, Asian, and Indian elements. Fortuny's gowns and evening cloaks were instantly recognizable by their pleated looseness reminiscent of the kimono or sari. His luminescent dresses and scarves bore classically inspired names such as Delphos, Knossos, and Peplos.[3] Casati valued Fortuny's work for its distinctive artistry, and she was especially fond of his velvet capes and mantles. Altogether, these magnified elements of cosmetics and clothing, coupled with her height and thinness, gave the Marchesa a macabre beauty.

Now all was in place for the curious Venetians to receive their city's newest and possibly most eccentric denizen. The mistress of the Palazzo dei Leoni finally made an unforgettable entrance into local lore on the Piazza San Marco. Clad in a Fortuny cloak of antique red brocade, she wore a thick gold necklace and a black fur cap. At her side strolled the contrasting greyhounds, both bedecked with turquoise collars. From behind followed Garbi, in turban and waistcoat, carrying a parasol of peacock feathers high above his mistress's head. At that moment, Luisa astounded Venice and earned the singular epithet "La Casati."

Back in Rome, Camillo Casati did not seem particularly distressed by the desertion of his wife. Her bold decision to rent the Venetian palazzo solidified the fact of their severed ties, although they would not separate officially for another four years. The Marchese continued his duties at the Roman Jockey Club, spending the rest of his time at the Villa Casati at Cinisello Balsamo or on horseback at the hunting château in Cusago. With her mother in Venice and her father engaged in his pursuits, nine-year-old Cristina was sent to an extremely strict French boarding school in a Catholic convent.[4]

In 1910, Gabriele D'Annunzio became the first writer of her circle to base a fictional character on Luisa Casati. This flamboyant creation would appear in one of his most highly praised novels, *Forse che sì forse che no*. Although the Marchesa's influence on D'Annunzio was evident in numerous instances, Isabella Inghirami is his clearest attempt to capture her unusual persona on paper. The novel's main female character is described in sensual detail, made more vivid by the author's ecstatically religious tone:

> She was enveloped in one of those very long scarves of Oriental gauze that the alchemist Mariano Fortuny plunges in the mysterious dyes of his vats and withdraws tinted with strange dreams. . . . She loved to enhance the freshness of twenty-five years with blacks and reds, she always darkened the eyelids around her bright irises, and sometimes bloodied her mouth with cinnabar. But her alchemy was much more complex, producing many other marvels. By what fire did she transmute the substance of her life into the beauties of such moving power? . . . The ordinary acts of daily existence—slowly removing her glove, allowing the doeskin to slip over the light down of her arm; sitting on the bed and taking off the long silk stocking, delicate as a flower that fades in an instant; taking the pins from her hat by raising her arms in an arc and letting the sleeve slip down to the curly gold of the armpit. . . . For all that she was so fragile, so supple, and so lascivious, she was akin to the great creatures of Michelangelo. . . . Her gowns lived with her body as ashes live with the embers. . . . She demonstrated how true it is that all enchantment is a madness induced with art.[5]

The book's title, *Forse che sì forse che no* (Maybe yes, maybe no), was taken from a fresco motto on the ceiling of the ducal palace in Mantua[6] and best typifies the unpredictable personalities of both the fictional Isabella Inghirami and her real-life inspiration. In a hidden jest, one of the novel's characters claims that a rival of Isabella is Luisa Casati. Although the Marchesa's penchant for fast automobiles and greyhounds remains intact, the invented double is plagued by episodes of incest and insanity supplied by her creator's fervid imagination. The writing of *Forse che sì forse che no* was an arduous task for the author, taking two years to complete before its eventual publication in 1910. D'Annunzio had originally conceived the idea almost a decade earlier, at the time of his initial relations with the Amman sisters. Francesca appears as Inghirami's sibling, Vana.

At the beginning of the summer of 1910, Serge Diaghilev registered at the Grand Hotel des Bains on the Venetian Lido. In attendance were Vaslav Nijinsky, his star dancer and ambivalent lover, as well as the scenic and costume designers from Ballets Russes, Léon Bakst and Alexandre Benois. Around the same time, Luisa met American dancer Isadora Duncan. Already in her early thirties, she was hardly a fresh talent but had been tracking Diaghilev in a persistent but ultimately failed attempt to join his meteoric company.

Overlooking the fact of the dancer's relationship to her societal rival, Winnaretta Singer, Luisa invited Duncan to a luncheon at the Palazzo dei Leoni. D'Annunzio joined them and, in typical fashion, began a seduction of this woman who possessed a figure more ample than the Grecian nymphs she so passionately wished to personify. Duncan would boast continually of her proud refusal of the rogue's advances on that afternoon and at all of their future meetings.[7]

One afternoon the danseuse arrived on the sunny sands of the Lido in one of her Hellenic outfits, shadowed beneath an oversized Japanese parasol. Duncan, as emissary for Luisa Casati, extended an invitation to the Russian quartet. Later that evening, their hostess, bedecked in an almost incalculable abundance of pearls, greeted them at the palazzo. However, according to Nijinsky's biography, written by his wife, Romola, "[There were] also others who swore that nothing more than a snake made up her costume that evening."[8]

D'Annunzio was again present, and attendants in eighteenth-century dress served Luisa's guests. After the meal, to the delight of all, Nijinsky and Duncan performed an impromptu pas de deux:

> Isadora clasped her hands behind her head, forcing Nijinsky to lead her
> by placing his hands around her waist. She became oblivious, lost in
> the beat of the waltz. With her eyes closed she allowed Nijinsky to
> guide her. . . . It was an unforgettable sight to see these two geniuses
> of the dance—each representing his art from opposite poles—waltzing
> madly around and, at that, waltzing rather badly. . . . As the last note of

the music ended, Isadora flung herself onto a sofa. . . . Everyone laughed and applauded. . . . Holding out her hand to Nijinsky in a gesture of affection, she said, "What a shame he wasn't my pupil when he was two. Then I could have taught him to dance!"[9]

Nijinsky then drifted about the palace until he was confronted by D'Annunzio. Not satisfied by the danseur's display, the dictatorial writer demanded, "Go on! Dance something for me!" Furious, Nijinsky responded, "Why don't you write something for me!" Matters may have been worsened by one of the Marchesa's pet monkeys that often imitated Duncan's dancing until its cage was covered.[10] Luisa's hopes for a splendid evening were ruined. Nothing so disastrous had occurred at a Casati soirée since an earlier incident in Rome, when one reveler's accusation of cheating at a parlor game almost culminated in a duel.

Luisa would more than compensate for the occasional failure of an entertainment with an incredible series of fêtes, but such spectacles would be achieved at a ruinous price. Dario Cecchi best described Casati's nearly mad quest to make real her recently unleashed dreams:

> Coré was a megalomaniac. Artistically and poetically a megalomaniac . . . the "Luisa Casati machine" . . . a creation made to lift tons of paper money, of checks, of titles, like bales of bound hay. She was a squandering mechanism. A machine that mashed lire, francs, pounds, and marks, as well as whatever else she chose to conquer—a work of art, a jewel, a leopard. Nothing seemed to be a matter of money. . . .
> It was money which flowed, that opened all the doors, which allowed Coré to obtain all that she desired . . . transforming itself sooner or later into a monstrous selfishness. . . . The precise notion of gathering all that one wants and desires at all cost to obtain is a complicated task. One must accept compromises. And Coré didn't even know what they were.[11]

Reckless of the future, Casati set about fulfilling her desires with a single-mindedness worthy of a sultaness from some exotic Arabian tale.

2

In an apparent dress rehearsal for the almost perpetual carnival yet to unfold at the Palazzo dei Leoni, Luisa hosted numerous intimate soirées and attended others as an unforgettable guest. At one party, she arrived bedecked in pearls and rare Egyptian lotus flowers. At another, her attire was described as a "symphony of white"[12]—a gown of ivory silk further adorned by veils and a bouquet of white orchids that was fastened on her breast by a ruby pin in the shape of a dragon. The memoirs of Mercedes de Acosta, infamous lesbian, femme fatale, and sister to Rita Lydig, present an insightful account of a meeting with Luisa during those fairy-tale years in Venice:

> I went to see the Marchesa Casati. I wanted to meet her because I had heard so much about her eccentricities. She received us in her garden, dressed in white with black strips of court plaster around and outlining her eyes. As she advanced to meet us she carried a lily in one hand, with the other she led by a chain a small lioness cub. I thought she was "bad theater," although her performance was not as "ham" as it would be now. These were different times, and people allowed themselves flights of imagination by dressing up as something they secretly wished to be. I myself often dressed up as a cossack or a Hussar, and once I went so far as to affect a Franciscan tunic—rope sandals and all—so perhaps I should not criticize La Casati, who evidently thought of herself as a virgin carrying a symbolic lily.[13]

On other occasions, Luisa garbed herself entirely in black. Unknowing guests would wonder if she was some stylish widow, but it was explained that her estranged husband was away hunting somewhere in Gallarate, Bracciano, or Britain. The two were seen briefly reunited at Italy's first International Air Circuit at Brescia in September 1909, joined by composer Giacomo Puccini and journalist Luigi Barzini. Gabriele D'Annunzio was in attendance as well, satisfying his current obsession with the airplane.

Luisa soon tired of the black and white color schemes that had become her fashion trademark. Once the popularity of Mariano Fortuny's creations resulted in increased sales to visiting society women, the Marchesa became less interested in their antiquated charm. Besides, there was not enough overt theatricality to be found in their streamlined elegance. What she required was the imagination and skill of a learned costume designer. Léon Bakst of the Ballets Russes was the obvious choice as Casati's next couturier. The immediate appeal of his stage work could be found in one critic's description: "A fantastic debauch of colour . . . the sets and costumes of Bakst burned with fiery light, dazzling oranges, brilliant blues, strident greens, and spewed exotic treasures before astounded audiences. Suddenly the barbaric East was in fashion."[14] The designer himself explained more succinctly: "I was born . . . in order to revive among my contemporaries the beautiful and fresh colour misunderstood and stifled for so long a time by people of taste."[15] Bakst once humorously told Luisa that his capability of achieving such a feat was due to having eaten tubes of paint as a child. Though enchanted by his fervid creativity, Casati found Bakst's personal manner uninteresting, an opinion that was not contradicted by the monotony of his droning voice.

When he was not working for the Ballets Russes, Bakst devised his most flamboyant outfits to fulfill the Marchesa's need for both fancy dress and domestic wear, although, at times, it was often difficult to discern any difference between the two. This was a reflection of Luisa's almost complete blurring of everyday life with the fabulous once she had settled firmly into her Venetian wonderland. The transformation from demure society wife to extravagant fascinatrix was no longer enough to satisfy her mania for illusion. Now even more outlandish disguises had to be constructed to conceal those beneath. It is nearly impossible to determine the precise number of *bal travesti* costumes and gowns Bakst conceived for his patron. One source states forty, whereas the artist himself once jestingly referred to their prolific collaboration as "deux têtes quatre milles."[16]

Although most of Bakst's designs for the Marchesa have not been discovered, a few survive to attest to his incredible imagination. Included among the most celebrated of these creations are his interpretation of a wide-belted *Arlecchino bianco* outfit, its sleeves, bodice, and legs embellished with oversized white pom-poms, complemented by swatches bearing the traditional variegated harlequin pattern, a face mask, black-buckled shoes, a tasseled stocking cap, and a wooden saber; another of an animal tamer with a macaw on one shoulder and a live ape on one arm; and yet another noted as *Danse Indo-Persane,* of multiple veils of blue and gold, a conical headdress ornamented with pearls, slippers curled at the toes, and attenuated golden talons for the wearer's fingertips. There is a photograph of Casati wearing this disguise while holding the hand of Boldini. Comically, the artist is standing on a raised dais to meet his hostess's height. Boldini was a frequent guest at the Marchesa's Venetian extravaganzas and would show his gratitude for her hospitality by sketching her romantically adrift in her opulent gondola. In 1912, Bakst, too, would pay homage to his patron by capturing her unique beauty in a pair of charcoal portraits.

But it should be noted that a showy outfit was not always relied on to cause quite a stir. More than one report details Luisa's unusual nocturnal promenades: her spectral form, totally nude within the folds of a voluminous fur cloak, leading her pet cheetahs by jeweled leashes about the Piazza San Marco. Accompanied by a black escort carrying a pair of blazing torches, she was illuminated for shocked onlookers. The Marchesa, described as wearing more perfume than clothing, would often use nudity to achieve a memorable effect or entrance during the coming years.

La Casati's au naturel nighttime strolls about the Piazza first stunned and then were looked for expectantly by tourists and local aristocrats alike. The

British writer Cecil Roberts witnessed one of these promenades: "[Casati appeared] death-pale, scarlet cloaked . . . exotic as an Aubrey Beardsley drawing. She was preceded by a Negro page that led a panther with a gold chain. It was sheer Tintoretto."[17] The Marchesa also caused a teatime sensation one afternoon when she appeared there wrapped in a tigerskin, its ferocious head atop her own. Such accounts broadened her scandalous fame, but it was Casati's masquerades that would make her an international legend. These costumed balls were meticulous in conception, lavish in execution, and almost mythical in the memories of their attendees. Soon, all of Europe's bon ton longed for an invitation to the spectacles at that strange ruin on the Grand Canal.

The Palazzo dei Leoni had been, by now, transformed into a sort of decadent amusement park. Mechanical songbirds trilled from gilt cages. Aromatic flowers and plants were cultivated in the garden to perfume the sometime foul-smelling miasma rising from the adjacent lagoons. A botanical setting for many festivities, the grounds of the palace were aglow nightly with torches and mysterious lights of blue and green while the trees were alive with the fluttering of the Marchesa's albino blackbirds, whose plumage was dyed whatever color would satisfy their owner's whim on that particular day. Classical statues, gilded with gold leaf, shimmered in the torch light in a dense forest of greenery. One servant's sole responsibility was to offer a continual supply of seed to one of Luisa's white peacocks so that it might stay on its perch, silhouetted on the sill of a window that overlooked the water.

But such feathered ornaments, along with the greyhounds and pair of cheetahs, soon became inadequate for Casati. Considerable additions to her menagerie would become so legendary that author J. B. Priestley described her as "the notorious Marchesa Casati who almost ran a zoo."[18] Now the palace's garden became home to primates of diverse sizes and breeds, multicolored parrots, and exotic felines such as ocelots and tigers. Luisa was not averse to sailing the canals with her pets, as recalled by Prince Alphonse Clary:

> In 1913, [Casati] brought me on a trip in her gondola. She was
> fantastically dressed, with a parrot on her arm, while, on the bow, a
> slave was minding two monkeys. When the gondola passed beneath
> bridges, spectators applauded.[19]

Besides the occasional irritable but isolated tête-à-tête between species, there were miraculously no unwanted escapes or serious harm. An English acquaintance, Mrs. Hwfa Williams, recalled in her memoirs Luisa's special sympathy with her unusual pets: "She was passionately fond of animals, and was one of those rarely gifted women who seem able to do what they like with the fiercest wild beast."[20] At one Casati soirée some revelers stole one of her cheetahs and paraded it about the Piazza San Marco. The stunt incited a reprimand from city officials.[21]

Apparently, the housing of such uncommon creatures had more than picturesque results. Once a large monkey was kept in a gold cage flanked by vases of lilacs in a salon of the palazzo. The floral scent could not dispel the odor emanating from the enclosure, and a repulsed visitor inquired why one would keep such a horrid-smelling animal. The Marchesa passed a lilac stem through the bars to the creature, which proceeded to clutch violently at the flowers, scattering them about in a purple flurry. Turning to her startled guest, Luisa replied, "Now do you see why I have a monkey? Don't you think that is beautiful? Isn't it like something in a Chinese painting?"[22]

Casati soon developed a fondness for snakes. One anecdote possibly reveals the beginning of this reptilian obsession. During a gondola voyage with Fortuny, Casati suggested, "Why don't we buy a serpent, Mariano?" Then, without pause, the Marchesa answered herself: "But in Venice there are none."[23] Casati set about correcting this perceived deficiency. In fact, her affection for her sinuous companions was such that she refused to travel without them and ordered satin-lined boxes from exclusive jewelers so that her pets might conduct their journeys in comfort. Increasingly larger snakes were collected until the Marchesa obtained a massive boa constrictor, named Anaxagarus, which would accompany her on future jaunts about the continent.

Luisa's mania for entertainment resulted in at least three masked balls: a Renaissance party, a Hindu party, and a Persian party (where guests were greeted by braziers, smoking with incense, and naked slaves striking gongs) as well as ten costumed water processions during a period of only six weeks.[24] An accurate chronology of these affairs is nearly impossible to determine. Nevertheless, numerous fascinating reports more than compensate for the lack of a reliable timetable. At a celebration held one summer night, when the heat became too much for her, the Marchesa announced, "I am suffocating!" Before a group of astonished partygoers, she seized a carving knife from a table and slit open the entire front of her dress. Then there was the fête at which she appeared as her girlhood idol, Sarah Bernhardt. Luisa suddenly flung an arm upward in an appropriately histrionic gesture and fell dead on one of the palazzo's black velvet carpets. Novelist Michel Georges-Michel tells what followed:

> She became whiter than her secret powders ever made her. She grew
> rigid. Everyone was frightened. Had she taken some strange drug?

Baron Panatelli, garbed as the Saviour, reassured everyone. He read the will of "Sarah Bernhardt" which desired that everyone should follow her body in a gondola, lighted with tapers, to the little cemetery of Attila, behind the Torcello lagoon.[25]

One of Luisa's lifelong friendships was with ballet and opera scenic designer Oliver Messel, who first met her in Venice:

[Casati] stood on the steps of her palazzo . . . with a leopard on each side of her in the mood of Bakst's *Schéhérazade*. The wild beasts took a good nip at the guests as they arrived, and two attendants dressed as Nubian slaves, dipped in gold, barely survived the exotic reception.[26]

This reminiscence refers to a mishap that has become falsely exaggerated among Casati legends. Variations of an incident in which servants nearly died by this strange method of suffocation were often suggested during the Marchesa's Venetian days, as well as during her subsequent stays on Capri and later in Paris. Although temporary illness was substantiated in a few isolated cases, no one actually died because of the bizarre body gilding.

Another notable, if somewhat dubious, report from this period had the Marchesa make "an entrance into a ballroom in Rome, which would have given Cecil B. DeMille the jealous jitters."[27] With an enormous boa constrictor wound around her several times, she was to have arrived in a chariot led by two leopards, nearly causing a riot among the other guests.

Not unexpectedly, such half-truths ensued from Luisa's extravaganzas. It was said that although many princes from Italy, Austria, Russia, and Persia attended her parties, few princesses would go because Casati's reputation terrified them. The gifted but self-destructive English painter Christopher Wood once offered a reason for Luisa's lack of female associates. The young artist's correspondence with his mother told how the Marchesa made certain that her companions were only animals and men: "She detests women, one never sees any with her."[28] A more likely reason was that Casati did not want to risk losing the absolute attention of her male admirers.

Further rumors soon flew. One concerned a young British nobleman who claimed, at one of Luisa's parties, that a particular unnamed English lady was the most beautiful woman in the world. At a signal from his infuriated hostess, her attendants seized the unfortunate guest, stripped him of his costume, and placed him on the palace's front steps, where he remained until he recanted his statement. Another story told of a handsome and mute Tunisian lord who was supposed to be the pleasure slave of the palazzo's weird mistress.

Society writer Gabriel-Louis Pringué recalled in his memoirs a first meeting with Casati at the Rezzonico Palace and one of her monumental bacchanals:

> The door to the room where we sat chatting suddenly opened. A dead woman entered. Her superb body was modeling a dress of white satin that was wrapped around her like a shroud and dragged behind her. A bouquet of orchids hid her breast. Her hair was red and her complexion livid like alabaster. [Her face was] devoured by two enormous eyes, whose black pupils almost overwhelmed her mouth painted a red so vivid that it seemed like a strip of coagulated blood. In her arms, she carried a baby leopard. . . . I was unable to resist the attraction provoked by this strange woman. She pointed a small diamond studded monocle on the other guests and invited them to a masquerade ball. . . . The party was to be given several days following in her palace on the Grand Canal. . . . At midnight [on the night of the party], she had gondolas driven by gondoliers carrying her livery come to get the two hundred guests to take them to the Piazzetta that the mayor of Venice had authorized her to occupy. . . . There was already an orchestra waiting there. Along the arcades some gigantic black men, dressed only in cloth of scarlet silk, were placed there every ten metres tied to one another by a golden chain which prevented the crowd from gaining access. . . .
>
> With a bouquet of giant white and black flamingo feathers twisted up in her lunar white satin, in a costume with a sash of black velvet, she grasped with one hand a bunch of black irises and held her favorite leopard on a leash with the other. The Marchesa Casati stepped off of her gondola to the acclamations of the crowd. The party was fabulous.[29]

Luisa's use of the Piazza San Marco for her own private ballroom was no inconsequential feat. Aided by both her wealth and her unique persona, she was capable of obtaining permission from Mayor Grimani of Venice, as well as the prefects and chief of police. As shown by Pringué, several Casati events were allotted a platoon of officers in dress uniform to protect the invited and maintain peace among spectators. To sway the government of an entire city must have been the fulfillment of a megalomaniacal dream. But the motivation behind allowing Luisa such exceptional carte blanche may have been of a more political nature. It has been suggested that the Italian government encouraged her parties as venues where secret diplomatic assignations among invited ambassadors and attachés could be conducted unnoticed.[30]

The Grande Ballo Pietro Longhi, an eighteenth-century masquerade held in the Piazza San Marco near the Caffè Florian during September 1913, may have been Luisa's greatest moment in Venice. Two hundred black servants in white wigs, red velvet dress coats, and ropes of pearls held candelabra to light the way to the tables that were scattered on the square. Arriving by gondola, aristocrats from Britain, France, and Italy appeared in baroque fancy dress with crinolines, powdered wigs, and embroidered waistcoats, as well as the traditional costumes of the commedia dell'arte. Many of these outfits had been commissioned from Léon Bakst, who also designed the uniforms for the Marchesa's servants. Fortuny's workshops provided the bolts of specially dyed velvets and silks. In his memoirs, Alex Ceslas Rzewuski recalled the event:

> Cordons of police . . . formed lines of vigilance at the entrances and exits on both parts of the Doges' palace and of the clock. All of the windows that faced onto the square had been rented out at a golden price. There were even spectators on the roofs.[31]

The fête's hostess made a grand entrance from the water, followed by a gondola-borne orchestra lit by countless Chinese lanterns. The Marchesa's appearance on the piazzetta was heralded first by flag bearers, trumpeters, and a trio of falcon handlers. Seemingly dressed as a Tiepolo deity, Casati wore an immense hoop-skirted gown of gold satin with a black lace mantle, its massive train held up by a pair of young footmen adorned with plumes. Her cheetahs, led by ropes of turquoise beads, followed at her heels. When Luisa materialized before the gathered guests and curious crowd thronging the Riva degli Schiavoni, everyone burst into thunderous applause.

Although it might seem impossible because of their frequency and time-consuming preparation, Casati's parties were not all that filled her years in Venice. Most significantly, she continued to patronize a number of portraitists. In 1911, she met the young Florentine artist Umberto Brunelleschi. His gouache portrait, *La belle rencontre*, depicts Casati nude except for blue stockings and shoes, a tall pale blue wig, and a navy blue mask. A blue and gold parrot sits on her shoulder, one of the mechanical songbirds is perched on her outstretched finger, and a gilded serpent is coiled around her right thigh. A pink and lavender greyhound stands beside her, and she is receiving an admiring bow from a Pierrot.

Guiglio de Blaas was another painter who idolized Casati on canvas. This Venetian artist had previously painted portraits of Anita Loos, Consuelo Vanderbilt, and opera star Lucrezia Bori. In 1913, de Blaas completed two oils of the Marchesa in commemoration of her most noteworthy fancy dress. Using the palazzo's garden as a backdrop, the first painting shows her costumed as Bakst's *Arlecchino bianco*. The other presents Luisa in her majestic eighteenth-century gown of gold satin and black lace.

During the next few years, the Marchesa would extend her travels far beyond Venice and her support to a group of new painters, designers, photographers, and composers. A rapacious need for novel experiences and aggrandizement would lead to her involvement with innovators of soon-to-be influential artistic movements. For many of them, Luisa became a Medusa-eyed figurehead, making possible their journey into the revolutionary art world of the twentieth century.

3

Late one evening, in the dimly lit comfort of the Vier Jahreszeiten Hotel in Munich, Polish-born pianist Arthur Rubinstein was visited by an unearthly specter. The young man had been finishing a letter to his family in a public salon, where he believed himself to be alone. Then through the darkness opposite him, a figure arose, later described in his memoirs as having mauve hair, painted eyes, and long, yellow teeth. Although Rubinstein does not reveal what immediately followed this seemingly supernatural manifestation, he would never forget that unsettling countenance, which caused him to actually scream aloud.[32]

Several years later, around 1910, the musician was traveling through Italy struggling to earn a reputation. A few private concert receptions had been arranged for some of Rome's elite by his friend and promoter Count Alexandre Skrzynski, an attaché of the Austrian Embassy at the Vatican. The Polish nobleman invited Rubinstein to meet an intriguing woman and together they drove to a large modern villa on the via Piemonte. A butler escorted them to their hostess. Rubinstein recalled what then occurred:

> From the way Skrzynski had talked about her I was prepared to find a
> blonde or dark beauty endowed with an irresistible charm, but when
> we entered her drawing room I could scarcely suppress an exclamation:
> the lady on a couch was the same ghost who had scared me so terribly
> by emerging from the other side of my desk in the dark writing room
> of the Vier Jahreszeiten hotel in Munich.[33]

The bemused woman had an excellent memory and recognized the musician. "Don't be frightened. I remember your scream in Munich, and I promise not to harm you."[34] The Marchesa Casati captivated Rubinstein: "She had a personality one doesn't forget (I don't mean to be sarcastic) and a remarkable intelligence. . . . That afternoon we became good friends, and we remained so for many years."[35] Luisa arranged a soirée musicale specifically to feature the young pianist, for which he was well paid. Rubinstein was impressed with the quality of the audience Casati had summoned:

> Aside from a scattering of illustrious names, she had gathered the
> real intellectuals, the real music lovers, the ones who are part of a
> concert public. . . . Skrzynski asked me to a lunch at the Grand Hotel
> on the day of my departure and gave me two thousand lire for the
> concert. . . . He also presented me with a lovely silver cigarette case
> with my initials in gold.[36]

Arthur Rubinstein remained grateful to Luisa for allowing him a debut that was considered to be an artistic achievement by all in attendance. Whenever he and Casati happened to be in Rome at the same time in years to come, a luncheon together was essential. Luisa's generosity helped solidify the musician's reputation at the start of what would prove to be a monumental career.

During the pianist's numerous visits, the husband of his patron was conspicuous by his absence. This was hardly unexpected. By 1910, the couple never maintained simultaneous residence in any of their homes. If Luisa was present in the Roman villa, Camillo fled to Cinisello Balsamo or the hunting fields of Gallarate. Although there were reports of a particular party given by the couple at the Palazzo dei Leoni in September 1913, very little evidence exists to suggest that the Marchese visited there with any frequency.

Each September during the Belle Époque, the favorite photographer of European café society would return for a season in Venice. Baron Adolph de Meyer and his inseparable wife, Olga, always took the small Palazzo Balbi-Valier on the Grand Canal. The two were linked not only by their individual homosexuality but by a voracious dependency on cocaine. But none of this detracted from the Baron's indisputable talent with the camera, producing impeccably composed and sensually lit black and white images. The luxurious sheen and underlying eroticism of his photographs led to enlistment by such fashion magazines as *Vogue* and *Harper's Bazaar,* to whom he also contributed articles on the beau monde's tastes and style. De Meyer's reputation expanded so greatly that by the mid-1920s he and Edward Steichen were the highest paid photographers in the world.[37]

It was inevitable that the de Meyers would eventually meet Luisa Casati while vacationing in Venice. With her inventive imagination to guide them, the couple planned several dinner parties. At an especially surrealistic soirée, one of the guests was a life-size male wax figure. A later report contended that in place of a heart, the mannequin contained an urn, which held the ashes of one of the Marchesa's former lovers.[38] This necrophilic rumor is clearly reminiscent of Luisa's inspiration, Cristina Trivulzio. It was a satisfying delight for Casati to know that Trivulzio's macabre aura had been passed on to her.[39]

Luisa was eternally captured by de Meyer's camera in 1912. Among the surviving images is a study of its seated subject, cigarette holder in hand, as she leans toward the photographer over the back of a chair, slyly smiling in her anti-Gioconda fashion. Luisa later presented D'Annunzio with a print of this portrait, on which he inscribed the dedication "Flesh is merely spirit betrothed to Death." The framed picture was kept near his bed, where it would be found after his death.

Another de Meyer image shows Luisa full length, posing near a doorway and wearing one of her lengthy strands of pearls. The final two are close-ups: one is extremely dark and mysterious, the other the single most revealing photograph ever taken of this extraordinary woman. A later critic would make an insightful appraisal of this image:

> The photograph of the fiercely eccentric Marchesa Casati is a direct assault on the viewer, a type of confrontation that was new in de Meyer's portrait work. . . . Casati's gaze in this image is compelling, she stares us down, the eyes dominating her strong face. Her body is enveloped in a dark cloak that gives us no clue as to her sexual identity.[40]

Unlike de Meyer, whose admiration for the Marchesa began in Venice, Alberto Martini already esteemed her when they met again around 1912. Now that he was in the city for an extended stay, it took little time for artist and muse to meet once more—and both shared a desire to deify Luisa. A contract was created by which the artist would become a sort of "court painter" for his new patron. In his autobiographical writings, Martini recalled the day of the agreement's signing:

> I went to the lawyer and drew up a regular contract with deadlines and advance pay and traveling expenditures. . . . The contract was signed by all parties, in duplicate, in the hottest of chambers. The Marchesa came in . . . shining with Byzantine majesty in a costume of gold and pale red . . . she was twinkling with gems and pearls and shining crosses. Her immobile eyes were like enamel.[41]

The weird fruit of this pact would be produced over a period of more than two decades. Luisa was exceptionally pleased with the arrangement, by which her gallery of portraits would be considerably augmented. In addition to numerous minor sketches and representations, one dozen major portraits were completed. Martini depicted Casati in the guise of many extraordinary real-life and fictional characters and types, among them Joan of Arc, an

Amazon on horseback, and La Camargo, the prima ballerina of the eighteenth century. These portraits have been lost, but fortunately others have survived.

Among the extant images is a 1925 pastel of Luisa dressed in the gilded armor and plumed helmet of Cesare Borgia, with her pet boa constrictor curled at her feet. Martini based the dagger she holds on the authentic weapon from Casati's personal collection, which had once belonged to the Renaissance tyrant. Luisa would also embody Medusa in a startling drawing of her disembodied head, soaring against a night sky. In another image, *Portrait de la Marquise Casati dans mon atelier a Paris,* she is wielding a magnifying glass as she browses through a collection of unframed canvases in Martini's Montparnasse studio. Numerous other sketches and unfinished designs by Martini include one of Luisa before the Palazzo dei Leoni with a gondola nearby and a cheetah at her side, as well as a pen-and-ink drawing of her in fancy dress, strumming a banjo.[42] Another shows Casati gliding through the Venetian waterways, sporting an impossibly domed hat beneath which a white oval, pierced by two gaping holes, represents her face. Obviously, the latter chilling detail was of prime importance to Martini, who described the Marchesa's foremost facial features as "giant black eyes, bigger than life, because she made them appear enormous. So much so that they seemed to be a mask. The artificially dilated pupils gave an unreal appearance to her eyes, like those of unsurpassed Egyptian sculptures."[43]

Luisa's unnaturally widened pupils were the result of her habitual use of belladonna eyedrops. Also known as atropine, this tincture is derived from the roots and leaves of the deadly nightshade plant. Even so, tiny brown flacons of it were de rigueur on the dressing tables of many turn-of-the-century women. The clear liquid would not only expand the pupils but make them sparkle as well. Although its hazardous side effects would become well known, they did nothing to diminish its use by Luisa. What was most significant were the drops' effect on her most prized physical attribute, and her daily toilette included this dangerous ritual for almost the remainder of her life.

Alberto Martini's most remarkable portrait of Casati is his 1912 *Un lent réveil après bien des metempsychoses,* a title derived from Verlaine's poem "Kaléidoscope." Also known as *Nocturnal Butterfly,* this immense pastel, over nine feet tall, was subsequently displayed at the Esposizione Internazionale of 1914. It shows Casati standing near the edge of a moonlit Venetian lagoon, her slender figure slowly transforming into that of a butterfly. In fact, her right arm has already changed into a brilliantly patterned insect wing. In his memoirs, Martini recounts the work's creation, which seemed of great interest to his patron's feathered pets:

I had to work on two ladders joined together by a marquee. Parrots
would climb up on top of it with their beaks. A huge bird from
the Grand Canyon flew up to the top of the ladder where I was
balanced. . . . The show must have seemed very entertaining and
acrobatic.[44]

The portrait's theme of metempsychosis—the transmigration of the soul
at death into another human or animal form—is particularly relevant to
Casati for obvious reasons. With her flamboyant imagination and plentiful
fortune, she had obtained the power to become whatever she desired. Such
authority was a rarity, especially among women, of any class at this time.
Certainly by now, the cocoon of the nondescript Luisa Amman had been
utilized and discarded.

Martini's memoirs contain an account of Casati's ever-changing persona
and often incalculable moods:

The Marchesa . . . lived partly as a slave to her dreamworld. She was a
great artist, but not understood by the common people or even her own
friends, who were jealous spectators of her artistic successes. She had two
venues: her palaces and her aristocratic circles. They served as stages where
everyone was usually an actor, but when she made her entrance, they
automatically became spectators or background extras. She scorned banal,
mundane criticisms and the ambiguous praise of her friends. But she was
pleased with herself for the success she always obtained. . . . Her golden
hair, waving like the mane of a lion in the wind, took on a Medusean shape.

"Give me a lion's head," she used to say to me conceitedly during her
poses. She looked at herself in the many mirrors with a focused, severe
glance. "I see myself, I feel as if I am a lion." . . . "You are a metamorphosis," I told her, with my sense of calmness that she considered
disconcerting. "One day you want a Medusa portrait. Today, a lion. Every
other day are you something different? Yesterday is dead; tomorrow is a
mystery. You'll jump out of bed tomorrow morning and in the mirror
you'll see some new revelation. In fact, the other day, you talked to me as if
you were inspired by the Phoenix. I think you want to play with fire."[45]

The relationship between the two was sometimes a turbulent affair. Martini once incurred Casati's wrath when he asked to display his images of her
in France:

Several of my friends, some of whom included the directors of a large
art gallery, wanted to have an exhibition of the portraits I had painted
of her. They tried for a year to obtain them, but in vain. The Marchesa
was not above protesting that my art was not commercial and that she

would never permit her portraits to be used in such a show. In that way, I lost a fortune because curiosity about her was huge at this point.[46]

Luisa's insistence in this situation was an ironic reversal of her earlier fury toward Boldini when he disallowed the reproduction of her 1908 portrait. She castigated Martini: "What is fortune compared to the dignity of art. Nothing!"[47]

A monograph on the work of Alberto Martini contains several allusions to Casati's skills as a poet.[48] It is probable that this claim was culled from Peggy Guggenheim's autobiography, *Out of This Century: Confessions of an Art Addict*, which suggests the same. Whereas Casati may have dabbled in verse on occasion, no examples are extant. Lady Moorea Black, Luisa's granddaughter, doubts such unsupportable literary aspirations: "I find it nearly impossible to believe that she wrote poetry. The Marchesa did not even keep a diary. For her, all art was visual. What mattered was the image."[49]

While still trapped in the confines of his Parisian debtor's prison at the Hôtel Meurice, Gabriele D'Annunzio met the Russian Prince Paul Troubetzkoy. The young man was living in the French capital and continuing an already illustrious artistic career as a sculptor. Such society friends as Boldini, Montesquiou, Leo Tolstoy, and soon D'Annunzio himself commissioned his bronze statuettes and busts. Even Rodin arranged for a sitting. Luisa, too, posed in 1913. The finished piece, one of Troubetzkoy's most noted, shows her standing in a short-sleeved dress, adorned on one shoulder with a large flower, while caressing the muzzle of one of her greyhounds.[50] In addition to the bronze, the sculptor completed a pencil sketch of Casati and an oil portrait.

Held during the months preceding World War I, the Esposizione Internazionale d'Arte della Città di Venezia of 1914 included a pair of works depicting Casati. On a pedestal in the sculpture hall stood Troubetzkoy's bronze, and close by was Martini's masterwork of the half-human butterfly. A request by Guiglio de Blaas to show his pair of Casati portraits was denied, for it was judged that the model was already well represented at the event.

An unknowing observer at the Esposizione might have assumed that the fabulous insect of Martini's portrait had taken wing purely from his own imagination. But the Marchesa's excessive visual attributes, as well as her behavior, were in reality as strange as those of the painting. Thus, it is not difficult to understand why numerous gondoliers passed through her employ before she found one sympathetic enough to endure her grand designs.

Never a contrary word would pass from the lips of Emilio Basaldella about the unusual requirements of his appointment as private boatman to the mistress of the ruined palazzo.

Luisa's desire for outrageousness soon affected the mandatory uniform of the devoted Basaldella. The Marchesa's tastes in her gondoliers' outfits evolved over the years. The eighteenth-century dress coats, vests, and powdered perukes were now reserved only for the most ostentatious parties. For daily use, the boatmen were garbed in the traditional costume of the Venetian oarsman—white shirt, tight knee-length breeches of blue with white stockings, and black leather shoes with gold buckles.

Since Basaldella was an accomplished gondolier, Luisa became concerned when his skills suddenly began to falter, causing her to keep a tight grip on the boat lest she tumble into a canal. She soon learned that the cause of her oarsman's distraction was a young girl, Italia Paoluzzi. From a wealthy family of the Giudecca, Italia's beauty had been apparent since girlhood, but her protective father was not impressed by the status of his daughter's suitor. Taking an interest in the young lovers' well-being and, more important, in securing the continual services of her gondolier, Luisa set out on a crusade to sway the girl's family. What followed was a mountain of letters extolling Basaldella's virtues. Italia's family received a barrage of notes, all written in the Marchesa's flamboyant hand on her Venetian stationery, which was engraved at the top with the winged lion of San Marco.[51] Confronted with these constant pleas for their daughter's happiness, as well as knowledge of Casati's dramatic retelling of the romance to her society friends, the parents recanted. Emilio Basaldella wed Italia Paoluzzi on April 25, 1914. The couple would remain gratefully indebted to the Marchesa for the persuasive battle she so successfully waged on their behalf.

About this time Luisa's gondola was guided to Murano, the Venetian island renowned for its skilled glassblowers. In one of the isle's galleries, the Marchesa became reacquainted with an artist she had once met briefly on an earlier Parisian sojourn. Roberto Montenegro was a young illustrator from Guadalajara, Mexico, whose pen-and-ink drawings most closely recall the decadent work of Aubrey Beardsley and Harry Clarke.[52]

While browsing in one gallery, Montenegro purchased a black vase with handles in the shape of dolphins. Just as it was about to be transported to his gondola, an assistant from the shop made an unexpected proposition. It was explained that another customer, a stylishly dressed woman, was so intent on possessing the object that she offered Montenegro any of the gallery's other items, even one of greater value, in exchange. Intrigued, the artist agreed and then met the persistent purchaser: "She was a tall woman, thin, covered in fur and wearing a hat with a veil of black lace which shaded the part of her mysterious face where her eyes sparkled. With a perfectly outlined smile, she extended her hand to me and asked my name."[53]

The loss of the vase would be more than compensated for when Luisa invited him to dinner the following evening. Before leaving the gallery, the Marchesa presented the artist with her card and inquired into commissioning a portrait. At the appointed hour, Montenegro made certain to adhere to the lady's wishes:

> The following night, as arranged, I took a gondola. It was 8:00 in the evening when I arrived at her palace. There was a great wall with a small entrance way through which the gondola could barely fit and a narrow canal which led to the house between the gardens and trees, where one could see classical statues, gilded and indirectly lit. There were ruined marble railings covered with carved flowers and fruit. The house itself could hardly be seen, through its covering of climbing vines. . . . Within was the great salon; walls, carpets, furniture, decorations, doors, all in gold, a gold of lost brilliance—a pale, aged color. The lady, dressed in a manner rare and eccentric, but elegant, presented me to the guests, the Director of the Academy of Fine Arts, a Russian prince, and other notable men. The supper was splendid, the service excellent, the conversation pleasant. I was overwhelmed with questions about my native country of Mexico. At 2:00 in the morning the party ended, but not before the Marchesa told me when she could pose.[54]

Montenegro completed the portrait of his androgynous-looking subject, who is shown modeling a Persian costume by Poiret on the steps of the Palazzo dei Leoni and holding a split pomegranate in her hand—a fruit closely linked to the Kore myth and a possible symbolic reference to Luisa's D'Annunzian name. A masked footman stands at attention near the Marchesa's feet, offering a bowl brimming with what might be fancifully drawn human hearts. Luisa was enthralled, so much so that she ordered the illustration made into personal Christmas greetings printed on gold paper. This portrait would also become an integral part of a further adventure in Paris.

4

The mountain of traveling bags and trunks that belonged to Luisa Casati, their exteriors upholstered in black velvet and leopardskin, were never idle for long. Their owner's wanderlust demanded them even during her seasons on the Grand Canal. This was hardly surprising since such journeys would allow access not only to varied scenery but also to something just as essential. The Marchesa had an insatiable need for new audiences to astound once the previous ones had been exposed to her theatrical pyrotechnics.

It has been claimed that it was Casati herself who helped popularize St. Moritz as a winter destination for the haut monde. Until the early years of the twentieth century, the Swiss town was known primarily for its beauty during the warmer months. But the Marchesa was entranced by this mountainous locale as it lay beneath blankets of snow, and what better place to survey this than from a suite at either the Montreux Palace or Carlton hotels. Luisa, of course, would improve the decoration of these rooms with her own taste. Brocaded hangings were hung from the walls. Velvet cushions and bear- and tigerskins were strewn about the floor, and tables were laden with a collection of crystal balls and black magic paraphernalia.

During the daytime, Casati and her fellow guests would take to the Alpine slopes. Although not proof of her athletic prowess, a photograph shows Luisa in a fur coat and Cossack hat, wielding a ski pole. After nightfall, the Marchesa was fond of sleigh rides in homage to those enjoyed by one of her childhood idols, "Mad" King Ludwig of Bavaria. She would fly through the powdery drifts, encased in ermine, in a sleigh drawn by a team of white horses.

In St. Moritz Luisa met Prince Adalbert of Prussia, a Royal Marine officer and, more important, a son of the Kaiser. Author Michel Georges-Michel relates what occurred one afternoon when Casati became infuriated because the prince chose to take a carriage ride with a noted beauty, the Marchesa di Rudini, instead of herself.[55] Luisa demanded that racehorses be harnessed to a private carriage and told the coachman to follow the couple. The horrified driver was then ordered to commit the offense of actually passing the prince. When the coachman expressed his concern, the Marchesa screamed, "Pass! I want to make him mad!" During the third pass of the prince's carriage she shouted prophetically, "That young man is very handsome, but he has no taste! He will end up as a traveling salesman!" Very shortly after World War I, Prince Adalbert would indeed earn his living selling automobiles.

From such locales as St. Moritz, Casati found pride in her ability to lure Gabriele D'Annunzio from the arms of his current mistress to her own side. As was her custom, Luisa would send him a summons scrawled in gold ink across a sheet of black parchment, crested by a death's head and a rose. The poet responded to one such command in the early months of 1913 by notifying her of his imminent arrival. The Marchesa mobilized the staff of the Carlton Hotel in preparation for D'Annunzio's whims. She did much to impress on them the high honor they would be receiving by the presence of this genius. Besides an amorous interlude with Casati, the writer achieved another union at the Carlton, which would bring him additional fame. He would meet Giovanni Pastrone, a pioneer of Italian silent cinema, and together they would collaborate on the film epic *Cabiria*.[56]

During the Venetian years, Luisa returned often to the villa in Rome to visit her sister and the Padulli children. Francesca had remained very fond of the Marchesa and took her eccentricities in stride. She gave little credence to any criticism or seemingly impossible gossip she heard about her younger sibling. But Francesca's view of the distant relationship between Luisa and her own daughter is not known. For most of the year, Cristina was still sequestered in her Catholic boarding school in France. Holidays brought the girl little relief under the equally severe eye of her efficient fräulein. Even more difficult was the Marchesa's insistence on attiring the near adolescent in the bonnet and dresses of a much younger girl until about her thirteenth birthday. This was especially painful considering Cristina's inheritance of her mother's height. Presumably, the illusion of a younger child lessened the advancement of Casati's own age.[57]

Although this remote connection between parent and child was not unusual among the elite, both Luisa and Camillo appear to have taken minimum interest in their daughter. This dismissive attitude was exacerbated by the Marchesa's extreme self-centeredness, which also compromised her closeness with her sister. During this time, Francesca contracted a virulent form of meningitis, which left her disfigured.[58] Even though the two visited amicably enough when both were in Rome, Casati ceased inviting her elder sister to any public soirées, where the external image was paramount. It is possible that this cruel decision may have been retribution, even if unconsciously so, for the jealousy Luisa may have experienced from Francesca's beauty many years before.

One such event would surely have been the fancy dress ball held on April 9, 1913, at the British Embassy in Rome, hosted by Sir James Rennell Rodd, the British Ambassador to Italy, and his wife, Evelyn. Many of the almost five hundred guests took part in a series of costumed processions. Casati attended the masquerade on the arm of Prince Liechtenstein, the navel attaché to the Austro-Hungarian Embassy. As the centerpiece of the sixth procession, she was dressed in gold as "a sun-goddess as conceived by Bakst," accompanied by gold-painted attendants and a peacock on a lead.[59]

These displays of outrageous ostentation did little to endear Luisa to either the Casati or the Amman families. She was well aware of her status as a pariah among almost all of her relatives. Begrudgingly, both groups were forced to acknowledge the Marchesa for her title and wealth. More important, neither family wanted to be accused of severing ties with this very public figure. Better to let her accomplish the same by her unpredictable and narcissistic actions. Except for Francesca, no Amman ever visited any of her residences.

With all of the Marchesa's perpetual international sojourns, it would be Paris, the center of European artistic life of the Belle Époque, which would act as the backdrop for her most flamboyant displays. These spectacles would prove to be of even greater extravagance than the surreal parties at the Palazzo dei Leoni or the masquerades on the Piazza San Marco. Many of Casati's public appearances in the French capital became legendary. At one party, even the most exquisite beauties were overshadowed by sheer theatricality: costumed as Lady Macbeth, Luisa was dressed completely in black, with a wax replica of a bloodstained hand at her throat, clutching a dagger. An even grislier scene was arranged around Casati's entrance into her box at the Paris Opéra. Crowning her flaming hair was an entire set of white peacock tail feathers, while blood, applied beforehand by her chauffeur from the freshly slit neck of a chicken, flowed over the pale skin of her right arm. This vision reportedly caused several female observers to faint.

At one performance of the Ballets Russes, Luisa shocked all who saw her, for she was dressed in a gown of egret plumes that, as she moved, molted in clouds of snowy down, leaving its wearer almost naked by the evening's close. Upon leaving a party another night, the artistic bon vivant Sir Francis Rose entered Casati's limousine after mistaking it for his own. He retreated in terror when greeted in the darkness by the gold-painted face of its occupant surrounded by a writhing headdress of stuffed snakes.[60] Casati had taken to wearing such wigs for effect. If her visage was not already unique enough, she now complemented it further with coiffures of green, gold, black, and even tiger stripes. For further adornment she sometimes affixed gilded ram's horns to her temples, as she did at a dinner given by the Baron Maurice de Rothschild.[61] During more subdued moments, Luisa could be seen along the Parisian boulevards attired in a black velvet dress by Madeleine Vionnet, a tigerskin top hat, and black eye patch.[62] She shopped the rue Royale with live marmosets scampering about her shoulders or with a miniature crocodile on a lead, and she once attended the races with her white greyhound, which had been dyed blue for the occasion to match the feathers in her hat.

As these carefully staged exhibitions attest, Casati's tendency toward the outrageous now began to teeter on the absurd. Perhaps this continual need to outdo herself, and any possible feminine rival, was rooted in a growing sense of insecurity. Her title as the undisputed empress of flamboyant tastes along the Grand Canal could be more easily challenged in such a cosmopolitan city as Paris, filled with other affluent and much younger beauties. Still, she had her admirers.

"Medusa or tigress, she smiles as though she would bite."[63] This apt and reportedly affectionate description of Casati by the Comte Robert de Montesquiou illustrated their growing bond. The Marchesa would become one of the few women in Montesquiou's circle to receive the exceptional status of "goddess." Such reverence was earned by the individuality of her personal aesthetic and unique vision, which was an appreciated contrast to the traditional beauty and manner of almost every other woman of the beau monde. This theatrical audacity also protected her from the wit's pernicious tongue and pen. She was even the occasional focus of Montesquiou's poetry.[64] A dabbler in watercolors, he paid additional homage to his friend by painting her in the guise of the Queen of Sheba.[65] Montesquiou and his Peruvian lover, Gabriel de Yturri, would often act as Luisa's *cavalier servants.* Well acquainted with the costly frivolities of Paris, they soon presented Casati with the Comte's list of the most aesthetic—and most expensive— shops. This included the establishment of artisan René Lalique. From him, the Marchesa ordered pendants, belts, and diadems set with sardonyx, moonstone, and topaz, along with emerald pins with which she studded her hair.

The acerbic Comte was on the select guest list when Casati held a dinner party for the deadliest wits in Paris. Boni de Castellane, Jean-Louis Forain, and the artist Boldini also accepted invitations. Although to the world they appeared the best of friends, each was petrified to be the first to leave the table that evening, knowing that he would be immediately dissected by the remaining others. This absurdity finally resolved itself when all four departed en masse.

In the years between 1912 and 1914, Luisa was considered the top patron of the city's premier couturier, Paul Poiret. Only Ida Rubinstein, star of the Ballets Russes, spent a comparable fortune for his fashions. Casati was said to have been the first woman to wear the designer's minaret robe and then his hobble skirt. Poiret dressed Luisa as the personification of her beloved black arts for a particular fête: this outfit of funereal black and intense emerald green was further embellished with black pearls and tassels and was surmounted by a helmet adorned with black plumes, beneath which was a wig dyed a vivid green. Such startlingly macabre costumes earned the Marchesa the sobriquet "la Vénus du Père Lachaise."[66]

Casati's occult interests led her to seek out numerous séances and supernatural soirées. In the company of D'Annunzio, Luisa was a frequent guest of the Baroness Ernesta Stern. The doors of the Baroness's apartments at 68 Faubourg Saint-Honoré were open to every form of psychic, fortune-teller, and medium. At one session, an elderly sorceress predicted a career of considerable success for D'Annunzio. The poet was thrilled at the time but then disappointed when, soon enough, almost the reverse of this promising prediction came to pass. Besides denouncement of his work by both the Vatican and the Archbishop of Paris, D'Annunzio was closely involved with the disastrous 1911 theatrical production of *Le Martyre de Saint Sebastian,* starring Ida Rubinstein as the tortured holy man. D'Annunzio had written the book for a score by Claude Debussy, and Léon Bakst was commissioned as scenic and costume designer. *Saint Sebastian* debuted in Paris, where it ran for only twelve days. After a successful opening night, the remaining performances were attended by pathetically small audiences, which found the work tedious. Both author and composer were angered when critics gave Bakst's designs and Rubinstein's balletic posing the production's only positive accolades.

Luisa had been present at the premiere of *Saint Sebastian.*[67] For some time afterward, she tried to assuage D'Annunzio's humiliation. The writer also took solace in his dogs, kept at a kennel near Meudon. It was rumored that he fed them on prime cuts of meat and old Cognac. Casati often accompanied him there, where she was entertained by the dogs' trained antics. Perhaps D'Annunzio's admiration for these beloved pets came from their loyalty, an attribute he treasured, more so now that he was convinced the rest of the world reviled him. D'Annunzio believed the same allegiance of Coré. As the changeable public and a succession of demanding muses passed through his life, Luisa Casati was a constant—never expecting more from her misguided hero than he was able to give.

5

Another steadfast, although platonic, relationship continued by the Marchesa was with her portraitist Giovanni Boldini. Their previous feud forgotten, Luisa often visited her elderly admirer at his studio in Paris. Boldini was now part of her charmed circle. Even so, there was still the infrequent spat, usually because he refused to appease Casati's egocentric behavior. Then all communication between the two would cease for a while before the painter would relent with a remorseful note. One read with an almost pleading naïveté: "Worry is making me sick. Telegraph me, but don't cut me out. I do not ask for more."[68]

These minor duels resulted mainly from Luisa's incessant demands for another portrait. Besides her verbal needling, Boldini was inundated with stacks of written requests accompanied by photographs of her, costumed elaborately. Then there were the suggestions, intending to inspire him: why not depict her in harem pants, maybe as a fur-clad Russian, or better still as a seductive Salomé or a sinuous Salammbô? A letter once arrived from St. Moritz containing a photograph of Casati in an exotic outfit of Asian influence. Not wanting to become another of her court painters, Boldini was able to mollify the insistent Marchesa by the use of careful diplomacy as exhibited by this response to her Eastern conception: "The oriental costume is splendid; the only criticism I can make is that your heels are too high. As if you were not grand enough! And, besides, an oriental in heels! They never wore those!"[69]

But Boldini finally undertook a second portrait. The new oil was much more fanciful in execution and design than the one of three years earlier. Begun in 1911, the canvas depicts Casati in a manner more closely aligned with her own perception of herself. She is shown in profile, tightly sheathed in a gown of silver, while crouching felinely on a mountain of fur cushions. She wears a black headband adorned with peacock feathers, which blend with additional plumes that are falling on her exposed back. Casati posed for the portrait with her pair of black and white greyhounds, but Boldini, over the next several years, would continue to alter the image until the canines were painted out entirely. In this way, the picture contains no distraction from the opulent siren who catches the viewer in a sideways glance.

Of a deceptively simpler artistry was the popular and satirical pen of French caricaturist Georges Goursat. Known to the reading public of *L'Illustration* magazine by the pseudonym SEM, he took special delight in lampooning upper-crust society with his work. Goursat maintained a close friendship with Boldini, whose 1901 portrait of the illustrator showed him in a striped suit and bow tie while holding a straw boater. Still, Boldini would not escape SEM's prankish pen, and the painter's height and rotundity became the constant brunt of numerous drawings. But this was not all: Boldini's passionate interests in the history and uniforms of Italian soldiery were widely known. Once learning of this, Luisa sent him an elaborately plumed helmet.[70] In his enthusiasm, Boldini naïvely modeled the headpiece before a group of friends, which included Goursat, at Maxim's in Paris. What followed was a hilarious SEM drawing on the back of one of the restaurant's menus, showing the undersized painter almost swallowed up by the helmet and its drooping feathers.

Boldini quickly introduced Casati to Goursat, who would portray her in several caricatures of a less sarcastic nature. The most detailed depicts her waltzing furiously with Boldini. Goursat took comic advantage of his subjects' incompatible physicality. Tall and slender, Luisa is presented in a parody of the pose she took for Boldini's first portrait of her. But unlike the 1908 oil, ropes of pearls swing out behind Casati, reminiscent of the ones that scattered at her first encounter with the artist in Venice. The sketch further exaggerates Boldini's shortness, requiring him to clasp his partner behind the knees to lead her about the dance floor.

During her frequent stays in Paris, Luisa became acquainted with the work of Jacques-Émile Blanche, one of the most popular of all French portraitists. The small, rotund painter was the son of an esteemed physician who ran a private clinic for the treatment of madness and who counted Casati's childhood inspiration the Comtesse de Castiglione among his patients. Blanche's sitters included such celebrated figures of the international arts as Proust, Debussy, James Joyce, and Virginia Woolf. Russian dance stars Nijinsky, Karsavina, and Ida Rubinstein also sought him out to immortalize them on canvas. Although he never finished a portrait of Casati, Blanche's study of her holding a lily was later exhibited in a major retrospective of his work.[71]

The Marchesa met many intriguing figures associated with the Ballets Russes through her continued acquaintance with Diaghilev. One of the most notable was Jean Cocteau, then a young artist and writer. Luisa's out-of-the-ordinary style and inclinations were immediately appealing to Cocteau's avant-garde vision. In a letter to his mother dated March 3, 1913, he declared Casati to be "le beau serpent du Paradis terrestre."[72] The lasting impression Luisa left on the artist would only intensify with their subsequent meetings during the coming years.

Several references imply that Casati actually appeared on stage with the Ballets Russes. Unfortunately, Diaghilev left no corroborative evidence to support this as fact, nor is Luisa's name listed in any of the company's programs. But a 1914 telegram from the Ballets' patron Robert de Montesquiou to Casati at her Roman villa queries, "If Mme Casati would agree to take on immediately the role that was discussed for her, I think I could assure what sincerely seems to be today capable of providing for her during the present London season the opportunity of a sensational presentation—renewable as well."[73]

The mystery is further enhanced by a costume design by Bakst entitled *La Marchesa Casati en costume romantique masculin*. This piece was later displayed at an exhibition bearing the following catalogue description: "Celebrated for her beauty and the extravagances of her costumes, Luisa Amman, the Marchesa Casati, was a friend of Bakst who persuaded Diaghilev to have the Marchesa appear in *Le Dieu Bleu*. He designed to this effect for the production one costume dated 1912."[74] Another clue is supplied by the memoirs of Mrs. Hwfa Williams, which seem to verify Luisa's participation, on at least one occasion, with the Ballets Russes:

> It was known that Diaghilev, the famous impresario, had offered her any amount if she would only go in a ballet. This sounded so very impressive that we all expected a wonderful exhibition from her. What was our amazement to find that she did not dance at all! Diaghilev had wanted her for the sake of her marvelous silhouette.[75]

Williams's remembrance seems more conceivable than the idea that Casati performed with the world-renowned corps de ballet. Except for her keen appreciation for the art form and large collection of programs, Luisa never seemed to have been attracted to dance as a serious performer. There were exceptions, however. The autobiography of the Comtesse d'Orsay mentions Casati's rendition of a Persian ballet during a ball at her villa in Rome, where she danced before scenery designed by Bakst while flanked by a pair of nearly nude men, painted gold, who remained motionless through-out her performance.[76] In August 1912, the Paris edition of the *New York Herald* described how with "un art consommé et un rythme exquis," Luisa performed a similar exotic dance to the music of Moussorgsky at a charity fête at the Palace Hotel in St. Moritz. A few nights later at a dinner and dance at the same hotel her interpretation of a scene from Stravinsky's *L'Oiseau de Feu,* partnered with a G. Izvolsky, occurred; the couple won first prize. Casati was also said to have offered an unusual contribution to an event to benefit a Roman charity during the early years of World War I: her dona-tion was supposedly a dance for which she wore little more than a black velvet rose.

If Lord Berners had been in the audience for this incongruous scene, he would have applauded most vigorously. But then again, this current intimate of Luisa might have neighed or barked just as well. The self-made universe of Gerald Tyrwhitt-Wilson was as tilted as it was titled. Unlike a similarly eccentric family, the fourteenth Lord Berners possessed an equal genius for the arts and elaborate practical jokes. A critically praised land-scape painter and novelist, Berners had also studied music with Stravinsky and Vaughn Williams, becoming one of only two English composers to be directly commissioned by Diaghilev. In addition, he managed to hold the post of honorary attaché to the British embassy in Rome. The Berners home, a Palladian-style manse known as Faringdon House near Oxford, was often the scene of absurd pranks, to the bewilderment of family and friends.

Casati and Berners became sympathetic cronies, as noted in *Memoirs of an Aesthete,* the autobiography of Sir Harold Acton: "The companions of her choice were albino blackbirds, mauve monkeys, a leopard, a boa constric-tor, and, among Englishmen, Lord Berners."[77] It is possible that the two had first met when Berners was in the Italian capital. Along with Casati, he too had attended Sir Rennell Rodd's costume soirée in Rome in 1912, disguised as a horned satyr, complete with tail and gray fur. Berners spent the evening terrorizing the daughters of the Marquis d'Alcedo.[78]

Unlike Berners's madcap antics, the deviltry of Luisa Casati sometimes tended toward the sinister. This was certainly the case for one particular childhood obsession that resurfaced at this time. Luisa had already exhibited a passion for human replicas, as proven by the Venetian dinner she had arranged at which the Baron and Baroness de Meyer's table was honored by the appearance of a life-size male mannequin. Two similarly strange companions would soon join this figure. During this period Luisa came to own a wax model of Mary Vetsera, the pitiable heroine of the Mayerling tragedy so often recounted by Contessa Amman to her daughters. This perfect recreation was purchased from a Viennese erotomaniac, who had had it made specifically to satisfy his fetishistic desires directly following the deadly affair. D'Annunzio's confidant André Germain described his encounter with this uncanny mannequin in his book *Les fous de 1900:* "[Casati] loved surprises. She would open an armoire and within you would see the Baroness Vetsera reproduced perfectly in wax. . . . The poor woman seemed in a strange way to be alive and the prisoner of this somewhat cruel Marchesa."[79] Luisa became so obsessed with the Mayerling incident that she made a pilgrimage to the notorious Austrian site, but was disappointed to discover that the tragedy had been commercialized by the sale of books and postcards, popularizing it in much the same way Verona exploited the legend of Romeo and Juliet.

Even so, Casati herself was not averse to drawing attention to the more ghastly aspects of the murder of the unfortunate Vetsera. Nino d'Aroma relates in *L'amoroso Gabriele* the story of Italian socialite Dora di Rudini's encounter with the bizarre mannequin:

> Dora arrived around eight in the evening and found the house of the Marchesa disturbing, half-immersed in darkness. [Casati] appeared in a black velvet robe, tight and constricting as if dressed for mourning, with large, white, death flowers on her chest. They began conversing in the dining room when Dora realized that, already seated at the table in front of one of the three settings with a bit of a bent face, was a feminine wax mannequin, the size of a human. In all seriousness, the Marchesa introduced the inanimate guest. "Dora, dear, allow me to present to you the young Baroness Mary Vetsera!" Dora, assuming that Casati was joking, went on as if nothing was out of the ordinary. But, when she looked into the face of the waxen mannequin, she saw that on the temple of the immobile Baroness . . . there was a bloody wound and she realized that the face of the statue bore an astounding resemblance to the real version of that tragic imperial lover.
>
> Dora commented: "To me, that spectacle of blood went the wrong way. With the light intentionally scarce, that wax face with the bloody wound clotted on her temple made me crazy. I felt compelled to get up, ready to leave. At the door, I realized that the two butlers who were to serve us were dressed funereally."[80]

A second wax figure was built as an exact mirror image of the Marchesa herself. It was created in the same Neuilly workshops that manufactured the half busts displayed in the windows of the finest coiffeurs and milliners. The mannequin's eyes of green glass matched Casati's, and its carrot-colored wig was fashioned, it was said, from her own hair. Although never verified, Luisa supposedly allowed a full plaster cast to be made of her naked body for the sake of verisimilitude. Not only was this figure given different dresses for each dinner appearance, but both owner and paraffin twin had to be garbed in the same manner. The doll maintained a place at the dinner table and a private boudoir at the Palazzo dei Leoni, where it was on display in a massive crystal case when not amusing its mistress. It could also be called on to execute wickedly humorous pranks. A dinner guest was completely unnerved upon joining Luisa and her double at the table. Since neither Marchesa made the slightest movement throughout the meal, it was impossible to discern the real from the illusory.[81]

Casati often brought her double to Paris for dress fittings. Based on the costume worn by the Marchesa in her portrait by Roberto Montenegro, a matching silver metallic fabric and pearl outfit was designed for the figure by Paul Poiret, prompting D'Annunzio to comment, "One for the wax and one for the flesh, one for the living and one for the dead."[82]

D'Annunzio had been always attuned to Casati's most personal caprices. Provoked by the man-made and finely attired doppelgänger, the poet began making notes in French for a short work to be titled *La figure de cire,* of which only a few fragments survive.[83] The hallucinatory narrative centers around a D'Annunzian male hero who becomes obsessed by his mistress's wax replication. His sensual delirium leads to the woman's murder, whereupon the figure comes to life to take the place of the deceased original:

> I am not afraid—when I strangle Coré, the Wax is there. The
> identities of the corpse and of the Figure are always seated and dressed
> in matching gowns. All of a sudden the Figure gets up. The Wax is
> alive, as if the last breath of the strangled woman passed into the
> frightening copy.[84]

In addition to a plot line reminiscent of Poe's *Ligeia, La figure de cire* offers several moments of suggestive sexual sadism:

> I am in a gondola. I am crossing the canal. I am approaching her
> palace. A fine rain falls in the shimmering violet moonlight. The green
> door of the low tide. The splashing of the water against the stairs.
> I see gold lacework shine in the windows. The striped carpet leads
> down to the water. Something white, lunar.

She is there, with her shining teeth between her hard lips. She has her silver costume with her pearls. The wide silver pants, the neat pearl blouse, the splendid helmet, the white vertical feather.

I open it. I put it down. I find it, kneeling in front of her. I find, in the sumptuous metallic material, that other, somber mouth. She is hot, almost burning. "All for you!" My heart stops. I have nailed it down in a silver coffin. The world is vanishing.[85]

In dealing with this lurid prose, one can make a variety of suppositions about the relationship of its two easily identifiable characters. In addition to *La figure de cire*, on which no commentary exists from either D'Annunzio or Casati, there survives a series of suggestive telegrams sent from a variety of countries throughout their lives. Luisa's missives range from the surreal ("I have a ferocious turtledove") to the elegiacally macabre ("Coré is dead because she wished to approach the gods—her heart has fallen asleep forever").[86] Her confidant might respond by sending an equally mystifying note or a photograph of himself surrounded by his greyhounds. But several of the telegrams refer specifically to Luisa's effigy. Bizarrely sensual in tone, those by the Marchesa are powerfully evocative: "Leave the wax figure in the crystal case and come watch the lagoon through the golden windows" and "The glass worker has given me two great green beautiful eyes like the stars—do you want them?"[87]

These fragments of unfinished fiction and correspondence endure as erotic puzzle pieces in the most supportive and complex alliance of Luisa's entire life. At one point in *La figure de cire*, the narrator tells Casati's fictional counterpart perceptively: "You have the face that allows a woman to hide her soul."[88] Gabriele D'Annunzio was possibly the only man capable of seeing beyond this barrier to true intimacy.

6

Besides their feeling for the bizarre, Casati and D'Annunzio shared a passion for lavish surroundings. Just as he would do while in Paris, Luisa resided in the city's most prestigious hotels—but only once her suites had been transformed to meet her strange aesthetics. Sofas and chairs were draped in leopard- and tigerskins. A boutique's worth of jade, gold, and alabaster bibelots cluttered tabletops. There was even a gilt cage containing a tiny mechanical bird, which when wound up would chirp and flap its gem-studded wings. Both the Hôtel du Rhin and the Princess Hôtel had endured her visits, but the Ritz was the Marchesa's main choice of address during extended stays in Paris. Since her first visit in 1908, Casati's eccentricities had become so infamous that they earned her the dubious distinction of being called "the Medusa of the Grand Hotels."[89]

The staff of the Ritz, as guided by its indefatigable maître d'hôtel, Olivier Dabescat, was adept at satisfying the fancies of even the most daunting guests. During earlier visits, Luisa had descended on the hotel with a few traveling trunks and a pair of greyhounds. Now, she made her entrance with a tower of luggage and pets with more individual dietary needs. Dabescat would personally provide live rabbits and fresh meat for Casati's boa constrictor and cheetahs whenever they joined her, and their mistress often demanded breakfast during afternoon tea. If these or other requests were not met with expedient proficiency, the staff would be the recipients of the Marchesa's fury. Her unpredictable behavior ranged from wandering the hotel's corridors at all hours of the night to flinging priceless jewels from an upper-story window during one of her tirades, which the exasperated concierge had to recover from the sidewalks of the place Vendôme.[90] One evening the serene atmosphere of the hotel was shattered by the screams of a guest who had discovered Luisa's snake in his bathtub. The serpent was captured and dutifully returned to its doting owner.

D'Annunzio called frequently on his Coré at the Ritz. Through him Casati was introduced to Catherine Barjansky, wife of the celebrated Russian cellist Alexandre Barjansky and a noted sculptress in her own right. The young artist's forte was exquisitely rendered but vaguely bizarre wax figures, which prompted an immediate commission. In her autobiography, *Portraits with Backgrounds*, Barjansky describes the Marchesa at their first meeting:

> I saw a woman who was more a work of art than a human being . . . she wore long Persian trousers of heavy gold brocade, fastened tightly around her slim ankles and held by diamond bangles of fine workmanship. Her feet were encased in gold sandals with high diamond heels. Her deep décolleté ended where her gold-draped sash began, her beautifully chiseled breasts were veiled with valuable laces. On her shoulders was a short cape of powder-blue velvet with chinchilla on the collar and on the short, flowing sleeves. Huge pearls were in her ears. An immensely large black pearl on one hand, an equally large white one on the other. A string of pearls encircled her slender neck several times. Her fingers played nervously with the long hair of a jet-black Russian borzoi, lying at her feet, while a white one was stretched out by the fire. She smoked cigarettes out of a long black mouthpiece studded with diamonds.
>
> She was an apparition out of the *Thousand and One Nights*, but, curiously enough, she did not look unnatural. The fantastic garb really

suited her. She was so different from other women that ordinary clothes were impossible for her.[91]

Several sittings were necessary for the completion of the Marchesa's miniature replica. The suite's once elegant salon soon resembled a haphazard atelier, the rugs littered with discarded clumps of wax and wire. Luisa studied the artist's painstaking technique as the doll took on her unmistakable countenance and sinuous shape. It was then that she decided her diminutive double should be as opulent as the original. So, at times assisted by D'Annunzio, Casati scoured the Parisian boulevards in her Rolls-Royce for boutiques carrying antique lace and genuine jewels to adorn the icon.[92] Barjansky wrote astutely of Luisa's childlike but obsessive interest in the entire process:

> [The doll] was a new toy, a purpose in life for a few weeks. She wanted me continually with her. It was her habit to occupy herself entirely with people until she had drawn from them all that was unusual and interesting and then to drop them entirely. When in later meetings with her in other countries I asked about the friends whom I had seen with her, she would dismiss them with a shrug. Their day was over. But she had great charm, much imagination, and regarded the world in an amusing and original manner. It was never dull where she was.[93]

In her autobiography, the sculptress also relates an incident that illustrates how Luisa's perennial search for artistic representation could, on occasion, become troublesome. It seems that a popular but unnamed portraitist of the time hoped to advance his reputation by having the Marchesa sit for him. If this was not possible, he ventured to say that the lady might simply purchase one of his canvases instead. Although Casati did visit the artist's studio to see his work, he could not sell her a single painting. Infuriated, the painter planned revenge. Shortly afterward, there was displayed in the window of one of Paris's most prominent galleries a large oil of a nude woman with writhing scarlet tresses, posed with two Russian wolfhounds—one black, the other white—and a mechanical bird within a gilded cage. Perceptive viewers recognized the Marchesa at once. There appeared to be only one method of stopping the spectacle. Much to her annoyance, Luisa was forced to purchase the canvas for an exorbitant amount.

Barjansky's wax figure was soon finished, to the delight of its inspiration. With insight, the artist said of the Marchesa: "She had an artistic temperament, but being unable to express herself in any branch of art, she made an art of herself. Because she possessed no inner life nor any power of concentration, she sought wild ideas in her external life."[94] Although possibly true of Casati, Barjansky would have to admit that another fellow artist in their circle had achieved a distinctive manner in both the personal and professional aspects of his life.

Born Hans Henning von Voigt, the artist answered only to the single appellation of Alastair. Poe's baroque tales, the erotically dark poetry of Swinburne and Baudelaire, and the sensuous illustrations of Beardsley stimulated his talent with pen and ink. Alastair would never achieve Beardsley's enormous fame, possibly because of a style much more imbued with the sexually grotesque. As he defined his individual artistic style, Alastair adopted a physical persona evocative of the commedia dell'arte. With costumes of billowing satin, black skullcaps, and ivory makeup, the artist came to resemble a diabolical Pierrot.

When the outré pair met during the early months of 1914, Alastair received a revelation that would last his entire life. He believed Luisa to be the living embodiment of the gallery of fantastic women he had created on paper. From that moment onward, Casati's unmistakable likeness prowled through Alastair's imaginings until his death in 1969. She can be recognized in his character designs for Ashtaroth in *The Sphinx* and Herodias from *Salomé,* both by Oscar Wilde, as well as Swinburne's Messalina from *The Masque of Queen Bershabe.* Luisa was elated with Alastair's near-religious devotion to her image. In thanks, she held exhibitions of his work in her homes in Rome and Venice. Philippe Jullian's later assessment of Alastair's work would probably have pleased both the German artist and his muse: "His drawings—more cruel than Beardsley's—could illustrate a fashion magazine in Hell, with the Marquis de Sade as editor-in-chief and La Casati as its only model."[95]

Luisa's fascination with wax replicas led her to the Berlin studio of German artist Lotte Pritzel. One art journalist described Pritzel's Kultur dolls as "delicate orchids in human form, outgrowths of a neurotic mind."[96] Standing about a foot and a half tall, these figures modeled in colored wax were adorned with rich fabrics and jewels. More baroque and overtly erotic than Barjansky's dolls, the pseudo-religious poses of Pritzel's creations gave them an added aura of blasphemy. The resultant commission produced a strange wax Madonna of Casati, crowned and semi-nude, offering up a crystal orb beneath a reverential gaze.

After more excursions between France and Italy, Casati returned to her suite at the Ritz in the summer of 1914. The foremost topic of conversation in the French capital was the recent assassination of Austrian archduke Francis Ferdinand and his wife, Sophie, in Sarajevo. Luisa's closest associates confirmed the widespread speculation that war was imminent. D'Annunzio attempted to convince her that there was no need to worry, although in truth he was anticipating a full-scale battle. His fears soon proved to be correct. By the end of July, Austria declared war on Serbia; Russia and Germany soon entered the fray. Then in rapid succession almost all of the world's major powers went to war. Italy maintained its neutrality.

Unaffected by the international unrest surrounding her, Luisa rang for breakfast during the late afternoon of August 4, 1914, but neither waiter nor concierge answered her call. The hallways seemed deserted, and even the elevator was not running. Infuriated, she ran down to the main lounge to discover that the Ritz was filled with soldiers in full uniform. The Belle Époque had just expired—and it had done so without her permission.

Luisa's fellow guest Catherine Barjansky witnessed the pathetic event: "I found the Marquise Casati screaming hysterically. . . . Her red hair was wild. In her Bakst–Poiret dress she suddenly looked like an evil and help-less fury, as useless and lost in this new life as the little lady in wax. War had touched the roots of life. Art was no longer necessary."[97]

The Basilisk's Stare
1914-1919

If you asked me what I came into this world to do, I will tell you: I came to live out loud.
　—*Emile Zola*

In art, only the bizarre is beautiful.
　—*Charles Baudelaire*

Many of the seemingly unconquerable beauties that reigned until the beginning of the war never again regained their previous places of honor. Such commanding women as Rita Lydig, Liane de Pougy, and Cléo de Mérode faded like wilting lilies or were ruined outright without funds and adulation to support them. Similarly, the shimmering Salomés painted by Gustave Moreau and praised in the writings of Jean Lorrain and Robert de Montesquiou had lost their seductive appeal for a public whose thoughts now were concerned with survival. For people in the arts, those without the ability to adapt would be condemned to the past. While Boldini retired to the beaches of Nice, SEM became a war correspondent at the front lines and Poiret joined the French army.

But Luisa Casati was determined never to succumb to a fate involving either hardship or anonymity. She relied on her transformative skills to reinvent herself once again. In doing so, she aligned herself with artists who mourned little for the Belle Époque's world of symbolism and snobbery.

As one of the earliest avant-garde art movements of the twentieth century, fauvism would be the touchstone for the boldness of the expressionists and a catalyst for the development of abstract art. It had evolved several years earlier in opposition to the highly prettified output of the salon painters and the soft ethereality of the impressionists. The fauvists took the concepts of such postimpressionists as van Gogh, Gauguin, and Cézanne to even further extremes of color and form. Vivid greens, blues, crimsons, and yellows were slashed across their canvases to create images defined by a vivacious spontaneity.[1]

One important member of the fauvist group was a thin and bearded Dutchman named Kees van Dongen. The female form, either nude or fully clothed, was the artist's preferred subject matter. Taking endlessly varied poses, van Dongen's women exude an undeniable eroticism. Their creator once stated, "I exteriorize my desires by expressing them in pictures. I love anything that glitters, precious stones that sparkle, fabrics that shimmer, beautiful women who arouse carnal desire."[2]

Fauvism as a unified movement had already disappeared by 1914, but some of its individual artists, such as Henri Matisse and Raoul Dufy, had developed major reputations and lucrative careers. The same was true of van Dongen, who held successful exhibitions in Paris and abroad. When World War I began, van Dongen's wife and child were unexpectedly trapped in Holland. Not long afterward, the artist met Luisa Casati. Attracted by the intriguing nature of his work and growing fame, she had sought him out for a portrait. The first documented reference to Casati by van Dongen appears in a letter written in 1914 to critic Félix Fénéon: "I know La Casati.

Her type is immediately agreeable to me and I would be very happy to paint her portrait."[3] Casati's commission would result in not one but seven, and possibly more, portraits.

Le Sloughy Bleu and La Vasque fleurie are two full-length oils painted between 1914 and 1917 and characterized by van Dongen's vibrant color schemes. In them, the Marchesa is reflected in large mirrors. Her nude figure is pale, elegantly tall, and graced by elongated limbs. Casati's greyhounds are included as well. But within van Dongen's animistic universe, the dogs, their mistress, and even their surroundings are infused with sensuality. Another portrait renders Luisa in profile, her bright white face, neck, and shoulders in direct contrast to her dark coiffure and the painting's vivid blue background. Executed sometime between 1915 and 1920, van Dongen's Femme en blanc depicts Casati, in another full-length pose, in a long white gown and elaborately buckled shoes before an expanse of black, white, and yellow. L'Amazone, from the same period, shows Luisa in full riding habit astride a rearing horse. A further canvas presents her standing beside a nighttime lagoon as a gondolier rows by, the background lit by both the Marchesa's fiery coiffure and the distant lights of Venice.

Simply titled Luisa, van Dongen's seventh portrait of Casati was painted in 1921 and is the most impressive of the series. The subject is nude from the waist up against a Venetian backdrop, tinted a pinkish-orange; a gondola floats before a skyline that features the domes of the San Marco cathedral and the Campanile. The Marchesa dwarfs these landmarks by commanding the painting's foreground. Her skin is a luminescent green beneath a helmet of russet hair. One critic noted, "Van Dongen reverses reality. The water of St. Mark's Basin is pink. Luisa, naked, is green. The woman/landscape."[4] The reason for van Dongen's choice of a Venetian scene in which to portray his model was more than just an homage to her reputation as that city's most infamous resident—it was also out of gratitude. In spring of 1921, Luisa shared the sanctuary of the Palazzo dei Leoni with him following an artistic scandal. Back in Paris, the painter was at the center of a storm of savage press when he exhibited his portrait of the revered writer Anatole France at the Salon de la Nationale des Beaux Arts, depicting the then seventy-seven-year-old grand man of French letters as realistically aged. One critic even sarcastically compared the likeness to that of a Camembert cheese. Van Dongen stayed in Venice with Luisa for the remainder of the summer, returning to Paris only to become entangled in another uproar over his portrait of actress Maria Ricotti.

Although not documented by the artist as such, at least two other un-dated works by van Dongen may depict Casati as well. Their subjects' resemblance to her is more than reminiscent of the artist's previous renderings of this easily recognizable model. One simple pencil sketch shows a woman enveloped in a fur coat and Cossack-style hat, strolling before a Parisian jewelry shop. The second image is a horizontal oil of a reclining woman, in turban and jewels, whose greenish skin tone almost matches that of the 1921 Venetian portrait.

Luisa's charms evidently stimulated more than the artist's painterly talents. The two became lovers for a brief but passionate period during which van Dongen referred to her as his "naked sorceress." He informed his dealer that he did not want to sell any of the Casati portraits. In *The Fauvist Painters,* author Georges Duthuit gives a particularly unsavory summation of the relationship between the artist and his model:

> It will never be known in what doorway, behind what scenes, Van Dongen encountered that woman, the Marquise C., who was to mark his work and life with her ruby claw, cash down. All that remains is the dazzlement of that apparition, compounded of face powder and sulphur. . . . Van Dongen was in a position to be impressed by her. . . . Shod in caviar, bathed in floods of champagne, her hair sleek with the sweat of the poor, this ghoul . . . attained without knowing it a nauseous allegorical grandeur.[5]

It was through the Marchesa's associations that the Dutchman would be introduced to French and Italian society. No secret was made of their affair as evidenced by van Dongen's inclusion of four of Luisa's portraits at an exhibition of his work in Paris at the Galerie d'Antin during March 1917—*L'Amazone*, which served as the cover illustration to the exhibition catalogue; the pair of full-length nudes; and a still untraceable canvas, *Chez la marquise Casati.*

Although van Dongen had an irreverent spirit before his affair with Luisa, the more extravagant aspects of his personality were enhanced even further by it, particularly his fascination with costume parties. Van Dongen hosted several *bal masques,* where his fancy dress included a devil and an Arab. But his choice costume was as the Roman deity Neptune, a disguise in which he appears in two self-portraits. Van Dongen would also become a frequent guest at Casati's Parisian fêtes.

Luisa had reached her midthirties during her artistic and romantic association with van Dongen. By this time, she had already earned a reputation as a seductive femme fatale, no doubt inspired mainly by her appearance, disposable wealth, and proclivities for the occult. Untrue but fabulously weird rumors circulated about her as a result. She relished the legends of the many doomed suitors who, after being denied her charms, committed suicide. Casting her as a high-society Circe, rumor revealed that the various additions to Casati's menagerie were in fact previous admirers transformed into beasts. The Marchesa's animals added to her carnal image by proving her powers as a dominant female whose very caress could calm the most savage creature. The erotic seminudity and constant attendance demanded of her muscular black servants likewise fueled gossip that they were her lovers. Luisa was known, however, to frequently persuade her gondoliers to divulge the amatory peccadilloes of her aristocratic British friends.[6]

Although documented through intimation only, Casati's sexual life may have been unconventional but it was certainly not inordinately scandalous. No plethora of deceased paramours existed, nor were Romanesque orgies conducted at her Venetian palazzo. Unlike the openly promiscuous *grandes horizontales* of the now faded Belle Époque, Luisa made her conquests through the art gallery rather than the boudoir. Regarding this contradictory aspect of her grandmother's life, Lady Moorea Black surmised that "sex was not the object of her affairs and relationships . . . in them, I believe, she sought admiration more than any other fulfillment."[7]

Luisa, however, could be a sexual provocateur. Exploiting a strange visage and androgynous figure, she had already become notorious for using nudity as a way of taking attention away from even the most beautiful women. This calculated exhibitionism went as far as adopting specific fashion accessories popular among the elite lesbian community of the day. For example, Luisa would wear a gold bracelet about the left arm just above the elbow and one around the right ankle. She used this bit of stimulative theater for a brief time, and Martini was ordered to include it in the butterfly portrait of 1912. But unlike such active lesbians as Ida Rubinstein or the Princesse de Polignac, there is intriguing evidence to suggest that Casati may have shared their inclinations at least once in a notable episode several years later.

Although Luisa seems oddly asexual—more obsessed with outward appearances than inward desires—there were those moments when her sexuality seemed taken to extremes. This was notably the case for the physical aspects of her liaison with Gabriele D'Annunzio, which, at times, bordered on the sadistic. In fact, the poet frequently called his mistress "the Divine Marquise" in reference to the infamous Marquis de Sade. In his biography of D'Annunzio, Philippe Jullian claims that this "homage to de Sade" was an enticing allusion to the couple's unusual sexual practices and is not unfounded.[8] The following suggestive fragment appears in D'Annunzio's diaries: "The evening at Saint-Germain-en-Laye, the stinging kiss on the neck, the mad return to the hotel, the red mark which she shows."[9] On numerous occasions, especially once after the couple's passion had been consummated in a gondola, Luisa was proud of displaying the resultant bruises of their lovemaking. One observer at a party noted that the Marchesa, in place of flowers or jewels, wore the black-and-blue marks of her lover's teeth on her neck. She attended another soirée with undeniably swollen lips. It was later discovered that they had been bitten so fiercely by D'Annunzio that they had bled. It is unlikely that Casati committed such excessive acts with van Dongen or her other lovers.

Luisa had learned well over the years how to maintain her own independence with such a demanding lover as D'Annunzio. Philippe Jullian aptly explained:

> La Casati was too independent to live in the wake of D'Annunzio, as
> so many others did, and to disappear into obscurity, madness, or even
> the convent; she always met D'Annunzio as equal to equal, always
> knew how to amaze him, and how to vanish before he could become
> accustomed to her follies.[10]

The romance between the poet and his muse would eventually become one of an *amitié amoureuse*. But although each became involved with a variety of lovers, they remained faithful to each other as unconditional friends. D'Annunzio's relationship with Casati was the longest and most emotionally intense he shared with any woman. Regardless of her wildest eccentricities, the writer never wavered in defending her against vicious gossip. In his own words, Luisa would remain forever as "pureness personified."

2

The fauves had expressed themselves by transforming the ideas of previous art movements into their own vision of colorful savagery. But a new, more blatantly reactionary group of artists refused to recognize the past in any way except for its total obliteration. Only through such a complete destruction of earlier notions could a foundation be laid for a fresh way of perceiving the world. They believed it was time to replace the defunct gods of obsolete modes of thought with ones more appropriate to the volatile times in which they lived. Naming themselves the futurists, they officially heralded their revolution with Filippo Marinetti's first "Manifesto del futurismo" published in *Le Figaro* on February 20, 1909. These guidelines included the deification of power, speed, and machinery, and, most controversial of all, the praise of war and ruination of feminism.

Although originally conceived as a literary movement, futurism rapidly expanded to include painting, sculpture, dance, photography, fashion, film, and even cooking. Three-dimensional works were constructed of such previously unorthodox materials as plastic, rubber, and cardboard, which clearly represented recent technologies. But regardless of the medium, the futurists'

Conte Alberto Amman, from a portrait by Felice Zennaro

Contessa Lucia Amman, from a portrait by Felice Zennaro

*Luisa Amman, ca. 1886.
Courtesy of Conte Edoardo
Amman.*

Luisa Casati and daughter Cristina, ca. 1902. Courtesy of Conte Edoardo Amman.

Casati at a foxhunt, ca. 1903. Courtesy of Conte Edoardo Amman.

Camillo Casati on horseback, ca. 1910

Gabriele D'Annunzio, ca. 1910

The Marchesa Luisa Casati,
by Adolph de Meyer, 1912

Palazzo dei Leoni, Venice, 1912

Casati with one of her pet cheetahs, Venice, ca. 1912

Un lent réveil après bien des metempsychoses,
by Alberto Martini, 1912

Casati (center) in Bakst's Arlecchino bianco *costume at one of her legendary
masquerades, Venice, 1913*

Portrait of Casati in eighteenth-century fancy dress by Guiglio de Blaas, 1913

Casati, ca. 1913

Pen and ink portrait of Casati by Roberto Montenegro, 1914

La marchesa Casati con gli occhi di mica e il cuore di legno, *by Giacomo Balla, 1915*

goal was to make a myth of the modern. The canvases of founding members Carlo Carrà, Giacomo Balla, Umberto Boccioni, and Fortunato Depero illustrated this concept by exalting any man-made item or human physical element evocative of motion. Dynamically fragmented images of spinning wheels, speeding automobiles, planes, and trains were intended to provoke a sense of velocity and vitality from the spectator.

But even within the most avant-garde artistic communities there were those who were wary of beliefs that ennobled "militarism, beautiful ideas worth dying for, and scorn for women." Caroline Tisdall addressed the latter in a study of the movement: "It was fundamentally an attack on the sentimental and romantic treatment of love and women as epitomized by the adulterous heroines of D'Annunzio."[11] So it would be with some irony that the futurists would eventually acclaim Luisa Casati, the embodiment of the D'Annunzian woman, as their most potent muse.

The Marchesa was already well acquainted with Filippo Marinetti by the time he published his manifesto in 1909. Her continually evolving persona fascinated him. Their friendship was proven graphically when Carlo Carrà painted a portrait of the movement's outspoken founder in 1911. Fractured by slashes of scarlet and black, the futurist leader is shown working at his desk. Marinetti himself later attached an actual handwritten note onto the painted desktop, which read, "I dedicate my portrait painted by Carrà to the great futurist Marchesa Casati with the languid eyes of a jaguar that has just swallowed the iron bars of its cage."[12]

Luisa soon cultivated relationships as friend and patroness to other members of the movement. According to Marinetti, her collection of futurist works included "three plastic sculptures by Boccioni competing with some of Russolo's violet dynamisms and some yellow cyclones by Balla."[13] Another was a full-length portrait of herself wrapped in fur, attributed to Boccioni. More certain are several pieces noted in a catalogue of Boccioni's complete work, which assign them to the "collezione della marchesa Casati."[14] Sculptor Aleksandr Archipenko also later confirmed that Casati had purchased one of his works at the Biennale di Venezia of 1920.

Before joining the futurist group in 1910 as one of its earliest members, Giacomo Balla had already achieved a well-grounded career in the arts. He was the first of his group to render the image of Luisa Casati in accordance with futurist ideals. *La marchesa Casati con levriere e pappagallo* was the first of three portraits completed by the artist; the pen-and-ink drawing depicts its subject's singular eyes, peering out from a kaleidoscopic tangle of swirling forms and black triangles, accompanied by her pet parrot and white greyhound. The second work, a full-color oil titled *Fluidita di forze rigide della marchesa Casati,* shows Luisa lost among a dynamic series of geometric shapes. But Balla's three-dimensional portrait garnered the most acclaim. Named *La marchesa Casati con gli occhi di mica e il cuore di legno,* the 1915 bust was fashioned from painted wood and cardboard. Below copper shapes representing hair was a large pair of eyes formed from sheets of mica. Luisa's smiling lips were represented by red swirls that stood out from her white face, and a scarlet wooden heart dominated the lower-left portion of the artwork.

Faithful to the futurist manifesto, Balla designed the piece to move. The spectator, by turning the figure's heart, could make its eyes pivot and appear to blink, as described by a report from its first exhibition:

> The public did not miss laughing uproariously in front of the work. Moreover, the visitors of this futurist exhibition enjoyed themselves enormously in pulling the elements which worked the eyes of the Marchesa, thereby changing her expression.[15]

The work was subsequently featured on the cover of the March 30, 1919, issue of the Italian periodical *il Mondo* in conjunction with the Esposizione Futurista in Milan. The Casati bust would later become a part of Marinetti's personal art collection. Luisa was so impressed with Balla's artistry that she commissioned him to design the costumes and décor for one of her extravaganzas.

Originally from Trentino, Fortunato Depero developed his artistic skills while an apprentice decorator for the Esposizione Internazionale in Venice. After meeting Marinetti in Rome in 1913, Depero abandoned an outmoded symbolist style for that of the futurists. The artist soon began to apply futurist ideals to theatrical commissions, including those for the Ballets Russes. In 1917, another commission brought him to the island of Capri, where he met the Swiss poet Gilbert Clavel.

Depero's friendship with Clavel led to the creation of a series of theatrical presentations financed by the poet. But the imaginative sets and music for their *Balli plastici* were not intended for human actors—instead, Depero devised a troupe of strikingly original marionettes. He described the resultant abstract effect as "perspectives of constructed landscapes. Mechanized flora and fantastic architecture having a metallic crystal style. Plastic and mobile wooden characters painted very bright colors."[16]

Depero's *Balli plastici* debuted on April 15, 1918, at the Teatro dei Piccoli in the Palazzo Odescalchi in Rome for a run of eighteen performances. Under the direction of Vittorio Podrecca, and with musical supervision by Alfredo Casella, the puppeteers of the Gorno dell'Acqua company controlled the tiny "actors." Among the brief vignettes presented during each performance were *L'orso azzurro,* set to music by "Chemenov," a pseudonym for Béla

Bartók, and *L'uomo dai baffi*, with music composed by Casati's friend Lord Berners.

Luisa's infamous expanding menagerie may possibly have inspired another of the *Balli plastici*, called *Il giardino zoologico*. This particular piece, with a book by Francesco Cangiullo, utilized music by Maurice Ravel and featured marionettes enumerated by Depero as "green monkeys, blue bears, metallic snakes, and flying hinged butterflies."[17] Presented especially for the attending Diaghilev, the darkly humorous scenario involves the escape of ferocious animals at a Parisian zoo during a newlywed couple's visit and the horrific pandemonium that follows.

In his autobiography, *L'alcova d'acciaio*, Marinetti recounts the events at Casati's villino on the via Piemonte preceding the premiere of the *Balli plastici*:

The door opens: a handsome black servant dressed in a most elegant tuxedo. In the atrium, it smells like a church. Maybe incense? No. Aquatic plants. There's a wild, sharp, sweet perfume that accentuates the bodily whiteness of a mutilated statue in the shadows. I'm in the library with lots of old gold. . . .

Enter Swift. Like a hot flash of lightning, the white greyhound quickly sits down, curled up deep in a white armchair. . . . Swift seems like the white cord that holds down the imagined sails of this house, the ship of dreams. . . .

A wide musical cadence of perfumes and rumbling announces the beautiful Marchesa. . . .

[She has the] face of a bleached tiger in a clear intrepid moonlit night. . . .

"Do you know my parrot from the equator? His name is Bra-cadabrà."

In the dark corner, a white, yellow, and green arabesque parrot was perched. He screeched:

—Bra-cadabrà, Bra-cadabrà, Bra-cadabrà!

The screams of the parrot tie the colours of his feathers to the red of the Marchesa's hair to the black of her eyes and of her nostrils, to the blood red of her mouth, and the celluloid white, red, and green tie of her friend Balla who enters, singing:

"Bra-cadabrà, Bra-cadabrà!"

Before going out, the Marchesa puts a strange ring on her pinky finger. It balances, suspended on three tiny chains, a microscopic incense holder with a grain of smoking incense.

We go out. Her car is fast.[18]

An exhibition of Depero's work had also been arranged in the foyer of the theater. During their association, the artist completed at least three portraits of Casati—an ink drawing, a charcoal sketch, and a watercolor.[19] Quite conspicuous among the canvases on display that evening were several depicting the event's Swiss producer. During the viewing, Luisa circulated among the attending Roman elite, praising her friend's paintings while swinging the little burning censer from her finger. Lord Berners followed closely in her wake of smoky perfume, miming expressions of overzealous ecstasy before the baffled onlookers.

With her singular personal style and involvement with such provocative artists, it is to be expected that Casati would be cited in the gossip notices flourishing in the periodicals of almost every major city at the time. Eugenio Giovannetti's column, "Satyricon," was one of the most notorious. He once offered the everyday person a rare look into the Marchesa's private world. Highly unlikely at best, his description still provides a taste of the period's sometime sardonic side:

> The Marchesa Casati, an intelligent and refined woman, prides herself on her "avant-gardism." She is, in the eyes of the public at large, the spirit protector of all the cubists and futurists and avant-gardists of all colors and races. . . .
>
> This is what is seen in the piazza. But, whoever actually enters into the house and the parlor of the Marchesa Casati sees something entirely different. Everything is beautiful. Everything is chosen with the finest taste. But, alas, everything refers to a more peaceful past. On the walls, you can see nothing of Balla or of Carrà or of Archipenko. Instead, you can see a portrait, as magnificent as any other, painted by Boldini and other paintings done in a purely classical style. And what happened to all of her boiling avant-gardists?
>
> If the Marchesa were to invite you to lunch, you would have the key to this little mystery. At the end of the lunch, when the usual discourses of the aristocrats begin, there is always someone who asks: "And, Marchesa, what of your futurists? Where have you put them?"
>
> —Do you really want to see them?—the Marchesa would then say, with a little smile
>
> —Come with me!
>
> Guided by the Marchesa, the gay brigade climbs several flights of stairs, passes down some hallways, and stops moving only at the threshold of a small, dimly lit and sinister room that seems like the room in which Bluebeard hid and collected his cadavers.

—Come in—says the Marchesa.—Now I'll shed a bit of light!

The moving brigade steps forward and looks around. Right there are all the horrible rebels of art. All are topsy-turvy, forgotten, and dusty, hanging from the walls like heinous cadavers amidst a strong odor of mildew. One by one, the brigade recognizes them and attacks them with mad laughter. . . . the Marchesa kindly bows her head and smiles in tacit approval.

The moral: The Marchesa Casati is an intelligent and refined woman, but artists must not give too much trust to their aristocratic protectors.[20]

Of course, this scathing report inadvertently reveals Giovannetti's complete prejudice against the avant-garde. More important, it presents a depiction of Luisa unsubstantiated by any other documentation before or after its supposed occurrence, and one at odds with those remembrances of the more reliable Marinetti, among others.

Inspired by the success of the *Balli plastici,* Marinetti believed it necessary to make futurist forays into other media by writing additional manifestos. The "Manifesto della danza futurista" was dedicated to the Marchesa when it was published on July 8, 1917, in the periodical *La Italia Futurista.* Indeed, Marinetti had conceived and written the piece in her villa in Rome, which would also be the setting where Marinetti arranged a private performance of a pair of Balla-designed ballets, *Macchina tipografica* and *Invenzione meccànica,* for Luisa and the visiting Diaghilev. Léonide Massine, one of the star dancers and choreographers of the Ballets Russes, staged a private performance set to Eric Satie's piano compositions, *Gymnopédies,* there as well.[21]

Along with other members of the Ballets Russes, the Marchesa also met Pablo Picasso. The Spanish artist accepted several invitations from the troupe's patron, such as one for a party on April 2, 1917. The fête was held in the white marble hall of the Roman villa. Positioned at the fireplaces that flanked both ends of the massive room, servants in waistcoats and powdered wigs continually tossed handfuls of copper filings onto the flames, transforming them into blazes of vivid green that bathed the hall in an eerie splendor.[22]

Luisa became reacquainted with Isadora Duncan in Rome during the war years. Duncan resided in a room directly next to that of D'Annunzio at the Hotel Regina. One evening, she accompanied him on his almost nightly visits to Casati's villa. With the inclusion of several contradictory embellishments, just what occurred there was told in the danseuse's autobiography, *My Life:*

I went to the palace and walked into the antechamber. It was all done out in Grecian style and I sat there awaiting the arrival of the Marquesa, when I suddenly heard a most violent tirade of the most vulgar language you could possibly imagine directed at me. I looked round and saw a green parrot. I noticed he was not chained. I got up and leaped into the next salon. I was sitting there awaiting the Marquesa, when I suddenly heard a noise—brrrrr—and I saw a white bulldog. *He* wasn't chained, so I leaped into the next salon, which was carpeted with white bear rugs and had bear skins even on the walls. I sat down there and waited for the Marquesa. Suddenly I heard a hissing sound. I looked down and saw a cobra in a cage sitting up on end and hissing at me. I leaped into the next salon, all lined with tiger skins. *There* was a gorilla, showing its teeth. I rushed into the next room, the dining room, and there I found the secretary of the Marquesa. Finally the Marquesa descended for dinner. She was dressed in transparent gold pajamas. I said:

"You love animals, I see."

"Oh, yes, I adore them—especially monkeys," she replied, looking at her secretary.

Strange to say, after this exciting apéritif, the dinner passed off with the utmost formality.[23]

But if the meal itself may have been described as uneventful, what followed was more characteristic of Duncan's hostess: "After dinner we went back into the salon with the orangutan and the Marquesa sent for her fortune-teller. She arrived in a high, pointed hat and witch's cloak, and began to tell our fortunes with the cards."[24] The clairvoyant predicted that Duncan's influence would spread globally, and under the protection of the angels she would lead a charmed life, living to "a great age." Then the fortune-teller turned to D'Annunzio:

You will fly in the air and do terrific deeds. You will fall and be at the gates of death. But you will go through death and go by death and will live to great glory.[25]

As the future would prove, that evening's prophecies played themselves out in an intriguing fashion. Isadora Duncan would achieve immortality, but the prior drowning accident of her children, her ex-husband's subsequent suicide, and her own macabre demise at the age of forty-eight, strangled by a scarf caught in the wheels of a Bugatti, would become as legendary as her artistic triumphs. It would be the seer's words about D'Annunzio that would come to pass with uncanny accuracy.

3

In 1914, the Marchese and Marchesa Casati legally separated. During the war, Camillo distinguished himself by rising to the rank of major in the Italian army under General Luigi Cadorna. British artist Sir Oswald Birley would later paint a portrait of the Marchese in full-dress uniform. At the time of the couple's separation, the decision of selecting a single parent with whom to live was imposed on their thirteen-year-old daughter. Cristina chose her mother, who would continue to keep her in the French boarding school. Ironically, in view of Luisa's overwhelming narcissism, this particular establishment was of the strict Roman Catholic variety, demanding the abhorrence of physical vanity. Even in the privacy of the bath, pupils were required to don shifts to avoid nakedness.[26] Cristina eventually left this rigorous institution for Oxford University, which Casati allowed only with the condition that her daughter reside in a private house under the careful watch of a governess.

During this time, the motion picture had developed into a form of entertainment that would help define the entire twentieth century. An imaginative hypothesis by Philippe Jullian describes the possible connection between the screen siren and Luisa Casati:

> This Art Nouveau sphinx unfolded her black wings to become the vampire of the horror films. . . . This malefic vision of La Casati in sumptuous, disturbing costumes dominated by black velvet, jet embroideries, mantillas, and black gloves with pailletted fingertips blossomed on the screen. . . . With their dead-white faces, their black-encircled eyes, these figures emerged from the Orient Express or Carpathian châteaux or New York townhouses, sowing despair in the wake of their black flower-embroidered trains. Impassive beauties draped in stoles of monkey fur, they fingered their ropes of pearls or the jade earrings that descended to their shoulders. All these were the younger sisters of Casati.[27]

The most notorious vamp of the silent screen was Theda Bara. In 1915, Bara portrayed a character whose appearance and associations with the art world were not unlike Casati's. It is probably more than coincidental that the script for Bara's film, *The Devil's Daughter,* was based on *La Gioconda,* an early stage play by Gabriele D'Annunzio. But unlike the verbose Italian author, the Fox Film Corporation found no difficulty in condensing its convoluted plot to a single line: "An artist's model wreaks vengeance on the male sex for their wrongs, then goes mad."[28]

Such entertainments were only momentary diversions from the realities of the Great War, which continued unabated. With so many nations dangerously unbalanced—a time of turmoil and superhuman causes—the world had finally become D'Annunzian. Much to his disappointment, the writer had to become a bystander as all his efforts to join the fight were denied. Past fifty and lacking any experience in genuine warfare, D'Annunzio visited the Parisian troops, on whom he exercised his increasingly belligerent rhetorical skills. But it took a telegram bearing just two words from Eleonora Duse to rally him to action. The note read, "Change wings." On the morning of May 4, 1915, D'Annunzio's self-exile ended when he again set foot on native soil. As a tireless orator and scribe for the people, he became the country's indomitable voice.

Finally recognizing his power over the troops, the Italian government agreed to D'Annunzio's requests to become part of the action. The writer was not assigned to one particular corps but instead was shrewdly rotated between the navy, infantry, cavalry, and air force to best utilize his galvanizing presence among the men. One French airman recalled the almost surreal image of the dapper D'Annunzio, climbing into an airplane wearing patent leather, high-heeled boots after delivering an address in a mess hall to both soldiers and cooks.

Luisa became linked once more with D'Annunzio in Rome. It was at this time of modern warfare that the intimates turned to centuries-old occult arts. The stroke of midnight on June 20, 1915, found the pair among the ruined tombs on the Appia Antica, attempting to raise the spirits of ancient warriors. Philippe Jullian stated, "It was never known what answers these amateur necromancers received, but one can imagine the diabolical attire that the marchesa must have invented for such a ceremony."[29]

According to author Tommaso Antongini, one of D'Annunzio's closest friends: "[Casati] cultivated the magical sciences with such diligence and passion, as to keep as houseguests—sometimes for months or years—seers and sorcerers, just as the princes of the Renaissance always kept their astrologers and jongleurs at their side."[30] It is not known with what degree of true reverence Casati and D'Annunzio enacted their pagan beliefs; quite possibly they simply enjoyed the atmospheric thrills to be had during such arcane theatrics.

On January 16, 1916, a seaplane in which D'Annunzio was flying was forced to land on a sandbank. During the ensuing commotion, he collided with the machine gun mounted before his seat. Once evacuated to a hospital, it was determined that he had completely lost sight in his right eye, and the left eye was in danger as well.[31] To save it, the doctors ordered a cure that entailed two conditions D'Annunzio abhorred: total darkness and complete immobility. Accepting the incarcerating requirements for his recovery, he departed for Venice. There he stayed at the Casetta Rossa, a small redbrick palazzo on the Grand Canal.[32] Directly across the water lay the glittering ruin of the Palazzo dei Leoni. Reduced to noting his thoughts on slips of paper with a pencil, D'Annunzio completed the haunting *Notturno*.

Described by its creator as a "commentary of shadows," *Notturno* is not so much a linear narrative as a series of vivid memories connected through association. These remembrances range from baroque images of death to the most mundane of daily occurrences. Florid accounts of funeral processions via gondola to San Michele, the Venetian island-cemetery, are offset by passages devoted to recapturing the scents of flowers or the melodies of particular pieces of music. There are simple but touching recollections of past paramours, such as the vision of Duse gathering violets during a soft rainfall in Pisa. Soon D'Annunzio's thoughts inevitably turn to his lover across the lagoon:

> From there on the Canal, the palaces of the beautiful and famous women lay quiet and abandoned. All the windows of the Da Mula Palace are closed, and the decrepit house of Coré has more than ever the appearance of an enchanted ruin. The cypress overlook the great poles on which the carpets of virgin vines hang.
>
> From that stairway, which now is a shadow of velvet, in a full-mooned summer's evening that seems so long ago, a masquerade came out, led by a white Harlequin that always carried a blue parrot on her shoulder and one of those little panthers on a leash . . . a confused clamor comes from Saint Mark's basin. . . . And the masquerade that returns with its cloaks, with its three-pointed hats, with its drums? Are the wigged servants ready to appear at the top of the stairs with their golden lanterns?[33]

D'Annunzio's description of the Palazzo dei Leoni as lying "quiet and abandoned" was not simply for picturesque effect. The Great War had unmoored its mistress from a seemingly endless routine of Venetian spectacles. Moreover, in war-torn Europe, it was becoming increasingly difficult to gather enough of the elite to be dazzled at such events. Instead, Luisa chose to drift among her favorite cities. Parisian stays at the Ritz and the Hôtel du Rhin supplemented her visits to Venice and Rome. On occasion, the Marchesa's impulsive travels took her far beyond the continent. More than one report described her appearance at a performance by prima ballerina Anna Pavlova in Lima, Peru, outfitted in leopardskin and a helmet adorned with black ostrich plumes.[34]

Luisa's obsessive journeying was curtailed for a while when her right arm was broken after a fall at the Roman villa. What followed was a bothersome convalescence in the Italian capital. As an antidote to her ennui, the Marchesa discovered a new way of keeping in contact with D'Annunzio, who was still undergoing his own recovery in Venice. Visiting friends were required to pen Luisa's messages to the poet on her personal calling cards, which would then be sent northward. This idea accomplished the dual purpose of providing Casati with well-wishers to quell her loneliness and an able hand to complete her correspondence.

Although the poet appreciated these affectionate tokens, they could not alleviate the tragedy of his mother's recent death and the miseries of his own injuries. After further recuperation, D'Annunzio's patriotic spirit flourished and he traveled throughout Italy delivering speeches to rally the people. By September 1919, the battles of World War I were over. Even so, D'Annunzio was not satisfied with what he perceived as the government's refusal to aid the populations of its annexed lands. The enraged nationalist led a modest army of deserters to take back the northeastern port of Fiume, which had been lost to Yugoslavia. D'Annunzio occupied the city for sixteen months as its "lyric dictator" before the Italian government ended his reign. Eventually, he took possession of a remote villa on the shores of Lake Garda, which became known as Il Vittoriale. This had been arranged with the cooperation of Benito Mussolini, who, knowing the poet's seductive verbal power over the populace, wanted to keep him in safe isolation. The leader of the radical fascist movement also bestowed the writer with overblown titles and placating medals for valor. Alone and cloistered, Gabriele D'Annunzio would transform his villa prison not only into his own gaudy tomb but into a shrine of decadent excess.

4

While Italy's warrior bard was absorbed in self-mythmaking on the battlefield, Luisa conspired to do the same through the patronage of a new set of artists. In 1915, as she wandered through Nice, the Marchesa met the symbolist illustrator Gustav Adolf Mossa. Known for his macabre pastels and watercolors of mythical harpies, lethal femmes fatales, and malefic Pierrots, he executed what is perhaps the single most frightening image of the eccentric Italian. In the center of the drawing, her disembodied head soars toward the viewer with kohled eyes lost in shadow and parted lips rounded in a silent shriek. A more earthbound vision of Luisa is an oil by the Paris-based American expatriate Mrs. Leslie Cotton, known for her renderings of Lady Diana Cooper, Prince Youssoupov, and Queen Elizabeth, the Queen Mother. Cotton's traditional portrait of the Marchesa presents its sitter as a chic high-society hostess wearing a simple but revealing white ensemble. As for the succeeding trio of artists to immortalize Casati, each would produce a masterpiece.

In the winter of 1918 at a luncheon given by British writer and artist Clare Sheridan at her London home, sculptor Jacob Epstein encountered Luisa Casati for the first time. Since his emigration from New York City to England, Epstein's craft had gained him infamous notoriety. In 1907, his large-scale, nude human figures, which adorned the British Medical Association building, caused outrage and were in peril of being destroyed. Then, just a few years later, a similar furor erupted around the artist's design for the monument marking Oscar Wilde's grave in the Parisian cemetery of Père Lachaise. In addition to an elaborate Egyptian headdress and a pair of art deco wings, the tomb's nude male figure bore a prodigiously large phallus. After repeated vandalism, the cemetery was forced to place a bronze fig leaf over the targeted and ultimately memberless area.

Epstein recalled Casati as a "very striking looking lady" in his autobiography, *Let There Be Sculpture,* and recalled how she drew his attention away from other guests who were vying for a commission from him: "The Marchesa had strange tastes. . . . She would argue for any perversity rather than countenance normal behavior. In art, of course, her taste was also for the perverse."[35] Never one to hesitate in her continuing quest for self-glorification, upon being asked by Epstein when she could sit for him, Luisa suggested the very next day:

> The Marchesa arrived in a taxicab at two o'clock and left it waiting for her. We began the sittings, and her Medusa-like head kept me busy until nightfall. It was snowing outside, and a report came in that the taxi man had at length made a declaration. He did not care if it was Epstein and if it was a countess; he would not wait any longer. On hearing this, Casati shouted, "He is a Bolshevik! Ask him to wait a little longer." He was given tea and a place by the fire and shown the bookcase.
>
> The winter light had failed, and I had many candles brought in. They formed a circle round my weird sitter with the fire in the grate piled high to give more light. The tireless Marchesa, with her overlarge blood-veined eyes, sat with a basilisk stare; and, as if to bear out her epithet of "Bolshevik" her taxi man picked out for himself *Brothers Karamazov* to read, and ceased to protest.
>
> The Medusa-like mask was finished the next day.[36]

Considered one of the sculptor's masterpieces, the unique quality of Epstein's achievement has been pinpointed: "Cast in bronze, some magical touch in its modeling retained the memory of candlelight glimmering in the eyes."[37]

The personality and work of Ignacio Zuloaga y Zabaleta, who was raised in Spain's untamed Basque region, could not be more at odds with those of

Epstein. Possessed with a penchant for the bizarre and beautiful, Zuloaga's appreciation for Luisa as an unconventional model is readily apparent. Although he began work on her portrait in 1918 when he was living *la vie bohème* in the Montmartre district of Paris, the canvas was reportedly completed, signed, and dated in Rome in 1922. This life-size portrait of the Marchesa has been noted as one of Zuloaga's most uncanny, and possibly grotesque, images in an already outlandish oeuvre. The artist characterized its subject as a "nocturnal phantasm in strange elegant dress."[38] Zuloaga's Casati is depicted in a Spanish Manola costume of red silk and black lace. In one black-gloved hand, she holds a fan that prominently features the reclining nude in Goya's *La Maja Desnuda.* Glaring sardonically at the viewer, Luisa is posed against a dusky backdrop of Montmartre's famous windmills.

The portrait's most important showing was at the Seconda Biennale Internazione Romana of 1923, alongside works by Degas, Matisse, and Picasso; it was also a centerpiece at the artist's solo exhibition at the Reinhardt Galleries in New York City the following year. Casati maintained a friendship with Zuloaga even after he established several homes in the Spanish cities of Madrid, Zumaya, and Paedraza. In fact, while visiting him in 1924, Luisa sent a telegram in Spanish to D'Annunzio, accompanied by a copy of the portrait. She concluded it by writing, " . . . *todo mi admiración al gran D'Annunzio. Coré.*"[39]

During a Parisian sojourn between 1918 and 1919, Luisa joined friends for a continual round of parties and social events. Fellow revelers included Cécile Sorel, Paul Poiret, the Baron and Baroness Adolph de Meyer, and Maria Ruspoli. Having become the third wife of the Duc de Gramont, who was more than forty years her senior, Ruspoli now spent most of her time at the couple's home on the Champs-Elysées. There the Duchesse conducted afternoon *thé dansants,* which became famous for their lively mix of bohemian artists and the most aristocratic members of the beau monde.

A tall and handsomely bearded Welshman attended one tea in February 1919. By this time, Augustus John was as well known for his successful artistic career as for his eccentric lifestyle. John had studied at the famed Slade School of Fine Arts in London before accepting a teaching post at the University of Liverpool. But this restrictive assignment could not satisfy his wandering soul. A friend entranced him with the mythology surrounding the quixotic existence of the Romany gypsies, whereupon John filled a horse-drawn caravan with art supplies and an ever-growing family to travel throughout the remote countrysides of England and Wales. The artist had also become infamous for his sexual appetite, which was satisfied in the arms of numerous women.

Augustus John was living in France following two years of service as a major in the Canadian army. After documenting Canada's war effort in Europe, he had been requested by the British government to provide an illustrative record of the current Paris Peace Conference. John spent much of his time there subsequently completing portraits of visiting dignitaries. Traveling alone, he found a home in the apartments of Don José Antonio de Gandarillas on the avenue Montaigne. Associated with the Chilean delegation, Tony de Gandarillas, in the words of Philippe Jullian, "knew everyone"[40] and was described by his occasional lover, the young artist Christopher Wood, as a "chittering, charming, childish, and always cheerful small monkey."[41] This rakish little bon vivant held open the doors to Parisian society for John.

At the fortresslike house of the Duchesse de Gramont, John was helping himself to a glass of port when another guest arrived. The artist states what followed in his autobiography *Chiaroscuro*:

> A lady of unusual distinction had entered. Her bearing, personality, and peculiar elegance seemed to throw the rest of the company into the shade. . . . The newcomer wore a tall hat of black velvet, the crown surrounded by an antique gold torque, the gift of D'Annunzio; her enormous eyes, set off by mascara, gleamed beneath a framework of canary coloured curls. . . . She moved about the ball-room with supreme ease, while looking about her with an expression of slightly malicious amusement. Our eyes met. . . . Before leaving I obtained an introduction; it was the Marchesa Casati.[42]

Luisa soon became a frequent guest at the parties given by John's host, de Gandarillas, where she exhibited a particular gift for wicked sarcasm, as John noted: "She had borrowed from the colloquial some important additions to her vocabulary, which, used with judgment, considerably enhanced her powers of expression, more especially when these were employed in the dissection of her friends' characteristics, mental, moral, and physical."[43] Whereas Casati's bizarrely enhanced visage inspired John's artistic sense, her "perfect naturalness of manner" amused him to laughter, often causing him to refer to her as "a child of nature."[44] At the same time, he was well aware of how she could easily become "a spoilt child of a woman."[45]

John's biographer Michael Holroyd best described Casati's allure to the artist: "Taken in small draughts, her presence, with all its malice and extravagance, intoxicated him."[46] The two became lovers for a brief but intense period, which would establish a lifelong friendship. Holroyd explains with perceptive frankness their attraction to one another:

"He painted like a lion," sighed Casati. "Le taxi vous attend," he writes to her from Paris. "Venez!" They flung themselves towards each other, but the romance, a brilliantly casual performance, seemed sadly under rehearsed. Sex was not the real attraction between them. Casati took other people's admiration for granted, using it as an orchestration to her life, a perpetual chorus singing invisibly while she stood on stage alone. Otherwise love-affairs threatened to interfere with her passionate self-love. . . . As an exhibitionist she needed partners only for her audience. Yet somehow John felt a kinship with her. Like him, she was outrageously shy, concocting, in place of real life, a pantomime.[47]

During excursions to London, the pair frequently attended a variety of soirées and dined at the city's most fashionable restaurants. Their favorite was the Hôtel-Restaurant de la Tour Eiffel on Percy Street near Tottenham Court Road. Augustus John once described to his friend, eccentric writer Osbert Sitwell, a curious afternoon he and Casati spent with the effete novelist Ronald Firbank:

I once presented [Firbank] to the Marchesa C—— at the Eiffel Tower; and we lunched together, all three. He then proposed we should all go to his rooms in Brook Street, but on the way deposited us at Claridge's and on some vague pretext disappeared himself. The Marchesa and I were becoming rather bored (it was between hours), when Ronald reappeared with an enormous bundle, which he unfolded in his rooms, displaying a magnificent bunch of highly exotic lilies which he offered with many apologies to the lady. He also showed her, but did not give her, a complete edition of his works, luxuriously bound. Naturally she was enchanted, and proposed we should all go to America together without wasting a moment. The plan was agreed to, but somehow or other never came to pass.[48]

In early April 1919, John found himself without a residence when Tony de Gandarillas was required to return to London with the Chilean delegation. The Duchesse de Gramont rescued him by offering the use of a studio equipped with an apartment on the Quai Malaquais. While John proposed to paint her portrait in gratitude, he had already begun preliminary work on yet another, his first effort to represent Luisa Casati on canvas. In John's words, although the Duchesse and the Marchesa were "outwardly friendly," they were "spiritually at loggerheads."[49] Therefore, it was necessary for him to maintain careful scheduling of their sittings to avoid an unwanted and potentially ugly clash. As John explains in his autobiography, a mishap was inevitable:

It was necessary for me, as far as possible, to keep them apart. They did not seek each other; but a collision in my studio was to be avoided. I don't suggest they would have lost control of themselves, both being well brought up, but such a situation would only have led to awkwardness and as a third part I was taking no risks. . . . But once I blundered: I had, by inadvertence, made an appointment with both ladies for the same hour. One sitting, at least, must be cancelled: but now it was too late. I waited. The Duchess arrived first. I pleaded fatigue and the immediate need of fresh air: we went out for a walk by the river and leaning on the parapet under Notre Dame, we watched the barges pass slowly by. At last I judged it safe to return. I was feeling better. I found the Marchesa had come—and gone. The situation was saved.[50]

In light of John's blatant womanizing, another reason might be proposed for the artist's circuitous attempts with these ladies—the possibility of concurrent affairs with both of them. Indeed, his insistence on the women's incompatibility is suspiciously at odds with the fact that each maintained the other on her invitation list for parties in Paris and Rome for more than two decades.

Painted that spring, Augustus John's first portrait of Casati depicts her in a pose perhaps too obviously like that of da Vinci's *Mona Lisa*. The canvas features the Marchesa, seated against a landscaped background, with her folded hands on her lap. Beneath a helmet of hennaed tresses, she stares down the viewer. The overall effect seems a rather uninspired tribute to a woman once considered the "anti-Gioconda." John expressed his ultimate dissatisfaction with the painting by not finishing it. Although its creation was originally a routine commission between artist and patron, the portrait was finally presented to Casati, and the canvas bears the prominent dedication "To the Marchesa Casati from Augustus John" in red paint. Even so, after refusing to compensate John for the work, Casati promptly sold it to Gerald Napier Sturt, Lord Alington, another British admirer.

There would be nothing half-hearted in conception, execution, or criticism connected with John's second rendering of Luisa. In addition to its importance as a true twentieth-century masterpiece, this single image probably captures the physical aura and idiosyncratic personality of its sitter more vividly than any other painted work. In the words of Michael Holroyd: "For once, romanticism and irony were perfectly blended."[51] The Marchesa is posed against a backdrop of storm clouds and craggy mountains, which have been likened to both Alpine cliffs and, perhaps symbolically, Mount Vesuvius. Not unexpectedly, Casati confronts the spectator directly with a disarmingly mischievous smile. So important was this aspect to John that her mouth was repainted twice during the portrait's production. With hands clasped at her waist, Luisa is dressed in simple white pajamas, opened widely at the collar. What also strengthens the portrait's arresting quality is the deliberate contrast between its ambiguous background of frigid blues and greens and the fiery crimsons and vermilions that highlight the Marchesa's form and especially her coiffure. Most striking is the absence of the subject's characteristic use of cosmetics and costumes. Combining an assured technique and the brushstrokes of a lover, John proves these masks unnecessary in presenting a woman equally memorable without them.

Initially intended as a full-length work, John cut the canvas down at some point almost by half. Museum analysis shows a single bold brushstroke that bisects the entire width of the painting.[52] Perhaps the artist decided that a complete representation of Luisa's figure lessened the impact of her dominant countenance.

The painting was given an auspicious debut at the Alpine Club Gallery in London in early 1920. Entitled *War, Peace Conference, and Other Portraits,* the solo exhibition featured numerous canvases, including John's paintings of Princess Marthe Bibesco, the Duchesse de Gramont, and his friend the adventurer T. E. Lawrence. Critics unanimously hailed the Marchesa's portrait. One laudatory review in the May 1920 issue of *The American Magazine of Art* was highlighted by a full-page reproduction of the work. About this time, the British newspaper *The Outlook* published a satirical drawing by French illustrator Edmund Dulac caricaturizing John as he completes Luisa's portrait. A long line of society women are shown waiting for their turn with the pipe-smoking artist, whose arm is in a sling as a result of the assembly-line process.[53]

T. E. Lawrence made frequent visits to the Alpine Club show and later wrote numerous amusing letters to John, offering his thoughts and comments on the works:

> La Casati is very different to what I remember of her in your house . . . much more lively in colour, and not vampish so much. In fact I shouldn't object to living with her (the picture of course), though the Birm. F.A. Gallery say it would be bad for the women of the town to hang her there. It must be hot stuff if I remember Birmingham correctly.[54]

The portrait continued to both fascinate and challenge the adventurer, and he summed up its complex appeal: "I hope the Casati is there: vampire is the word I was trying to think about as I looked at her—only I couldn't think because she froze me. (Mixed metaphor: perhaps I meant Gorgon.)"[55]

Sir Evan Charteris, chairman of both London's National Portrait Gallery and the Tate, would subsequently own John's second portrait of Luisa before its purchase by the Art Gallery of Ontario in 1934 for fifteen hundred British pounds sterling. Art connoisseur Sir Joseph Duveen congratulated the Canadian institution on its wise choice:

> I consider it to be an outstanding masterpiece of our time. It is no exaggeration to say this will live forever, which is true of very few pictures of modern times. You have bought a masterpiece for practically nothing. . . . Such painting of the head, for instance, I have never seen surpassed by any artist, and you can safely place it for comparison alongside the great Velásquez, Giorgione, or even Titian! That is what I think of this picture.[56]

It is perhaps fitting that this particular portrait has received such lasting accolades. In its refreshingly unadorned representation, John's work may indeed reveal the essence of a woman deliberately obscured by her own flamboyancy.

Tigress on Capri
1919-1920

Capri . . . its rocks had sheltered the sirens; it had seen
Odysseus pass, and Aeneas; one of its oaks had put forth
unseasonal verdure in the presence of Augustus; Tiberius
had sought refuge there, and pleasures; the day Christ died
its lighthouse had collapsed into the sea. The island had
remained a place apart, a place of asylum and delights.
   —*Roger Peyrefitte,* The Exile of Capri

The Marchesa arrived on the Piazza from the funicular,
escorted by an effeminate *cicisbeo,* on whose arm one of
her own rested. In her other arm was a gilded gazelle. . . .
Presently an enormous buck Negro appeared, carrying a
blue parrot in a cage.
   —*Sir Compton Mackenzie*

1

The spring of 1919 would be tempered with tragedy. This year, marked by several personal and artistic triumphs for the Marchesa, coincided with a violent epidemic of the Spanish flu. At the Padulli villa on the via Goito in Rome, every member of her sister's family was gripped by fever. On April 24, 1919, Francesca died after being ill for only two days. She was thirty-nine years old. It is not known how deeply Luisa was affected by this loss. Francesca had been the single relation to offer unconditional support and affection during the previous tumultuous decades. But whatever Casati's emotional state may have been, her wanderlust now became an obsession. In Poland, she visited Lancut, the fantasy palace of Count Roman Potocki, and in France she was the guest of Prince and Princesse d'Orleans at the Château de Chaumont-sur-Loire, an enormous, forbidding structure that had counted Catherine de Medici and Nostradamus among its previous inhabitants.[1]

Around this time, Luisa attended the Parisian premieres of the Ballets Russes's production of *Le Tricorne* and Cocteau's *Le Boeuf sur le Toit*. She was also seen hunting in Hungary, fishing in Scotland, and dancing in London. Author Gabriel-Louis Pringué comments on the more colorful aspects of this last sojourn:

> I've heard (but not seen for myself) that, upon finding herself in the English countryside she had herself accompanied by an orchestra of guitarists and flautists, who during her walks would take turns, stepping out from behind the hedges that line her path, to sing songs to her. The peacocks, of which those gardens were full, seeing the Marchesa dressed in purple, with a halo of feathers, began to follow her, trying to court her, recognizing in the odd woman a certain divinity.[2]

While in England, Luisa was often among the irreverent, continental society cultivated by the Baroness Catherine d'Erlanger at her pair of London addresses—139 Piccadilly, Lord Byron's former residence, and Falconwood, a Palladian mansion located on the outskirts of the city. Known as "Flames" because of her vivid red hair, d'Erlanger often exercised dubious artistic talents as a portraitist, even persuading the Marchesa to become the subject of one small effort.

Casati was also a frequent guest at Faringdon House, the home of her friend Lord Berners and his mother. Their eccentric visitor arrived with an unexpected traveling companion carried in a glass case—her pet boa constrictor, which Mrs. Tyrwhitt thought looked rather famished. But its owner assured her that it had already eaten a goat that very morning. With a son noted for his own peculiarities, this foible did nothing to hinder Mrs. Tyrwhitt's admiration, and she commented to Berners: "I like her so much better than your other foreign friends."[3] The Marchesa's host became quite attached to the peripatetic snake, often supplying it with a dinner of personally caught rats. Also visiting Faringdon was the Duchesse de Sermoneta, who described Casati's latest fashion accessory and Berners's counterattack:

> Luisa looked even stranger in appearance.... She had now added eyelashes two inches long to her enormous eyes, and her hair was more flame-like than ever. She came down to supper in tight white satin trousers and announced her intention of visiting Oxford with us next day. We were all rather nervous about what she would wear on this occasion, but she mercifully arrayed herself in a huge black coal-scuttle bonnet and so many furs that not a single undergraduate glanced at her. At dinner I could not understand why the others were so hilarious, until I found that Gerald Berners was wearing a false nose which I, being extremely short-sighted, had not spotted, and therefore persisted in talking to him quite seriously.[4]

Fortunately the demure Duchesse was not present at a particular Sunday luncheon in Oxford to which Luisa wore white Turkish trousers, a tight jet bodice, shoulder cape, and enormous black hat, while carrying a walking stick as tall as herself. When offered a selection of liquors, she dismissed them as being too tame for her tastes. Instead, she startled the other guests by unscrewing the knob of her cane, from which she poured a glass of absinthe.[5] She inspired further comment while attending a boat race sheathed in a suit of skintight maroon leather. Even though the garment included a row of buttons down each side, it still caused observers to speculate how she ever got into it. Tales of such appearances became notorious enough to cross the Channel and be remarked upon in the pages of numerous popular French periodicals. The *Gazette du Bon Ton* dubbed Luisa "la reine de l'étrange" when she attended a performance of the Ballets Russes at Covent Garden. Casati arrived on the arm of Gerald Berners and soon the pair were involved in, as Berners later described it in his memoirs, an "absurd incident" when Luisa and the foppish Ronald Firbank loudly complained that each had spent the evening "leering" at the other.

During another stay in England, Casati's pearls were central to an event similar to the earlier mishap with Boldini—although this time the outcome did not lead to a lasting friendship. Following a party one snowy evening in London, Luisa was escorted back to her hotel by Count Hermann von Keyserling. This eminent German philosopher was, contrary to his ideologies, a notorious womanizer and renowned for his violent temper. As the couple exited the nobleman's car, he caught Casati in an amorous embrace. When she attempted to ward him off, one of her lengthy pearl necklaces was broken. While most of the priceless baubles were lost in the snow, the others were smashed underfoot by the rebuked count. Luisa never forgave him.[6]

Naturally, Casati required a valid passport to conduct her travels. Although she had one, it had been improved in a manner consistent with the vanity of its holder. It is not surprising that her date of birth had been changed to a more flatteringly youthful one, but even more idiosyncratic was the substitution of her identifying photograph with a tiny reproduction of one of her own painted portraits. It is amazing that this audaciously stylish maneuver was allowed without legal obstacle.[7] Elisabeth Chaplin, niece of the renowned nineteenth-century French painter Charles Chaplin, had executed this image. The same artist also rendered what might possibly be the most curious depiction of the Marchesa—that of her feet, elegantly encased in gold slippers. Alas, Luisa's passport alone must not have been sufficient for the officials during one journey. As described by Sir Francis Rose, she was saved from public embarrassment by the intervention of Abbé Meunier, the celebrated priest to high society, when he "prevented that veiled lady from being carried naked from her sleeping compartment at the frontier by the Italian Customs authorities for holding up the train by refusing to get out and open her luggage."[8]

During her visits abroad, Luisa continued to keep in touch with D'Annunzio by sending him postcards with intriguing comments. One bearing the image of Ireland's Castle Kylemore, where Casati was a guest of the Duke and Duchess of Manchester, rhapsodized, "I've been here in this enchanted castle. Oh how you'd like it here." Another showing the Ancient Egyptian division of the British Museum warns, "These are the two most powerful and evil mummies."

It is not known whether D'Annunzio received a postcard from Luisa's sojourn to India. In his memoirs, the celebrated Parisian coiffeur Antoine described the effect this excursion had upon his client:

> She came home from India with a passionate interest in tropical
> primitive life. She called me in consultation. "I know now what I am,"
> she said. "Since I've been in India I am sure. In another incarnation
> I was a tiger. Now I am a tigress. Look at me. Do you see?"
>
> To begin with, she had long, yellow-green eyes and her hair had
> been tinted yellow-red. Now I dyed it in streaks—stripes like a tiger's
> of black and tawny yellow. . . . She had cultivated a superb walk so that
> her lithe muscles really suggested a feline creature in the jungle.
> Dressed in long, black, clinging gowns with no corsets or underwear

and always accompanied by a tiger cub, she indeed gave the impression of a tigress.[9]

But after such globe-trekking jaunts, Casati discovered a destination that captured her baroque imagination.

At the time of Luisa's visit, Capri was a favored site of artists of all kinds. Poets, writers, and painters, as well as the simply privileged seeking solitude, migrated to the island for its warm climate, inspirational landscapes, and secluded grottoes. They would throng the once sleepy Latin town of Anacapri and the Marina Grande to take rooms with the locals or rent elegant villas overlooking the Tyrrhenian Sea.

Capri also attracted society's misfits. By the late 1880s, the island had become a tranquil haven for homosexuals of the haut monde. Escaping the laws that opposed their lifestyle, these wealthy expatriates could buy safety, seclusion, and amorous satisfaction in a panorama of ocean waves and lush greenery. Among them were Frederick, Lord Leighton, the repressed president of London's Royal Academy of Arts, and John Singer Sargent, the reclusively shy American portraitist, here capable of appeasing a secret passion for Italian pugilists; from Germany came armament king Baron Friedrich Krupp, whose prohibited desires scandalized the courts of the Kaiser. The island had even played host to the decadent nomad Oscar Wilde (who traveled under the pseudonym Sebastian Melmoth) and his beau, Lord Alfred Douglas.

Capri also gave safe harbor to a sizable and equally distinctive lesbian community. This included Faith Mackenzie, wife of Scottish author Sir Compton Mackenzie, who enjoyed an ardent affair with Renata Borgatti, noted pianist and aggressive womanizer. Kate Perry and Saidee Wolcott, a dedicated American couple, built the Villa Torricella and adorned it with a self-invented coat of arms. It was rumored that the sisters Wolcott-Perry, as they dubbed themselves, suffered the loss of several housemaids to the seductions of a wealthy Russian resident of Sorrento on the nearby mainland. The Princess Hélène Soldatenkov was often recognized on Capri by her preferred all-white, leather-belted ensembles and sparkling monocle. With indomitable charm, it was alleged, the noblewoman added these wayward serving girls to her own considerable household staff consisting of gardeners, chauffeurs, and grooms—all of them female. It is no wonder that Capri became known as the "Paradise of Vices."

In the early summer of 1920, the funicular from the Marina Grande deposited its latest passenger onto the Piazza Umberto I: the Marchesa Luisa Casati had descended upon Capri. No better description of this incongruous sight could be found than that in Roger Peyrefitte's *The Exile of Capri:*

Although the Capriots affected to be surprised at nothing, such a spectacle was not seen, even by them, every day. The Marchesa . . . wore an astrologer's hat from which depended long veils enveloping her person. Her face was plastered like a mountebank's. . . . She wore bells . . . in her ears. Her make-up, melting in the heat, ran in streams down to her dusty shoes. . . . She carried a crystal ball in her hands to cool them. One of her maids carried a bush made out of wrought iron and bearing pomegranates painted vermilion, and a label identifying it as a present from Gabriele D'Annunzio. There was a negro in charge of two leashed greyhounds powdered mauve, and a leopard. A heiduke kept his eye on three cages containing, respectively, a boa-constrictor, some parrots, and an owl. Innumerable trunks and suitcases were piled into a whole procession of *carrozelle*.[10]

Casati had also arrived in the company of the effete Prince Giovanni Battista Serra and the pair of gilded gazelles transported from the villa in Rome.

Luisa had previously met the famed Swedish physician Axel Munthe in Paris. Before Casati's arrival in Capri, Munthe had built a majestic villa, San Michele, on a mountain overlooking the sea. Although he now resided in the Torre di Materita on the island, he never parted with his villa on the cliff, which he often rented to visiting friends. Thus, there was no reason for him not to consent to the Marchesa's telegram from Rome, asking to rent San Michele during a future stay on Capri. Later panicked by the multitude of rumors concerning his potential houseguest's behavior, Munthe reconsidered and sent off a refusal, thinking no more about the matter. But, at least initially, the doctor did not understand that once Casati had decided on San Michele, even its rightful owner could not bar her from the estate. As told by Munthe directly to his close friend Swedish diplomat Count Knut Corfitz Bonde, the account of what followed is described in Bonde's book *A l'ombre de San Michele*.[11]

One morning, Axel Munthe was surprised to discover San Michele's gardener at the gates of the Torre di Materita. The man told his employer that a strange and very agitated lady, accompanied by a mountain of luggage and entourage, was demanding entry into the villa at that very moment. Munthe then remembered Luisa's telegram. Infuriated, he sent the gardener back to San Michele with explicit instructions to refuse entrance to the gatecrasher. The physician suggested suitable amenities at either the Quisisana Hotel by the Piazzetta or the Hotel Paradiso near San Michele. The gardener departed with his specific orders, and Munthe considered the matter closed. Then a heavy rain began to fall.

Later that afternoon, the entry bell of the Torre di Materita sounded with repeated insistence. Munthe greeted a young girl, soaked to the skin, who was obviously in a state of near hysterics. She was the maid to the Marchesa Casati, and she proceeded to tearfully entreat the physician: "For the love of God, Sir, please let the Marchesa enter San Michele! She is driving the hotel staff crazy because her baggage was left in front of the villa and now it's pouring. I plead you to let her into the villa!" Munthe refused to take responsibility for any unfortunate outcome because of Casati's rudeness. Indeed, he asked, why would he want such an unstable visitor in a home filled with priceless antiquities? The frantic girl was sent back to her mistress. That evening the bell was rung again. This time it was the manager of the Hotel Paradiso, who beseeched, "My mother-in-law died today at the hotel and now I have a demented marchesa staying there. It is really too much for me to handle! I ask you as a favor, please, can this woman sleep at your villa this evening, and tomorrow she will return to Rome?" Sympathizing with the desperate man's plight, Munthe relented against his better judgment. His only condition was that Casati's luggage should remain outside San Michele's gates. At last, all fell quiet on this humorless farce.

In hopes his unwanted guest had vacated the villa, Munthe walked to San Michele the following morning. Luisa was waiting for him at the gates. Worse still, the mountain of baggage was nowhere to be seen. Munthe's insistence on her taking leave of the premises was met with a willful smile and Casati's shocking reply:

> But weren't you the one to consent to my entry into the villa? Do you ignore the law? Didn't you know that when you let me into the villa you also gave me the right to stay here for as long as I please? My lawyers have been contacted and they are all ready to prepare papers.

The physician had been trapped by his original agreement. Italian law would support the Marchesa's actions because she possessed Munthe's written permission to lease San Michele regardless of his later change of mind. Worse still, the initial arrangement between the two might allow Casati's occupancy, if enforced, for years to come. Nothing remained for Munthe to do except hope for her quick departure. As expected, this was not to be. In a letter to a friend, Munthe expressed considerable vexation toward the possibility of Luisa's long-term tenancy: "The future outlook remains very uncertain and my desire to seize her by her red peruke and scalp her and fling her degenerated carcass over the precipice is stronger than ever."[12]

Luisa wasted no time in making herself at home in the hostage villa, transforming its once placid rooms to suit her bizarre tastes. Whereas its owner had once written, "I want my house open to the sun and wind and the voice of the sea, like a Greek temple, and light, light everywhere,"[13] shadows now fell upon San Michele. Ivory walls and windows were obscured behind golden curtains and heavy draperies of black velvet. Black carpets and animal skins hid the mosaic floors, while Munthe's collection of antiques was shut away to allow space for the Marchesa's ebony furniture. In a room now reserved for Casati's sorcery paraphernalia, a black sheepskin had been nailed to one wall and the others were adorned with quotations and proverbs handwritten in French with black paint. Only two objects originally belonging to San Michele remained untouched, probably because they appealed to its rampaging tenant. One was an oversized bust of Medusa; the other, an Egyptian sphinx of red granite perched on the villa's loggia, keeping watch over the Bay of Naples. Luisa was particularly fond of the latter as it was reputed to grant the wishes of those who touched its flank with their left hand.

Casati's choice of decoration reflected yet another visual transformation—and one at deliberate odds with the sultry summer season. Her wardrobe while on Capri consisted entirely of black. Swathed in gowns with immense cathedral trains, the Marchesa bedecked herself in jet rings and necklaces of black pearls. Even her typically crimson coiffure was dyed first a vivid green and then black. Soon gossip spread of Luisa's supposed celebrations of black masses in the villa and, like her childhood inspiration Sarah Bernhardt, she was now believed to be sleeping in a coffin.

Ironically, while all was made black at San Michele, Casati's attendant was gilded from head to foot. According to legend, the man collapsed during a particularly hot afternoon, his life saved only when Munthe managed to scrape away the suffocating gilt. Despite the report's questionable validity, which mirrors tales from Casati's years in Venice, Luisa's manservant would cause the physician some consternation. The titan required a specific daily diet of large quantities of poultry, which Munthe was to supply. Compton Mackenzie recalled the doctor's displeasure over the situation in his autobiography, *My Life and Times:*

> Munthe would tell me presently that her Negro servant was being an even greater problem for him than the Marchesa herself.
> "I have to find two fowls a day for him. He eats two fowls every day."
> "He'll probably eat the Marchesa's parrot if you don't keep him in fowls," I said.[14]

The colossus followed Casati everywhere, even when she was invited to dine by the Princess Soldatenkov at her home, the Villa Siracusa, in Sorrento. Guests were stunned when the man, stripped to the waist, maintained a silent vigil behind his mistress's chair during the entire meal. All the while, the Marchesa sat calmly at the table with a large snake coiled about one arm.

Such reptilian embellishments often garnered as much attention as the servant. At another party, a serpentine necklace of gold enhanced Luisa's ensemble. When an admirer inquired whether the piece was Egyptian in origin, its wearer smiled slyly—just as the necklace uncoiled itself before a roomful of dumbstruck onlookers. Another time, the sleeping creature was revived by the heat of the Capriot sun and caused a small panic after sliding from about the Marchesa's shoulders.

Although Axel Munthe, for obvious reasons, did not frequently socialize with Casati during her stay, others on the island found her a curiosity and accepted invitations to San Michele with enthusiasm. Sir Compton Mackenzie relates Luisa's unusual method of welcoming him there as a guest:

> Munthe presented me [to the Marchesa], and after studying me for a moment or two through a lorgnette she invited me to tea . . . [When I arrived] a gilded gazelle was standing on either side of the heavy front door, which was opened by the Negro servant, dressed now in blue plush tailcoat and breeches. The *cicisbeo* was fluttering about in the entrance-hall to say the Marchesa was waiting to receive me. . . . I passed on to the *salone* and went in. Surprise scarcely expresses what I felt when I saw my hostess lying on the big black bearskin in front of the huge fireplace. The reader may feel equally that surprise is hardly strong enough to describe his feelings when I tell him that the Marchesa was lying there with absolutely nothing on.
>
> "Ah, Mackenzie, I am glad to see you," she said, extending her arm for me to kiss her hand. "I must put on a wrap because we shall have tea outside in the pergola. Go you along now."
>
> I am glad that Augustus John immortalized the Marchesa Casati, but I sometimes wish that he could have seen her as I saw her that afternoon of early summer in Capri upon the black bearskin rug, so appropriately bareskin.[15]

Mackenzie grew fond of Luisa and invited her to soirées at the Casa Solitaria, where he was staying. Other evenings saw them together at the marionette shows at the Faraglioni Puppet Company or listening to a performance of Chopin's keyboard music played by Alfredo Casella. Luisa knew the pianist well since his involvement with her friend Fortunato Depero's *Balli plastici* in Rome a few years earlier. The futurist artist also had a studio in Anacapri, and Depero describes his reunion there with Casati in his autobiography, *So I Think, So I Paint*:

> The Marchesa Casati comes unexpectedly to my studio. She is accompanied by a Neopolitan prince and by a white greyhound elastic

as a feather. She wears shoes with mother-of-pearl heels. She is friendly and clever. After having examined my paintings, she chooses one depicting a vision of Capri with the Clavel Villa in the center.[16]

Then there was Diaghilev, who arrived on the island for a rest from the Ballets Russes with his new companion, Boris Kochno. They, too, were sure to call on Casati and Mackenzie.

The Marchesa made a new artistic acquaintance with Polish painter Jan Styka, renowned for his massive panoramas and religious-themed works. The previous year, the portly artist had relocated from Paris to Capri, where he converted the Villa Certosella into a studio and private museum. As a result of their association, Styka completed a portrait of a tousle-haired Luisa, garbed in simple robes.

Gabriele D'Annunzio also came to visit his Coré on Capri. In typical fashion, no sooner had Luisa been comfortably ensconced in San Michele than she deluged her intimate friend with telegrams and invitations. Finally, he arrived. In honor of his loyal muse, D'Annunzio had the villa's gardens filled with sparkling glass flowers commissioned especially for the occasion from one of Venice's Murano glassblowers. It was said that this gesture of affection cost the poet hundreds of thousands of lire. Evening hours on Capri would often find Casati as sole audience to D'Annunzio, who recited his own verse or sang self-composed songs. The volume of his serenading reached such intensity that the populace below became privy to these impromptu musicales as well. Luisa was hardly displeased by how such eccentricities were quickly becoming the main topic of conversation.

During one of Casati's seasons at San Michele, Capri's mayor, Edwin Cerio, gathered together an international assembly of dignitaries for what was called the Convegno del Paesaggio. The mayor had a grand vision of a future Capri vastly different from the decadent playground it had become. Though supposedly there to promote the island's possibilities as a utopia for rarefied cultural ideals, the foreign delegates' conduct instead upheld the more sybaritic aspects of Capri's reputation. As chance would have it, Luisa happened to witness one such scandalous incident.

A visitor from Great Britain, Hugo Wemyss, the honorable attaché in Diplomatic Service and brother of the Admiral of the Fleet, found the isle's lack of restrictions on homosexual practices more than liberating. Late one evening, the Englishman was engaged in an amorous encounter with a young Italian cabdriver at an idyllic, moonlit spot along the cliffs just below San Michele. Suddenly, from the balustrade above the clandestine couple, laughter sent the boy fleeing. Wemyss gazed upward to see Luisa standing alongside an authoritative-looking gentleman who was sporting a pointed goatee. With complete composure, the Britisher bowed before asking if he might join them. He ascended to the villa, where Casati greeted him and introduced His Excellency, Count Carlo Sforza. While the two men were shaking hands Hugo Wemyss realized his priapic tryst had just been witnessed by Italy's foreign minister.[17]

2

The owner of a residence below and to the east of San Michele would have appreciated the indiscreet liaison between the Englishman and his taxi driver. The Villa Lysis was home to Capri's most notorious exile, Baron Jacques d'Adelsward-Fersen, the scion of noble Swedish steel industrialists and a descendant of one of Marie Antoinette's lovers. In addition to writing homoerotic verse and forgettable novels, Fersen was the editor of *Akademos*, a Parisian periodical celebrating the male nude. The Baron's apartments near the Parc Monceau were the site of illicit assignations, disguised as refined literary teas, with schoolboys from the surrounding area. In 1903, Fersen, then only twenty-three years old, was arrested for the *corruption de mineurs*. Following the southern migration of other ostracized aristocrats, he, too, found sanctuary on the Island of Sirens.

In 1904, Fersen built the Villa Lysis. Young male Capriots constructed its whitewashed walls (decorated with leering satyr masks) and its Corinthian columns and verandas of blue and white tile to meet the Baron's specifications. The nobleman would share the new villa with his companion, a fifteen-year-old newspaper boy from Rome, Nino Cesarini. The gardens, overgrown with orchids, featured a life-sized bronze statue immortalizing the proudly naked Italian youth. Within the villa was a labyrinth of dimly lit chambers culminating in Fersen's inner sanctum—a private opium den more euphemistically called the Chinese Room.

Not long after her arrival, Luisa received invitations to the almost nightly parties at the Villa Lysis. She attended one soirée costumed in yards of gilded silk in the style of a Hindu.[18] Fersen applauded such displays of theatricality. He also shared her interest in the occult; it was rumored that Fersen was fond of celebrating mysterious pagan ceremonies with his intimates. Casati boasted of the rites she had participated in with D'Annunzio and showed the Baron her collection of spell books, some supposedly bound in human skin, on which she claimed the hair still grew.[19] Much to her disappointment, Luisa discovered that Fersen's black masses "had been at worst pink."[20] Even so, with her host Luisa concocted a ritual commemorating more earthly delights. A torch on the balcony of San Michele would be lit to signal her amatory satisfaction during D'Annunzio's visit. The flame could be seen across the valley from the Villa Lysis, where Fersen would ignite another to indicate the same with his own suitors.

Casati was soon ushered into Fersen's oriental temple of narcotics. In the world of the beau monde, where money could purchase any pleasure, drugs were no exception. Such hypnotics as the opalescent liqueur, absinthe, and the intoxicating fumes of ether had achieved great popularity during the early years of the Belle Époque. Cocaine then came into vogue. Its true dangers unknown at first, the innocuous-looking white powder soon found its way into the salons of café society. Exclusive jewelers such as René Lalique and Georges Fouquet were commissioned by their patrons to create tiny boxes and caskets of gold, silver, and enamel in which to secrete pocket stashes of the drug. Pinches of cocaine were dissolved in champagne, a certain demimondaine was known to spread a paste of it on toast points, and many gentlemen applied it as a topical aphrodisiac. In a short time, cocaine use was rivaled by morphine injections. Yet another prevalent narcotic was opium. Derived from the poppy flower, the potent drug was rolled into tiny balls, set alight on gilded needles by the flames of small oil lamps, and smoked in long wooden pipes.

It is certainly not difficult to imagine that Luisa dabbled in stronger narcotics than the belladonna she used in her illustrious eyes. She moved too closely in such circles not to have been at least an occasional user of these drugs. Such Casati intimates as the Baron and Baroness de Meyer and even D'Annunzio greatly admired the effects of cocaine. Her more recent friend Tony de Gandarillas owed his constant ebullience to more than a jolly disposition. According to Lady Moorea Black, the perennial partygoer was "absolutely embalmed"[21] on opium. Then there was Luisa's continual association with many dubious clairvoyants and occult practitioners who were known to peddle mind-clarifying philters to their clientele.

More than one source confirms Casati as a frequent guest to Fersen's Chinese Room. There, beneath the gaze of a jade Buddha, visitors would stretch out on mountains of pillows and smoke themselves into numbed pleasure. Roger Peyrefitte noted, "[Fersen] had the prestige of being an opium addict, added to that of having the best opium and the finest collection of pipes. La Casati hardly ever went outside of San Michele, excepting to smoke opium at the Villa Lysis."[22] Although there is no evidence that verifies her regular drug use, it is intriguing to consider its relationship to Luisa's increasingly bizarre behavior.

Baron Jacques d'Adelsward-Fersen's indolent indulgence continued for just another three years. On November 11, 1923, he committed suicide with dissolute panache by swallowing a lethal cocktail of champagne and five grams of cocaine. Scandal followed the aristocrat even after his death when his lover, Nino, was falsely accused of his murder. Finally cremated, Fersen's ashes were placed in a white marble urn and interred in the island's cemetery. Gazing down on the nobleman's resting place, the Villa Lysis would eventually fall into quiet ruin.

While on Capri, Casati became obsessed with the idea of traveling to Sicily. The purpose of this trip was far from recreational. The Mediterranean isle was home to a figure dubbed by the international press as the "Wickedest Man in the World," although Aleister Crowley preferred the more evocative title of the "Great Beast of the Apocalypse." By 1920, Crowley's exploits in the black arts were already legendary. During the spring of that year, he established the infamous Abbey of Thelema in Cefalu, a coastal fishing village on the northern part of the island. This center for select disciples of Crowley's sect eventually became the scene of blasphemous rituals and death. Luisa's temptation to dedicate herself to the occult madman was apparently short-lived, for she never journeyed to Sicily. The reason for her decision not to surrender her fierce ego to another is quite obvious: although devoted to the dark arts, the Marchesa's black masses were, in truth, just as "pink" as those of Baron Fersen. By surrounding herself with indulgent audiences, Casati could take center stage as the high priestess of her own haut monde coven. This was reflected in the magical details often incorporated into her parties on Capri. Hidden fans on San Michele's loggia would, on the flick of a switch, cause the palms to sway in their breeze. If heavy clouds hung over the villa on the night of a soirée, Luisa could conjure up an artificial moon that had been installed in the gardens. By this illusion, she proved herself victorious over the elements before awestruck guests, who viewed the luminescent orb as it was made to actually appear to move across the sky. Casati's residency at San Michele, and the marvels she performed there, became so well known that the international press began to refer to Munthe's villa as the Marchesa's own property.

It was not long before Luisa discovered that American expatriate painter Romaine Goddard Brooks was staying at the Villa Cercola close by San Michele. Here was an opportunity for a new commission—although the self-reliant painter would prove to be unlike any Casati had yet encountered. By the time of their first meeting, the dark-haired, pale-skinned Brooks had already lived on Capri for many years as a semi-recluse in a villa that had been formerly an abandoned chapel. Her tendencies largely lesbian, the painter had shared a marriage of convenience with homosexual poet and pianist John Ellingham Brooks since 1902. Under the guise of this proper union, the two lived separate lives on Capri until the latter's death seventeen years later.

Romaine Brooks's sexuality must have been somewhat malleable when she met Gabriele D'Annunzio at a Parisian luncheon in 1909. Bedazzled by his seductive wit, the artist was soon added to the poet's list of feminine conquests. He named her Cinerina, or "little gray one," in tribute to her favored palette of blacks, whites, and grays. She responded by painting two portraits of the writer. The affair lasted until Brooks began another with Ida Rubinstein, whom she called the "heraldic bird" of the Ballets Russes. Brooks subsequently met Parisian *saloneuse* Natalie Barney, and the two remained companions for nearly fifty years.

As soon as Luisa learned of Brooks's presence on the island, she invited her to dinner at San Michele. The artist would describe her admiring hostess as "a bit too sloe-button-eyed for my taste."[23] Still, she was flattered by the many additional requests for visits that flooded the Villa Cercola. Perhaps this effusiveness made Brooks hesitate when the inevitable appeal for a portrait arose. Hoping to evade what she knew would be a demanding task, Brooks invented a number of feeble excuses to avoid it. But the Marchesa was indomitable. When Brooks claimed she had no canvases, it was suggested that she paint on cloth or board. Brooks's refusal to travel to San Michele was greeted by Luisa's proposal to come to her instead. In fact, Casati was prepared to pose three days a week if necessary. Then, using a ploy she thought would surely kill the project, Brooks lied, stating that she only worked with nude models. Without hesitation, Luisa replied, "Very well; I'll be nude!"[24] Conquered on her own terms, the artist accepted her fate.

Preliminary work on the portrait began in early August 1920. In a letter to Natalie Barney, who remained in Paris, Brooks commented erroneously: "[Casati] has never been painted nude before. Her friends were astonished that she accepted so readily."[25] Luisa was not one to shy away from being represented nude, as proven by the work of Kees van Dongen. Ballets Russes designers Mikhail Larionov and Natalia Gontcharova and Russian avant-gardist Léopold Survage had all completed unclothed images of her as well.

Once the sittings started, Brooks continued to confide her troubles to Barney. At first, these letters were filled with both trepidation and hopefulness. On August 4, Brooks wrote to her lover: "I've begun the portrait of Casati—an immense life-size nude. I foresee with fear the amount of work this will demand of me. She has been most enthusiastic. . . . [The painting will be] a combination of rocks (silver and black) and her straight beautiful body. . . . *Adieu* to the moments of idleness and the joys of summer!"[26]

At first the Marchesa's erratic adherence to the scheduled posing sessions became an obstacle. Brooks wrote to an associate: "[The portrait] is very little done and I am not at all certain if it will be completed. She left now for Rome. Will she return? I don't know anything about it. The huge two-meter high canvas is filling up my atelier and is giving me the discomfort of being a painful work which will, perhaps, remain as it is."[27]

Casati did return, and the combination of the painter's diligence and Luisa's stamina proved Brooks wrong. Indeed, her correspondence to Barney hints at a budding flirtation between artist and patron: "La Casati is now applying herself to posing. . . . She is mad for the picture, which has taken over her imagination. . . . The work itself is very strong, a bit theatrical. . . . I have never had such an intelligent model. She is going to have an exhibition for this painting alone."[28] During this early phase of the project, Brooks was still capable of maintaining a mixed enthusiasm for Luisa, tempered by a growing attraction: "She's really a remarkable woman, all the same she is very much a spoiled child."[29] Containing satirical caricatures of Casati in their borders, her letters to Barney soon took on a disturbing edge. By September 19, Brooks wrote, "I am exhausted, I am losing weight, I am losing my hair, I am afraid, I need my rest."[30] Casati came to monopolize all of Brooks's time. Not only did she spend three days each week sitting for her portrait, but she also took the artist along on daily outings. Brooks did get a brief reprieve when an incapacitated Luisa took to her bed at San Michele with a toothache.

The likelihood exists that Brooks began experiencing conflicting emotions of desire and guilt toward the possible consummation of a sexual affair with Luisa. At this time, the artist began sending a barrage of telegrams to Barney urging her to come to Capri. Perhaps initially or at least in part, Brooks inferred the start of an intimate liaison with Casati as a maneuver to test Barney's responsiveness to such a situation. In addition, the artist remained wounded by her lover's former unfaithfulness with the self-destructive seductress Renée Vivien. But Barney did not act on Brooks's pleas, the immediate outcome of which remains enshrouded.

At last, the painting was completed. But what might have begun as a realistic representation metamorphosed into something at once grotesque and captivating. In a full-length pose against a background of jagged rock, Luisa is portrayed as a harpy perched in some desolate niche. Her pale, elongated, androgynous body is draped in a black, shroud-like cape, the falling pleats of which resemble the wings of a bat. Her hands are nothing more than talons. Brooks described her vision of Luisa as "a sort of fantastic bird on the rocks or a fallen angel with nothing human about her." When confronted by the finished portrait, Casati's only criticism was, "You did not make me beautiful." Brooks replied, "No, but I made you noble."[31] It is not insignificant to note that the only portrait Brooks ever painted of Natalie Barney during their half-century relationship was done within months of finishing the one of Luisa.

Casati was able to continue to vacation at San Michele during the ensuing years and even sublet it to her friends. At one juncture, an exasperated

Munthe attempted to evict Luisa with the assistance of Capri's undefeatable lawyer, Roberto Serena—but the man returned from a visit with the villa's immovable lodger totally enchanted and willingly conquered by her considerable charm and wit.

In any event, much to the relief of San Michele's owner, Luisa abandoned Capri—at least for that summer. Axel Munthe's grandson Adam Munthe summed up the doctor's final opinion of this exasperating tenant:

> As far as the Marchesa Casati is concerned, my grandfather found her uniquely irritating. . . . She sent crass fawning letters and he was bored to death by her histrionics, her refusal to pay rent, not to mention the moth eaten leopard she chose to parade with at the end of a diamond studded leash.[32]

After one of her stays, Munthe found a photograph of the Brooks portrait of Casati in a writing desk. He certainly had no need for such a souvenir. The doctor scoffed: "What do I want with a picture of Casati stark naked? I know her naked soul, and that's enough."[33] Munthe's annoyance was not lightened by the memory of Luisa appearing unannounced at his tower home, bearing the gift of a black velvet sack. One of Munthe's children emptied out its mysterious contents only after the Marchesa's exit. The bag held two genuine shrunken human heads and no explanation of any kind.[34]

The enigmatic relationship between Brooks and Casati did not end in the summer of 1920—nor would it preclude the involvement of Natalie Barney.[35] Just several months later in a letter to Marcel Proust, Barney noted that she had been invited by Brooks to share Christmas Eve dinner with her and Luisa at the Ritz in Paris. Then early 1921 found Brooks and the Marchesa together in London. Writing from Claridge's Hotel in Mayfair, Brooks's letters to Barney describe Casati's possessive nature and several nightmarish episodes of their stay:

> Darling—I do not think that I can stay here for very long. Certainly not if things continue as they are. As I feared, I have been dragged by La Casati into a whirlwind. . . . She is now buying, buying, buying, everything she sees. It is a real madness. Incredible!
> On the first day she was rushing to find a skeleton of an orangutan . . . and contented herself with a pale little canary in a black cage. Today it was the day of the balloons—six times larger than normal. The car was filled with these multicolored globes. She was seated in the middle of them like a terrifying dream, a cage on her knees with two large hoot owls, who looked about them with dread. Casati seems to object to almost everyone who could interest me.

Now, I'm at the end of my tether. She lives in an atmosphere which is absolutely the opposite of love. . . . She is unable to confront the abstract. She is an infantile spirit. . . . La C. bores me more and more. She wants me entirely for herself and runs down everyone else.[36]

Although it is not known what portion of the following months Brooks and Casati shared together, the artist sent a revelatory letter to Barney on June 15, 1921, once again from Claridge's Hotel:

Casati has gone for the day to Ascot. We had a tiff last evening and many interesting things were said on both sides. . . . I had simply been frightened at her desire to bring the coarser elements of male love into what was, as love between women should have been, delicate and beautiful. This last made an impression I think. We separated somewhat bruised on both sides.[37]

Following this emotional scene, Brooks remained at the hotel while Luisa found asylum at the home of the Princesse Violette Murat. An acquaintance of Casati, this lesbian noblewoman was infamous for her drug use and obsessive cleanliness, as well as for her pet white rat.

During the ensuing months the two reconciled and traveled back together to Capri in the summer of 1921. But this time Natalie Barney joined them there in August—a visit that resulted in Barney's poem "Isola di Capri." In the work, the writer insightfully describes Casati as "ever trying by strange disguisements to escape from the inner strangeness."[38] A few weeks later, Barney left for Paris once more. By mid-September, Brooks's last letters concerning Casati were sent to her lover. Their tone of frustration clearly signals the end of a temporary affair between painter and model. In these letters, Brooks expresses her eagerness to see Luisa leave the island for a stay in Naples—a plan foiled by rain. Finally, Casati convinces her to attend the Fête Sauvage she is giving before departing for Venice. Whether Brooks appeared in Luisa's suggested costume of loincloth and horsehair mane is not known.

Ultimately, Romaine Brooks's portrait of the Marchesa offers an intriguing puzzle. It is arguable that Augustus John was able to see past Luisa's outward eccentricities to the bewitchingly canny woman beneath. Surely, his vision of her had most likely been colored by their romance at the time. But as evidenced in her letters, Brooks never acknowledged such affection toward Luisa—a fact that she may not have wanted to admit even to herself. Meryle Secrest, Brooks's biographer, proposes: "Faced with La Casati's bitch-goddess, Romaine was baffled and took the fantasy for fact. . . . In Romaine's portrait [Casati] is desexed and has become a raging figure bent on vengeance."[39] Perhaps, then, the portraits by John and Brooks, painted only little more than a year apart, should be viewed together as displaying two very different aspects of the same complex model.

Regardless of what role her emotions played in its execution, Brooks did openly proclaim her dislike for the Casati portrait. But, interestingly enough, she never parted with it. Indeed, when Luisa asked for the work's price upon completion, the artist requested to keep it for herself. An admirer of the Marchesa who also desired the painting for his own collection was rejected as well. It is known that at least for a time the canvas was displayed prominently on one wall of Natalie Barney's bedroom in her Parisian home.[40] Although Brooks's memoirs note that the portrait was shown at an exhibition in the United States, no catalogue exists to corroborate this statement. Brooks spoke no more about the painting until almost fifty years later when she broke her silence in an interview with French author Michel Desbruéres. Tantalizingly enough, her words of protest are softened by a lingering appreciation:

> It looks like a [Félicien] Rops. . . . In place of feet, I made it look like claws. . . . I thought she would have screamed, but she said, you are a genius. . . . I also made the hands like claws. . . . I detested that portrait because it wasn't me. I never did anything theatrical. It's enormous. . . . She was very crazy, very eccentric, but with a great admiration for me . . . and she was beautiful. She was . . . worth the pain.[41]

In 1970, a fascinating discovery would be made upon the demise of Romaine Brooks in Nice at the age of ninety-six. Just two years prior, Brooks had not only ended her near half-century relationship with Natalie Barney but also donated her own paintings and drawings, scrapbooks, and a variety of writings from her personal collection, including an unpublished novel and an autobiography, to the Smithsonian American Art Museum in Washington, D.C. But beneath Brooks's deathbed was found a single rolled-up canvas—the portrait of Luisa Casati. Had the artist chosen to hide the image in such a nearby place for so many years in an ironic attempt to forget its painful creation? Or did Romaine Brooks still harbor a continued fascination with its subject? Then the portrait disappeared.

3

After her departure from Capri in 1920, new canvases depicting Luisa Casati became increasingly rare, with several notable exceptions. The avant-garde among wealthy patrons had begun to favor photography rather than traditional oil portraiture as a means of immortalization. Already captured by de Meyer's glossy lens, the Marchesa had yet to expand her portfolio of black and white images with those of a more artistically daring nature. In late 1920, a Spanish painter would create another work that portrayed Luisa as a sphinxian muse, but there was no doubt that the age she had inspired was becoming hopelessly outmoded.

"Atrociously decadent"[42] was how critics characterized the women painted by Federico Beltrán y Masses. After studying at the Barcelona Academy, the artist found his sitters among the beau monde of Paris, where he worked most of his life. Even so, almost all of his models, at least on canvas, exhibited the dusky sensuality of the painter's homeland. Beltrán y Masses described his first encounter with Casati in the society pages of *Aux Ecoutes* in a brief piece, "Une visiteuse nocturne":

> As I was falling asleep in my studio one night around one in the morning, my manservant José came to me in a frightened state after the unexpected arrival of a visitor—a woman in black velvet with a large silver dog. The lady, he claimed, appeared so strange as to make him wonder whether he was dreaming. Intrigued, I went downstairs. There I saw a woman with brilliant eyes accompanied by a slender Russian greyhound in a silver topcoat and pearl collar. A silent man, who I assumed was a lackey, stood behind her. The visitor introduced herself. "I am the Marchesa Casati. Two days ago in London, I saw one of your canvases, the *Maja Maudite*, and I have decided to be painted in the same pose as this woman. In my hands, I will hold a blue crystal ball given to me by Gabriele D'Annunzio. . . . Now, get your paintbrushes. I have only this night to give you." And the woman posed. Black lace covered her arms, her mouth was blood red, and her eyes seemed to widen from the darkness. . . . When the sitting was completed, the lady departed with her greyhound and follower back into the night.[43]

In Beltrán y Masses's portrait of Luisa, the classic Turkish harem odalisque is reinvented as high-society seductress. She is shown reclining, full length, on a divan before a ghostly ship in full sail, which the artist said represented his sitter's "nomadic and mysterious soul."[44] Casati's pleasure at adding the portrait to her collection unfortunately did not mirror some of its critical reception. Sir Harold Acton's memoirs contain the reaction of his artist brother, William, to a meeting with the Marchesa: "As soon as she saw my paintings she said I was the *one* painter she had been looking for, and so forth. After the horror that Beltran y Masses did of her I thought she might well hope for something more encouraging."[45] But Casati must have been satisfied with the Spaniard's talents, as two further commissions followed—one representing Luisa as a flaming-haired Leda with a swan and the other showing her caressing her pet serpent.[46]

Some artists did slip through Casati's grasp. Longtime friend and art critic Michel Georges-Michel documents an acquaintanceship between Luisa and painter Tamara de Lempicka during the 1920s. On several occasions, the famed art deco portraitist attended the Marchesa's Parisian *salons*. But de Lempicka never committed Luisa to canvas. Perhaps the pair were too equally matched in provocative and egocentric temperament for such a commission.

In 1920 sculptress Catherine Barjansky visited her former client at her villa in Rome:

> To enter [Casati's] house one had to cross a big garden, with golden deer near the entrance. There were roses, roses, and a mimosa tree in full bloom.
>
> As usual the Marquise Casati had created an unusual setting for herself. The door was opened by a tall dark butler in full uniform. Behind him a small, blond page, who looked like a miniature cupid, took my coat. The contrast was deliberate and designed to be amusing.
>
> In the hallway there stood on a high pedestal a life-size Egyptian statue of a woman. The Marquise had told me about this statue on our first meeting in Paris. She had bought it because, on taking all its measurements, she had found they were exactly the same as her own. In another big room there were enormous chairs, upholstered in pale blue brocade, with gold and silver cushions; wonderful fabrics; dark-shaded lamps; and flowers everywhere. In the center of the room, in a gold cage, was an enormous monkey, leaping and screaming. It smelled very bad.
>
> Beyond there was a small library, without windows, the walls entirely filled with books in gold bindings. And in the center of the room, absolutely motionless, sat the Marquise Casati, dressed as usual in a fantastic manner. On this occasion she wore a tight black velvet bodice, extremely décolleté, and a long pleated skirt of black and white wool—with a train.
>
> Her carrot-colored hair hung in long curls. The enormous agate-black eyes seemed to be eating her thin face. Again she was a vision, a mad vision, surrounded as usual by her black and white borzois, and a host of charming and utterly useless ornaments.[47]

Casati befriended another Russian exile in Rome in 1920. A former high-ranking member of the imperial court in St. Petersburg, Prince Félix Yous-soupov was infamous for masterminding Rasputin's assassination. Though equally notorious for his homosexual affairs, Youssoupov was married to the favorite niece of Tsar Nicholas II. Fleeing their homeland's revolution with a fortune's worth of jewels stitched into their clothing, the couple went on to open exclusive dress shops in Paris, London, and Berlin. But the Prince was not content to simply design elaborate ensembles for his well-heeled clientele. His flair for transvestism was apparently convincing enough to have once attracted the amorous attentions of England's Edward VII.[48]

During his stay at the Grand Hotel in Rome, Prince Youssoupov came to know Casati, as related in his autobiography, *En exil:*

> I had not yet made contact with the Roman people, when I found one morning in my mail an envelope on which the address struck me for the originality of the handwriting. It contained an invitation to dinner at the home of the Marchesa Casati.
>
> I did not know Luisa Casati except for her name, but her name was too well known in cosmopolitan society to not be familiar to me, and her reputation of eccentricity was too well established not to excite my curiosity. I seized the opportunity and responded to her. My expectations were going to be surpassed.
>
> In the room where I was introduced, a woman of singular beauty was [reclining] on a tiger pelt with translucent veils outlining her slender body. Two greyhounds, one black and one white, were sleeping at her feet. Fascinated by this picture, I hardly noticed the presence of a second character; an Italian officer had arrived before me. Our hostess raised her splendid eyes. They were so large that in her pale face, you could not see anything but them. With a slow and undulant movement, like that of a royal cobra, she offered me a hand decorated with rings of giant pearls. The hand itself was ravishing. I leaned in to kiss her, having fun in anticipation of an evening that already appeared to be interesting. Then, I learned the name of the officer who I did not notice until then because of my distracted attention. It was Gabriele D'Annunzio, the man who, out of everyone, I had wanted to meet. . . . Completely captivated, I was no longer conscious of the time and the evening flowed by like a dream.[49]

By the end of 1920, such regal introductions were becoming a rarity for Luisa. The elite world she had spent the previous two decades shocking and seducing was growing ever smaller. The financial and social effects of the recent war had diminished the narrow universe of the haut monde. Tastes were changing. Youth had become paramount. *Vogue* and *Les Modes,* the most reliable seismographs of French fashion of the time, featured short-skirted models with bobbed hair hidden beneath tight cloche hats. If this was not horrific enough to any aging grande dame, magazine articles instructed these gamines on how to dress elegantly on a limited budget. Many great couture houses of the past were forced to close their doors in London and Paris because of lack of patronage.

Nearly forty years old, Casati had little place in a world where ready-made had become all the rage. But instead of reinventing herself yet again, she began to retain those personal trademarks of the now faded salon set. The red hair, cadaverous pallor, darkly kohled eyes, and scarlet lips remained unalterable, giving her more and more the unsettling appearance of a Kabuki performer. There still endured an audience to astonish among the idle rich, including Sir Basil Zaharoff, notorious Greek financier and armaments contractor; Hugh "Bendor" Grosvenor, the enormously wealthy Duke of Westminster; Arturo López, heir to the greatest fortune in South America; and society millionaire the Baron Maurice de Rothschild. Another admirer was the Aga Khan III, who once asked Luisa to be seated next to him at a dinner to be given in her honor. She agreed—providing at least six seats were kept vacant on either side of her own, so voluminous was her gown for the event.[50] In Paris, Casati went to see Charlie Chaplin's *Shoulder Arms* escorted by Augustus John and Ricciotti Garibaldi, younger son of the famous Italian patriot, and she even captivated the well-known German boulevardier Otto Haas-Heye, who first glimpsed her one afternoon at the Palace Hotel in St. Moritz:

> [Casati] was wearing a long redingote coat, a big, cream-colored hat and had an enormous bouquet of Parma violets on her chest. I said to myself, "Is she ever ugly!" And then I noted how there was not the least bit of white in her eyes. Raven-black and huge, they looked straight ahead and were like no other. At that same moment it hit me like lightning, "She is absolutely beautiful!"[51]

Casati also continued to attract the devotions of a cluster of effete young and titled *cavalier servants*, including Prince Giovanni Battista Serra, with whom she had traveled to Capri; Prince Giraci; and the adoring Marquis Don Ranieri Bourbon del Monte. Of the last, Augustus John once commented:

> As for the Marquis Bourbon del Monte, too much of a faithful dog, she treated him like dirt. Once, unable to bear the sight of his face any longer, she ordered him out of the taxi: "Voilà la femme que j'aime," he said to me, in tears, as he obediently disembarked.[52]

John's excessive profligacy left him no room to comment jealously on his former lover's attentive swains. In fact, the artist once noted candidly: "There was an evening . . . when Count Carlo Sforza and I humorously disputed the favors of the macaronic wonder who sat between us, laughing delightedly."[53] On other occasions, John took pleasure in making lewd suggestions to Luisa, watching in amusement as she ran from the room shrieking "Porco!" and other infuriated epithets.

Also acting as an occasional escort was Ezra Pound. During earlier visits to Venice, the American poet became acquainted with Luisa through Gabriele D'Annunzio. By this time, Pound had settled in Paris where he soon began a lifelong relationship with Olga Rudge, the American concert violinist and musicologist. Rudge had encountered Casati separately while summering on Capri in 1921 with Renata Borgatti. It was in Natalie Barney's boudoir that Pound and Rudge first met, among other select guests being received—all beneath the fierce gaze of Romaine Brooks's portrait of Luisa.[54] Pound paid homage to the Marchesa in his poetic masterwork *The Cantos*. Inspired by a particular line in reference to her from D'Annunzio's *Nocturne*, Canto III contains a mention of "peacocks in Koré's house."[55]

Rome and Venice, once places of personal revelation for Casati, no longer afforded her the stage she required for fulfillment. The villa on the via Piemonte began to lose its charm, and stays at the Palazzo dei Leoni on the Grand Canal became increasingly less frequent. While D'Annunzio now held court in his shrine on the shores of Lake Garda, the Marchesa desired a sanctum of her own. A new venue was sought in which to continue exploring a thoroughly eccentric existence. Within the palace of a dead poet, Luisa Casati would prove herself capable of conjuring the most extravagant visions one final time.

Medusa in Pearls

1921-1927

There on the table lay a jumbled half-century of society artists and authentic geniuses who had imprisoned on their canvases her haughty eyebrows and Baudelairian pupils, immobilized the abandon or affectation of her gestures, molded in their clay her high cheekbones and breasts proudly set apart, and searched among their paints for the variations of light and time on her skin.
   —*Maurice Druon*, La Volupté d'être

Tall and gaunt with heavily made-up eyes, she represented a past age of splendor when a few beautiful and wealthy women adopted an almost brutally individualistic way of living and presenting themselves to the public.
   —*Elsa Schiaparelli*

1

Just outside Paris lies the pleasure palace of Versailles. This majestic shrine to the glory of the French monarchy was once the carnival ground of an earlier epoch. Versailles saw the excessive splendors of its creator, the Sun King, Louis XIV; the frivolities of famed courtesans Madame de Pompadour and Madame du Barry; the selfish extravagances of Marie Antoinette; and the megalomaniacal strategies of Emperor Napoleon. Rivaling the Royal Palace itself in grandeur are numerous outbuildings and pavilions. One of the most notable is the Grand Trianon. In 1899, this Italianate single-story structure, with a façade of pink and white marble, served as a model when the affluent engineer Arthur Schweitzer and his wife commissioned a private home built in Le Vésinet, the exclusive Parisian suburb about ten miles west of the city. The mansion's surface of pink marble would later determine the estate's name, Le Palais Rose. Ideally situated at the corner of the Allée des Fêtes and the rue Diderot, it included extensive grounds, various outbuildings, and prestigious lake views. Within only a few years, the financially ruined Schweitzer was forced to sell the property to the wealthy Indian industrialist Ratanji Jamsetji Tata for the reputed price of three pearls and one perfect emerald.[1]

In 1908, the Palais Rose was bought by Comte Robert de Montesquiou, who wished to retreat from the gossipy soirées and flamboyant parties of Paris to mourn his lover, Gabriel de Yturri, who had recently died from neglected diabetes. This seclusion did not hinder the nobleman from receiving frequent visits from such guests as Sarah Bernhardt, Debussy, Maurice Rostand, Rodin, and even D'Annunzio. By early 1921, decades of snobbish revelry and overindulgence had helped Montesquiou contract uremic poisoning, and, ironically, much of the Comte's last year would be spent not in the convivial atmosphere of his accustomed grand salons but in the antiseptically sterile wards of private clinics. Late autumn found the bon vivant peacock elegant to the last, bundled in furs and clutching the blue porcelain handle of his favorite walking stick on a final excursion to warmer climes. The man Marcel Proust once dubbed "the Professor of Beauty" died on December 11, 1921, at Menton along the French Riviera. For the remainder of that winter, the snows gathered about the vacant and shuttered palace, awaiting the arrival of its next inhabitant. Very soon, the dignified avenues of Le Vésinet would receive a shock.

Luisa Casati had purchased the deceased poet's home. During the thirteen years of Montesquiou's occupation, the Palais Rose had been crammed with a collection of aesthetic excess. Rooms overflowed with bibelots and Gallé glass vases filled with bouquets of the Comte's preferred blue hydrangeas. Even the gardens could not escape the dandy's exacting vision.

Landscapers had been hired to arrange specific groupings of trees, plants, and flowers so that a perfectly framed horticultural masterpiece might be viewed through each window. Behind the palace stood Montesquiou's rose-colored folly, the Pavillon de l'Amour, but even this could not compare to the garden's twelve-ton pink marble fountain adorned with water-spouting dolphins. This gaudy curio had once served as the bathing pool of Madame de Montespan, the celebrated courtesan from the court of the Sun King.[2] Now the Palais Rose would be transformed yet again to the specifications of its newest occupant—and made to accommodate the six train cars of marble slabs, assorted columns, and Egyptian alabaster vases with which she arrived.

Luisa stripped the building's interiors of their former ostentation. Walls were removed to create an immense ground level. The marble floor from the Roman villa, which had been used at the Palazzo dei Leoni as well, was installed. This was further ornamented with an alabaster sun that could be made to radiate by a hidden light source. According to André Germain, the house was now "almost empty, furnished only with . . . some curule chairs, and a collection of very beautiful medallions of the Roman emperors. It seemed to be waiting for some royal assassination."[3] As in the villa in Rome, the color scheme was dominated by black, white, and gold. Perhaps Luisa repeatedly favored such monochromatic design so that her own physical aesthetic might deliberately contrast for dramatic effect. One bathroom featured an oversized alabaster tub, supported on the back of gilded lions, the water of which flowed from the mouths of jade fish. In the corner of one salon stood a tall spire of curling horn, claimed to be that of a unicorn, and throughout the floors were covered with tiger and leopard skins.

These trophies nostalgically recalled Luisa's now greatly reduced menagerie. Besides several colorful parrots, all that remained of her private zoo were a tame cobra named Agamemnon and the prized boa constrictor kept in a crystal enclosure in the palace's foyer. For a short time, the Marchesa retained at least one of the cheetahs that had stalked her Venetian gardens. She would later hire a pair of Bengal tigers for a particular soirée; while their trainer hid nearby, the menacing animals lay about Luisa's heels as she greeted guests from the palace steps. It was reported how even the bravest of the male revelers, required to kiss their hostess's hand, were not reassured by the cats' leashed condition.[4] Then there was the addition to the more permanent Casati bestiary. The creation of a full-size, mechanical, stuffed black panther was commissioned from a Parisian taxidermist, and it soon became one of the mansion's most unique embellishments. Its purpose, Luisa claimed, was "to surprise my guests and disconcert burglars."[5] Controlled electronically, the creature was capable of moving its head and tail, lighting its green eyes, and growling ferociously. A newspaper report from 1926 claimed that the panther was named Toto and had once been one of Casati's most cherished pets. Much to her dismay, it was ordered shot after killing two men.[6]

A detached pavilion that Montesquiou had built as a library now contained books, bound in matching bindings of gilded leather, on magic and spell casting. More important, this structure, known as L'Ermitage, was converted into a private gallery devoted to the Marchesa's portraits. A precise count of its contents is not extant, although one report states that Casati owned more than one hundred thirty images of herself by 1923.[7] Canvases hung on the pavilion's walls, including those by Depero, Boccioni, Martini, Zuloaga, and the more recent odalisque painting by Beltrán y Masses. Boldini's 1908 portrait and such three-dimensional objects as Troubetzkoy's bronze and an ewer sculpted to resemble Luisa's face by Italian ceramist Renato Bertelli were on view as well. To inaugurate this narcissistic sanctum, Casati commissioned Spaniard José María Sert to paint her likeness. The artist was then enjoying great success as a specialist in large-scale murals that adorned the interiors of cathedrals and private homes, as well as such international luxury hotels as New York City's Waldorf-Astoria. Inspired by the monumental serpent in the Marchesa's foyer, Sert portrayed the reptile on a wide wall panel in the pavilion, where it joined its mistress, who was pictured as a nude Eve in the Garden of Eden.

An estate as imposing as the Palais Rose required an extensive housekeeping staff to maintain it. Casati hired another towering black man, Yamina, as personal chauffeur for the new midnight-blue Rolls-Royce, which was purchased to transport her on frequent journeys into Paris. A Tunisian, Mohammed Ben Abdullah, became Luisa's valet, and a Russian chef, Georges, held sway in the palace's kitchen.[8] A battalion of personal maids and gardeners were also at the Marchesa's call.

Casati was additionally in need of a new jeweler. The era of art nouveau had passed, and Luisa, disenchanted with the baubles of René Lalique, began patronizing the house of Cartier. On Casati's demand, proprietor and designer Jeanne Toussaint would often personally make the journey from Cartier's Parisian address on the rue de la Paix to Le Vésinet bearing the boutique's signature red boxes filled with a selection of emeralds, diamonds, and the Marchesa's favorite, oversized black and white pearls. In a letter to Louis Cartier, Toussaint confirmed how a curiosity observed at Luisa's home directly inspired one of her most celebrated design motifs: "The sight of that stuffed panther had confirmed me in my desire to create a panther-jewel."[9]

Finally, the building Casati referred to as her own "Palais de rêve" was completed. A celebration was essential to launch it properly, but in contrast to the sumptuous affairs for which she was renowned, the premiere event was an intimate luncheon. Among the select few to receive an invitation was Cécile Sorel. As fate decided, a torrential downpour occurred that afternoon. The actress's memoirs recount the tempestuous party:

> [Casati] invited us to visit the pavilion reserved for her numerous portraits and her nudes. Several servants had opened umbrellas to protect us from the storm that was raging while we crossed the garden. With a tight gold lamé dress on, the Marchesa walked through the pouring rain, wet as she was, in the freezing laminated corset that sapped away at her body heat. She offered her images up for our admiration. Then, without even drying off, she went back with us into the rooms.[10]

Returning to the dining room, hung with black velvet and lit by innumerable black candles flickering from the chamber's silver chandeliers, the Marchesa invited Sorel to perform a selection of recitations. Throughout the presentation, Luisa stood as rigidly as a statue in the far corner of the room, eerily illuminated by the candlelight, while, as Sorel noted, "drops continued to fall from her shoulders and gilded sides."[11] The guests departed beneath cloud-ridden skies and pounding rain. This disappointing baptismal fête for the Palais Rose would prove to be a harbinger of darker misfortunes to come.

Later that same year, Casati became obsessed with reuniting with D'Annunzio. She forwarded a telegram from her Roman villa, asking to visit the writer in his lakeside shrine. Although permission was granted, she never followed through on the proposition. D'Annunzio sent a note of concern regarding this unlikely absence: "Why, in these past days, has my imagination been continually occupied by Coré? I have not heard from her. I don't know where she is. . . . Several weeks ago, you offered me the opportunity of seeing you again. And I was left perplexed."[12] Although this correspondence was addressed to the via Piemonte, Luisa replied from the Alps: "Thank you dearest friend for the immense joy of this letter. I'd come down from the Olympic heights of St. Moritz just to see you in your harem—can I see you? Will you come to Seville with me in April? —Coré"[13] D'Annunzio declined on the excursion to Spain and it would be another two years before Casati finally accepted his invitation to the Vittoriale. Even so, the many months in between were not spent idly.

If Luisa was not to be found in St. Moritz or Rome, she might be seen along the place Vendôme in Paris. More fanciful was the rumor that she had joined Italian Duke Achille Lecca di Guevara on a round-the-world trip by airplane. Apparently, the Duke boasted to friends of how they had engaged in continual amorous activities during the entire flight.[14] Much more credible are the details surrounding the Marchesa's brief association with fashion designer Elsa Schiaparelli. The couturier had a boutique just across the place Vendôme from where Luisa was in residence at the Hôtel du Rhin. Schiaparelli was then gaining notoriety as the innovator of the provocative color "shocking pink" and as a dressmaker whose designs were admired and inspired by the emerging surrealists. The Marchesa, too, was still capable of delivering the unexpected, as related in the designer's autobiography, *Shocking Life*. Learning of Casati's latest visit to the French capital, Schiaparelli sent one of her employees to the hotel with a gift in an attempt to win her as a client. The salesgirl returned to Schiaparelli with an astonishing account: "She found the Marchesa in bed, fully made-up in the old vamp style, covered with a rug of black ostrich feathers, eating a breakfast of fried fish and drinking straight Pernod while trying on a newspaper scarf."[15]

Although she did not patronize Schiaparelli's boutique, Luisa would become part of surrealist history through the camera lens of one of its key figures. In 1921, American-born photographer Man Ray journeyed to Paris—the city that then became his permanent home. Through Marcel Duchamp, whom he had first met in the United States, Man Ray made friends with a group of struggling artists. Among them were the founders of the influential dada and surrealist movements, Max Ernst, André Breton, and Salvador Dalí. The following year, Man Ray's photographic career benefited from a fortuitous meeting when a chimerical visitor came to his far from regal room at the Grand Hôtel des Écoles. The artist's autobiography, *Self Portrait*, first sets the stage:

> I received a visit from a tall imposing woman in black with
> enormous eyes emphasized with black makeup. She wore a high
> headdress in black lace and bent her head slightly as she came
> through the door, as if it were too low for her. Introducing herself
> as the Marquise Casati, she expressed the wish to have herself
> photographed.[16]

Man Ray was quick to accept the offer and its subject's stipulation of being immortalized in her hotel suite surrounded by a collection of curiosities. After Casati's departure, the photographer began to prepare for the session: "I informed myself about her—she was famous in aristocratic circles, but considered rather eccentric."[17]

At last, Man Ray arrived at the Marchesa's suite, where she greeted him garbed in a silk dressing gown. Through eyes heavily ringed with dark makeup, she watched as the photographic equipment was arranged, seated at a table on which was displayed an artificial floral bouquet of jade and precious stones. The shoot continued until fate reportedly interfered significantly for both photographer and subject:

> When I turned on my lights there was a quick flash and everything
> went dark. As usual in French interiors, every room was wired and
> fused for a minimum of current. The porter replaced the burned-out
> fuses, but I did not dare use my lights again. I told the Marquise that
> I'd use the ordinary lighting in the room, but that the poses would be
> longer and she must try to hold them as still as possible. It was trying
> work—the lady acted as if I were doing a movie of her.
>
> That night when I developed my negatives, they were all blurred;
> I put them aside and considered the sitting a failure. Not hearing from
> me, she phoned me sometime later; when I informed her that the
> negatives were worthless, she insisted on seeing some prints, bad as they
> were. I printed up a couple on which there was a semblance of a face.[18]

Man Ray returned to the Hôtel du Rhin with the products of the session. Six images are known to have survived from this particular shoot. Each has a disarming weirdness, suggesting its model has been captured through some form of spirit photography. The first shows Casati peering through the rear glass wall of a vitrine containing her bouquet of jeweled flowers. On closer inspection, Man Ray can be seen at his camera, mirrored in the glass sphere held in her hand as if conjured up by the Marchesa. In the next, a variation on this image, Luisa holds the sphere to her face while standing in slight profile. In the third photograph, she is a mere reflection, visible in the window glass of an opened French door that leads out to the balcony. Posed by a large fishbowl, she appears in the fourth image wearing a gown with sleeves of pearls. The fifth portrait offers an unusual opportunity to observe Casati's raccoon-like eye makeup in medium close-up; just discernible around her head is a halo created by the outline of the same fishbowl set directly behind her.

But the last photograph revealed the unexpected result of the alleged electrical failure:

> [The image had] three pairs of eyes. It might have passed for a
> Surrealist version of the Medusa. She was enchanted with this one—
> said I had portrayed her soul, and ordered dozens of prints. I wished
> other sitters were as easy to please. The picture of the Marquise went
> all over Paris; sitters began coming in—people from more exclusive
> circles, all expecting miracles from me.[19]

In recent years, analysis of the archival plate of this particular image proves Man Ray's claims to have been more theatrical than true. The effect was achieved through deliberate double exposure. This single image of Luisa would become one of her most famous representations, and it has been credited as one of the first and most potent surrealist photographs.

In addition to the photographs, Man Ray completed a still life of Casati in 1924 using the *cliché verre* process. By this method, an image is created by scratching a drawing onto a coated glass plate that was then contact-printed on sensitized paper. The artist based this work on the triple-eyed portrait, and, in addition, surrounded his subject with a variety of objects.

Man Ray's photographs of the Marchesa, and the influential commissions stemming from them, gave him entry into a lucrative and artistically noteworthy career. He obtained highly visible work as a fashion photographer for such important magazines as *Harper's Bazaar, Vu,* and *Vogue.* Although he was an occasional guest at future extravaganzas at the Palais Rose, another thirteen years would pass before Luisa would pose again for Man Ray's camera.

2

As Man Ray feared, the success of Luisa's triple-eyed portrait created a demand among the elite for identical marvels. One member of the French aristocratic clique eager to visit Man Ray's studio was the Comte Étienne de Beaumont. This art and theater patron had aspirations of becoming an impresario much in the style of Diaghilev. The Comte had even founded his own ballet troupe. But de Beaumont's true notoriety was earned as a master of fêtes. Both he and his wife, Édith, ruled over the salons of Paris from their mansion on the rue Masseran for nearly three decades. The couple was most known for the annual Beaumont Ball they gave every year from the early 1920s until 1949.

Each of these Soirées de Paris was assigned a different theme, and guests were strictly instructed to arrive costumed accordingly. One event was proclaimed a Games Ball, at which revelers came attired as merry-go-rounds and domino pieces. At the Perrault Ball, the Comte appeared as Cupid. Sheathed in pink tights and feathered wings, he sought out potential victims for his tiny bow and arrow among a ballroom filled with assorted Sleeping Beauties and Prince Charmings. Merrymakers at the Kings and Queens Ball included couturier Christian Dior, costumed as a lordly lion; scenic designer Christian Bérard, in the corpulent form of Henry VIII; and artist Leonor Fini, in red finery and curling horns, as Persephone, Queen of Hell.[20]

Luisa became well acquainted with the de Beaumonts and was a frequent guest at their masquerades. Although the majority of her costumes for them are unknown, images and accounts document several of the most outstanding. A photo-portrait shows Casati, her hair flared out on end, holding a live snake draped across her shoulders. An unknown artist constructed a collage to commemorate the de Beaumonts' Sea Ball. Disguised as fish, shells, and cellophane-wrapped jellyfish, attendees "swam" beneath blue and green colored lights. Their host oversaw the festivities as a giant manta ray. Among the many guests, the collage depicts Luisa as a 1920s-style Venus having risen from the waters in an enormous shell. Gargantuan pearls are shown at her feet.

The Marchesa chose wisely when she asked her old friend Léon Bakst to devise an ensemble for a particularly notable ball held at the Paris Opéra House in 1922. For it, Bakst invented one of his most outlandish creations. It was so elaborate that it required drastic alteration before it was wearable. Known as either "The Queen of the Night" or simply as "Light," the original costume was to consist of a gilt hoopskirt decorated with stars and a train of translucent blue silk. Ultimately pants were substituted for the skirt to provide ease of movement. The headdress was an explosion of feathers and silver and gold tendrils adorned with celestial symbols. The entire outfit sparkled with genuine diamonds that the Marchesa further embellished with diamond bracelets and tiara. The actual execution of Bakst's conception could only be entrusted to the hands of a genius, so Casati commissioned Worth to create it—the very same Parisian fashion house that had designed her mother's gowns in which she enjoyed pretending as a child. Documented by several photographs, this fantasy cost the substantial sum of twenty thousand francs and took three months to complete.[21]

The *Gazette du Bon Genre* gave a vivid account of this fancy dress event known as the Bal Vénitien. Even though it was presided over by Luisa's actress friend Cécile Sorel as the embodiment of La Serenissima, the Marchesa became the evening's central attraction. Masked revelers gazed in wonderment as she made a legendary entrance rising upward on a golden disk. Suddenly, the darkened hall was set ablaze as the light of the surrounding lanterns reflected the network of diamonds and jeweled headdress worn by Casati. Witnesses swore that she was nude beneath the revealing costume. Carrying a large white lily, the Marchesa stood resplendent before an awed assembly that included Ida Rubinstein, Prince Karam de Kapurthala of India, and Parisian stage star Edouard de Max. Next, Étienne de Beaumont joined Luisa. Dressed completely in blue, the Comte presented her with a gold orb.[22]

Not designed by Bakst and far less successful was a costume worn at a subsequent fête given by the de Beaumonts. Cecil Beaton described it in *The Glass of Fashion*:

The Marquesa Casati decided to appear as an electrically equipped Saint Sebastian. She was to wear armour pierced with hundreds of arrows, each studded with glittering stars that were to light up when the Marquesa appeared. On the morning of the ball, she arrived . . . bringing a fleet of servants, an electrician, and stoves for boiling water to make cups of tea or coffee while the elaborate preparations for her appearance were in progress. . . . But at the moment of being plugged in a disaster took place: the costume was short-circuited, and, instead of being lighted up with a thousand stars, the Marquesa suffered an electric shock that sent her into a backward somersault. She did not recover in time to appear at the party, leaving a note . . . that stated simply, "Milles regrets."[23]

But a single hair-raising experience would never have hindered Casati from another attempt to amaze an audience. A supposedly similar mishap was reported at a different party. The Marchesa was said to have attended another masquerade at the de Beaumonts, this one designed by Pablo Picasso. In accordance with the cubist setting, Luisa appeared in an outfit of wire and light bulbs constructed to resemble one of the artist's drawings. This three-dimensional impersonation hardly passed through the entryway before its electrical cable became twisted, and Casati was nearly electrocuted. As awestruck revelers looked on, she crumpled within a cage of sputtering wires and flickering lights. Christian Bérard, who witnessed the catastrophe, described the fallen Marchesa as a "smashed zeppelin."

Such diversions as the Beaumont balls and their like offered too infrequent relief from the isolation Casati encountered at the Palais Rose. There did not seem to be a sufficient number of acquaintances to invite for gatherings of her own. Even if there were, the nearly hour-long drive to Le Vésinet from Paris hindered any willingness to travel there often enough to satisfy the insatiable Marchesa. Abandoned by her audience, she was reduced to more solitary pursuits. For countless hours, Luisa, garbed in less formal outfits of transparent mauve silk, raced through the countryside in her lemon-yellow Hispano Suiza[24] or her chauffeur-driven Rolls-Royce.

More and more frequently, she turned to stimulants when the days dragged too heavily. Both the intoxicating liqueur absinthe[25] and the smoky daydreams of opium soothed the lonely afternoons. But these insular spells could be broken by an odd excursion with a sympathetic, and usually unsuspecting, companion. Cecil Beaton related how Luisa's capricious motivation for one shopping excursion was in order to obtain an object of no particular specifications other than it was of the precise orange color she fancied at that moment. After what seemed to be visits to countless boutiques,

Casati chanced upon a Fabergé cigarette case enameled in the desired hue. Satisfied, the bibelot was purchased and the hunt for that day was over.

As further entertainment, Luisa gave parties for formerly prominent members of the Russian nobility, including the rakish Grand Duke Alexander Mikhailovich, past Admiral of the Russian Navy and brother-in-law to the late Czar Nicholas II. The Palais Rose provided them with a taste of the opulence they had enjoyed before their status as refugees. Some were known to abscond with items from their hostess's dinner table. At one such affair, Prince Youssoupov pilfered a jar of mustard among other trifles. When these accidentally fell from his pockets to smash on the floor, Youssoupov rallied from embarrassment by blaming Rasputin's ghost for still haunting him.[26]

To her acquaintance Sir Francis Rose, Casati was still at this time "as beautiful as a black panther and as terrible." He noted how the use of both belladonna and stimulants had made her eyes, so often concealed behind a veil, as flaming red as her hair. One evening, Rose accompanied Christian Bérard by invitation to the Palais Rose. The guests were escorted by liveried footmen directly to Luisa's bedroom, where they discovered their hostess enveloped in white tulle and crowned by an upside-down silver flower pot, adorned by a single white ostrich plume. Immediately, she commanded Rose and Bérard to join her where she sat on a vast green carpet made to resemble a grassy lawn. Casati had taken aesthetic outrage at the felt daisies that were scattered, among a variety of other wild flowers, about its expanse. Each armed with gilded scissors, the trio snipped away the offending blooms in what would prove an exasperating task. In keeping with Luisa's bucolic fantasy of the moment, they sustained themselves on foie gras and champagne served from a picnic basket presented by a black youth in fancy dress.[27]

Casati still attracted the interest of new artists. One was Adrian Désiré Etienne, who established a career under the pseudonym Drian. An associate of Augustus John, his distinctive pencil and charcoal sketches of French society women adorned the pages of such periodicals as *La Gazette du Bon Ton* and *Harper's Bazaar*. Drian would complete numerous drawings of Luisa in such guises as Sarah Bernhardt, the Sun, and a sphinx in the gardens of the Palais Rose, or as the stylish mistress of the Palazzo dei Leoni greeting guests disembarking from gondolas. One of these sketches is a clever study in self-referentialism. The Marchesa is shown posing for a portrait for Drian and the canvas being completed within the drawing mimics Augustus John's famed second portrait of Casati.[28] Drian also captured Luisa in two oil paintings. In one, a life-sized bust, she is attired in a simple white blouse and fur stole; the second portrays her as the virgin responsible for the capture of the unicorn.

Another confidant gained at this time was Count Knut Corfitz Bonde, the Scandinavian diplomat and friend of Dr. Axel Munthe. Bonde knew all the stories of Casati's hostile seizure of the Villa San Michele two years earlier. Even so, he became quite fond of her as noted in his book about Munthe's home on Capri:

> Coincidence had assembled us at a rich American artist's hotel room in the Faubourg Saint-Germain. We were only four at this luncheon, but regardless, the Marquise showed up in an embroidered gold dress possibly from the curtains of San Michele. As soon as she came in she caused perpetual agitation in the room, the sun hitting her from the garden blinds with a discrete elegance. She manipulated the conversation with a strong contralto voice. After having drunk a few cocktails she took off her black embroidered veil and unbuttoned the first few buttons of her black velvet cloak, revealing her strange beauty.
>
> We were served an enormous lunch in the dining room. . . . I had never seen such a voracious woman as the Marquise. She ate and drank without stopping. She talked about the latest Parisian scandals, citing names that were unknown to me. She talked about new art exhibitions, and novels that had just been published as if she had read them all. She talked about politics, as if she knew all the men of state, like she talked of frivolous matters. During her long monologue she agitated her long frail hands, ornated with heavy gold bracelets, which seemed to weigh her down.
>
> After lunch . . . she proceeded on citing a passage from Proust, analyzing each term. My companions took part in this discussion. But I was content with just listening without saying a word.[29]

When Robert de Montesquiou once described the Baroness Elsie Deslandes as the "ambassadress of the aesthetic movement in Paris," he did so with ample reason. Her salons sparkled with such wits as Oscar Wilde, Marcel Proust, Jean Lorrain, and the dandified poet himself. These guests were received as the Baroness lounged regally on a low divan while feeding a bronze statue of a frog a glittering diet of loose gems. But with the scattering and demise of her irreplaceable gallants, the triumphs of Deslandes became relegated to legend only. During her twilight years of increasing poverty, the tiny, rotund Baroness had gained a reputation for possessing divinatory powers of startling accuracy. Luisa was among those amazed at her precise predictions. One evening, Casati invited Bonde to her suite at the Hôtel du Rhin to witness the miraculous talents of the aging prophet. The writer arrived to find Luisa dressed in a white satin gown with ropes of pearls wound about her wrists. Deslandes was already present, as was Casati's escort, the young Marquis Bourbon del Monte. A small dining table for the quartet was arranged in the suite's front salon. Bonde recounts the repast in preparation for that evening's entertainment:

> What we each ordered was as diverse as each one of us. The Marquise devoured a raw steak and drank beer; the Baroness did not eat anything but drank large glasses of French mineral spa water; as for the two gentlemen it was the good ordinary French menu with champagne. The conversation topics were controlled by the women. After the meal, while we drank our coffees and smoked our cigarettes, the Baroness, as usual smoking and still drinking a lot, gave us little discourses, half-political and half-religious, of the future. . . . These were all very abstract and not attached to any time period.[30]

With unexpected generosity, Casati assisted Elsie Deslandes during her financial troubles. The Baroness's house was becoming increasingly empty as she was reduced to selling her possessions. About to be lost were the bronze figure of a lamb and a golden unicorn with onyx eyes and ivory horn. When Deslandes desperately sought a potential owner worthy enough to shelter the talismanic beasts, Luisa welcomed the pair into the Palais Rose.[31]

Luisa's assistance, however, had not been bestowed on her native land. By this time, a continual plague of paralyzing strikes and civil unrest was spreading throughout Italy. In his stronghold along Lake Garda, D'Annunzio was inflamed by this dire situation. The fascist revolution would take place on August 3, 1922, at which time D'Annunzio and Mussolini were hailed as saviors of the people. But ten days later, a bizarre occurrence signaled the downfall of the writer's career. During a soirée at the Vittoriale D'Annunzio toppled from a salon window and fractured his skull. The event still remains a mystery. Some attribute the fall to an accident, failed suicide, or even attempted murder. No explanation was ever offered by D'Annunzio himself. With brutal truthfulness, Philippe Jullian sums up the remainder of the writer's life from this point onward: "The date of 13 August 1922 marks a breaking-point in the life of the poet. Thereafter, he was to grow old without dignity in a sort of Escorial, a combination of opium-den, sacristy, and museum of plaster casts."[32]

3

Luisa requested a multitude of prints of Man Ray's surrealist portrait, and one quickly arrived at the Vittoriale. But the black and white picture received by D'Annunzio had been altered by the Marchesa. Either side of the

subject's neck was trimmed vertically, thus exaggerating its length to unnatural proportions. The result, resembling the bust of an art deco sphinx,
was then pasted onto a sheet of heavy paper. On one side of the head Casati
inscribed her affectionate name for D'Annunzio, Ariel, in purple ink, and her
own D'Annunzian appellation of Coré adorned the opposite side. Directly
below the image was written "La Figure de Cire."[33]

When D'Annunzio's exile to Lake Garda and Casati's seclusion at the
Palais Rose coincided, an intense emotion rekindled between the pair. After
years of receiving Luisa's penned enigmas, so often accompanied by reproductions of her innumerable portraits, D'Annunzio wanted to once more
become close to his Coré. In a poignant letter to Casati from February 1923,
the poet wrote:

> Dear, dear, friend, why does all that which comes to me from you
> touch me so much inside? Maybe because *we have not yet gotten to
> know each other.* Since that far off day when I first saw a subtle, young
> Amazon gallop right in front of me, in that wasteland of Gallarate.
> I remember it. Coré does not.[34]

In March 1923, D'Annunzio celebrated his sixtieth birthday. His muse
had turned forty-two less then two months earlier. Luisa, too, was now
suffering from a sense of diminishing powers, although not as severely, in a
world in which neither of them seemed as provocative as before. As of late,
it was not unusual for the Marchesa to find companionship only in the
many static works that represented her in her gallery. And now, for the first
time, an uncomfortable reality began to make itself known: Casati's finances
were becoming insufficient to support her flamboyant lifestyle. Most important, the purchase of the Palais Rose had not been a wise decision. Although
it suited her criteria as an ideal palace in some chic fairy tale, the mansion
was both too remote and too costly to maintain.

Luisa made a rare visit to her native city in early December 1923 to sell
off the Amman residence in Monza, the Villa Amalia, and all of her holdings in her father's cotton mills in Pordenone. Arrangements were also
proceeding for the sale of the villa in Rome. But even during this mission
to salvage an unstable monetary situation, Luisa made sure to reside at the
fashionable Hotel de la Ville.

From her suite there a telegram was sent to D'Annunzio, requesting
access to his shrine. With undiminished romanticism, his reply of December 5 claims that his thoughts of her led to a psychic episode: "Another case
of telepathy . . . last night between ten and midnight." This was followed
cryptically with "I both desire and dread seeing you again . . . from the
seventh day I will await you."[35]

Before Gabriele D'Annunzio occupied the Vittoriale, it had been an unassuming house, nestled amid olive groves on a hillside overlooking Lake Garda. The simple building was subsequently transformed by the poet's eclectic tastes into a utopia, where reality was forbidden to enter. Within its stuccoed walls was a maze of claustrophobic chambers crammed with cabinets, shelves, and vitrines, overstuffed with a confusion of mementos—nearly nine hundred ornaments cluttered one bathroom alone. Other rooms, all suffused with choking perfumes, were lined with showcases displaying yellowed photographs and letters, tarnished medals, and defunct uniforms. Plaster casts of Michelangelo's sculptures of male slaves stood guard in corners; the nude torsos were given a weirdly provocative sexual appeal by being painted in lifelike flesh tones and then clad in Poiret robes and tawdry theatrical jewelry. Another statue, a bronze of Saint Francis, wore an American cowboy's holster, complete with pistol.

Similar wonders, both unabashedly crass and sublimely elegant, continued throughout the villa. From a hook in the auditorium's domed ceiling dangled the biplane in which D'Annunzio had made wartime propaganda raids. A V-type Fiat, the vehicle used for the poet's entrance into Fiume, was parked beneath an arched canopy beside a yellow limousine. With its prow lodged in a sea of cement, the full-size cruiser *Puglia*, salvaged from the Italian Navy, became a garden outlook over the shores of the lake below, its decks vacant except for a platoon of cypress trees standing at attention. At times, its guns were heard across the water firing a salute to arriving guests. D'Annunzio often presided over this imaginary kingdom garbed in the brown velvet habit of a monk with a large cross of diamonds about his neck. An armed manservant in a uniform of gold or silver and a serving maid dressed as a nun attended to their sovereign.

Luisa entered this phantasmagorical setting for the first time on December 12, 1923. Its owner directed her into a boudoir known as the Leda Room, its name made evident by the bedstead carving of a nude nymphette being ravished by a swan. D'Annunzio's own sanctum was the Room of the Leper. The contents of this scarlet chamber imbued it with an atmosphere of religiously exalted profanity. Walls were adorned with a collection of women's satin evening gloves—trophies, D'Annunzio claimed, of "all those ladies who lost their heads."[36] A life-sized wax effigy of a bleeding Saint Sebastian stood beside a narrow bed, surrounded by framed photographs of the poet's past lovers. During her visit, one of Luisa's portraits by de Meyer was wisely placed in the forefront of other sepia-toned muses.[37]

The Marchesa arrived at the Vittoriale with an appropriate gift once belonging to another decadent poet—a ring previously worn by Lord Byron. Luisa's stay would last only two days before her return to Milan. There she found a telegram from D'Annunzio already waiting for her at the Hotel de la Ville: "Ariel is immersed in melancholy and battles against rancor."[38] Another telegram arrived the following day: "I have found a golden amphorette fallen from one of your necklaces—It is empty and there is not even a hope in the bottom—Ariel."[39]

Luisa eased the writer's loneliness, and her own, by returning to the Vittoriale by car at seven in the evening on December 24. It would prove to be a further rekindling of the magical times the two had shared. D'Annunzio made certain to escort her along one corridor lined with more than two thousand books. Here, the bindings of the books and all of the door facings were emblazoned with the inscription "Forse che sì forse che no," honoring the writer's novel of the same name inspired years before by Luisa. A Christmas Eve repast was laid in the dining room that night. It was an ideal setting, with its red- and gold-lacquered walls and black chairs. An art deco statue by Le Faguays of a rutting satyr pursued a nymph across the dinner table decorated with lace and wine glasses from Venice. Then D'Annunzio entertained his guest with an antique Russian marionette. The puppet, with its grinning face, was made to tell ribald jokes as it danced across the mountain of Christmas greetings that littered the poet's desk. Both Coré and Ariel enjoyed this special holiday immensely.

Shortly afterward, Luisa returned to Milan to finish the disposal of her properties. But there was a surprise when her luggage was unpacked. "The puppet with lead wires jumped out of my suitcase," she wrote D'Annunzio. Then she added with childlike hopefulness: "What should I do? Do I have to send it back?" The note ended with "infinite thanks for the Christmas—Coré"[40]

Spring 1924 found Casati at the Hagenbeck Zoo in Hamburg, Germany.[41] Here was the ideal boutique for Luisa to select a gift for her Ariel. The present's impending arrival was announced at the Vittoriale by a postcard dated April 24: "You will receive a tortoise from Hagenbeck. Put it in your garden."[42] Ten days later, the creature found itself in certainly much warmer and decadent surroundings than its former German home. D'Annunzio wrote to Luisa on May 6: "The tortoise has arrived surpassing in speed Coré, who maybe will arrive next year. . . . I work much and think of my far-off friend."[43] It was said that this note of gratitude was accompanied by D'Annunzio's reciprocal gift of a tame black alligator.[44]

The poet would have to console himself with memories, for Luisa did not respond to his request. Nor did she remain at the Palais Rose during the summer of 1924, when Paris served as the site for the Olympic games. Instead, Casati conducted an international race of her own. From Le Vésinet, she flew to Milan and Rome for further legal consultations. There was a visit to Lahage and a stop in Verdun to view the site of the legendary battle of the Great War. She traveled to Constantinople aboard the Orient Express and on to Kemel Pacha. Along the way, there was a stay in Budapest. D'Annunzio littered Casati's trail with telegrams in an effort to lure her back to the Vittoriale. "I maternally follow Coré everywhere as if I were Demeter," he wrote. "I welcome Coré to return right away to Hell where Hades awaits her."[45] But Luisa did not descend into Ariel's underworld. She was off to Venice.

Luisa's journey to the Palazzo dei Leoni was an unhappy one, for its purpose was to surrender this fantasy palace on the Grand Canal. Even so, she would make attempts to have the city declare it a national monument. It was only then that she contacted D'Annunzio with a lengthy telegram to gain his assistance on this crusade. With unending patience, D'Annunzio did his utmost to assure her of his belief in protecting the palazzo and its gardens, but Casati's quest failed. Several years later, the periodical *The American Weekly* noted that the palazzo had been transformed into "a gloomy government museum, considerably neglected."[46]

Again in Milan, Casati received yet another appeal to return to Lake Garda: "I have waited since 29 July . . . Leda's Room is ready."[47] Luisa accepted the invitation and arrived during the first weeks of August 1924.

Once more at the Vittoriale, the Marchesa was presented with a gift of an agate belt. She was also able to visit the tortoise as it basked in the gardens. Luisa asked what D'Annunzian name had been selected for the pet. Her dismay was considerable when she learned it was nothing more high-born than Carolina. Quick to soothe her ire, the poet attributed this choice to the gardeners. She was reassured when told that D'Annunzio himself used the more dignified name of Cheli, derived from the Greek word for tortoise.

Shortly afterward, Luisa resumed traveling at a furious pace. A trip to Spain was arranged to visit painter Ignacio Zuloaga, after which she returned to Italy to finish clearing away the remaining items from the Roman villa. Before the house's subsequent disposal, Casati made certain to have the Egyptian statue that resembled her transported to the Palais Rose. Soon, her depleted bank accounts would be replenished by the sale of the Italian homes and cotton holdings. Now yet another fortune would be at her disposal, but Luisa seemed unaware of the connection between the devastating financial setbacks that had necessitated the liquidation of her family's estates and her own careless spending.

Casati's costly indulgences in satisfying her obsessions would not be stopped. One that came to the forefront in 1924 was her lingering fascination with her childhood heroine, the Comtesse de Castiglione. Shopping sprees throughout Paris had produced a remarkable accumulation of objects once belonging to the mistress of Napoleon III.[48] These included fans, embroideries, portraits, books, and even saltcellars, as well as a pair of sandals that Luisa now wore herself. Two years earlier, she had loaned two gouache images of the Comtesse by anonymous artists to the Louvre for the exhibition *Le décor de la vie sous le second Empire*. Never content to be a mere collector, Casati would actually become Castiglione, even if just for a single evening.

The charity entertainments called Les Bals du Grand Prix were held annually at the famed Paris Opéra House. Held on July 3, 1924, the last of these spectacles was the Fête Espagnole, conceived as a night of fantasy at the home of the Comtesse de Castiglione. A thirty-two-year-old Russian designer, born Romain de Tirtoff, designed the costumes for the event. Settling in Paris in 1913 from St. Petersburg, Tirtoff took the nom de plume of Erté, an appellation based on the French pronunciation of his initials. The artist had soon found employment as an assistant to couturier Paul Poiret. On his own, Erté would later gain greater recognition as one of the most popular designers of costumes and stage settings for theater, opera, and the Folies Bergère.

Having met previously through Adolph and Olga de Meyer, together the Marchesa and Erté devised her entrance to the ball. For Luisa's costume as Castiglione herself, the artist created an enormous tulle and black lace crinoline scattered with diamonds. Erté designed equally elaborate fancy dress outfits of brocade, silver, and gold lamé for the noblewoman's entourage, which included Don Luis of Spain, son of the Infanta Eulalia, and his friend Antonio Vasconcelos; Baron de Meyer; Prince Nicolas Ourousoff, Erté's lover at the time; the artist himself; and a tiny monkey, complete with plumed hat.

After weeks of lengthy rehearsals under the time-beating stick of renowned ballet master and choreographer Leo Staats, the sextet was ready to make its appearance. In keeping with the evening's theme, the Paris Opéra had been adorned with Spanish shawls and gilded arches by designer Jacques Drésa. A cortege of torchbearers preceded Casati's entrance. Fearing fire, the Opéra's director had forbidden the use of any open flame, including candles, within the building. Casati met this restriction with her usual insouciance: "If the Opéra burns, I'll pay for the damage!"[49] The Opéra did not burn. But something even more unexpected occurred—Luisa experienced stage fright. Erté's insistent appeals were required to finally propel her forward into the auditorium and down the Opéra's grand staircase along a pathway strewn with rose petals. Her appearance was met with thunderous applause.

Femina described Luisa, the evening's central character, as "la belle marquise Casati." The magazine further elaborated, "After she had taken a seat on a golden armchair set with precious stones—almost a throne!—the festivities commenced."[50] But not everyone was impressed with Luisa's impersonation of the Comtesse, as seen in André de Fouquières's memoirs, *Cinquante ans de panache:*

> [Casati] had a certain fatal air with those prominent eyes of hers. They
> were like those of an insect. . . . As a comedienne without a theatre, she
> passed her life performing for others and even more so, for herself, in
> the roles of the characters her imagination could give birth to. . . . But
> on the night the Marchesa Casati dressed as Castiglione . . . she
> appeared either too painted, or not enough; arrogant, but nervous . . .
> under her helmet of hair braided in the Byzantine style. She came
> out from some imperial sepulcher. She was a strange image: archaic,
> precious, and savage at the same time. She was not the gallant
> Castiglione of the then-recent history, but a creature of dreams, an
> emanation of the legend. Instead of an evocation, she was a spectral
> apparition. . . . Undoubtedly, only a few of us knew that the cameo
> bracelet, the black onyx medallion, and that rose mirror that she held
> had truly belonged to the Comtesse de Castiglione.[51]

The task of immortalizing Luisa in this latest incarnation was again entrusted to Alberto Martini. His pencil portrait depicts her, eyes hidden behind a half-mask, arrayed in Erté's ensemble and Castiglione's personal effects. Executed in 1925, Martini's portrait was presented at the XV Biennale Exhibition in Venice the following year.

Erté himself would pay obvious homage to the Marchesa in a gouache entitled *The Portrait* that depicts a cluster of whispering admirers gazing at an oversized oval canvas hung from a pair of massive tassels. The painting's subject is a tall, thin woman in an outré outfit of white gauze and pearls, crowned by an aigrette of egret plumes. The wall on which the portrait hangs is decorated with sprays of roses, the artist's possible clever reference to the Palais Rose.

By the time Erté wrote his autobiography nearly a half century later, the designer had dressed some of the world's most opulent women. Even so, he would remember Luisa with great insight and wonder:

> The Marchesa was, in fact, a shy person. Her eccentric behavior was a
> cover for her shyness. I think this is true of many eccentric people. She
> was certainly the most extravagantly odd woman I have ever met.[52]

4

The year 1924 heralded the beginning of dramatic changes in the personal life of Luisa Casati. While on her trip to Budapest, she obtained a long-overdue divorce from her husband. With this act, some sources claim, the Marchesa became the very first Italian Roman Catholic divorcée. According to the gossip pages of *Aux Ecoutes*,[53] Camillo assumed all blame for the legal action in order to pursue a marriage to a Greek woman, although this has never been substantiated. The publication stated that Luisa would accept the terms of the settlement only if she could keep her married title and surname. Camillo acquiesced to what proved to be a shrewd gambit on the part of his ex-wife, for the notoriety she had given the name continued to provide her with a prestige still potent enough to open many doors. The Marchese was more than relieved to be free of a spouse with whom he had little interaction during the past decade, but even more, he was eager to protect his own financial security from the ravages of Luisa's extravagance. It was even rumored that, at one point, he attempted to have her declared legally dead to avoid responsibility for her debts.[54] Just as in the legal separation of 1914, the couple met once again over the desks of their Milanese attorneys. The Marchesa requested no alimony and Camillo offered none. Following the proceedings, Camillo remained in the Casati villa at Cinisello Balsamo while their daughter moved on to Britain.

Never completing her degree in English literature at Oxford, Cristina married Francis John Clarence Westenra Plantagenet, Viscount Hastings, the future fifteenth Earl of Huntingdon, in a private ceremony on October 21, 1925. Both were twenty-four years old. The couple's attempts to keep the wedding a secret were foiled by more than one newspaper.[55] An ominously ambiguous notice appeared in the *Times* of London on October 29: "We are authorized to state the marriage contracted by Viscount Hastings and Miss Casati last week at a registry office in London was without consent, approval, or knowledge of his parents or family." Whereas there would be no reason for Luisa to object to such a beneficial union, one can suppose that at least a small portion of Hastings's clandestine actions may have been the result of his mother-in-law's notoriety and his family's response to it. Indeed, a report on the nuptials in the *New York Times* described the Marchesa as being "well known in artistic circles and a clever exponent of the tango."[56] But Hastings's parents' ire, especially that of his father, was more likely a reaction to the young couple's reputed communist sympathies. At the time of their marriage, Hastings had been making a name for himself as a painter of notable talent. Very soon, the couple abandoned England for exotic adventures in Australia, Mexico, and the South Seas.

With financial stability regained at least temporarily, Luisa was intent on reinstating herself into the glamorous ranks of Parisian society—but by this time, the social landscape had been altered irrevocably. Casati's style, regardless of its timeless outrageousness, was now considered dated. Even her close friend Baron de Meyer commented in the bon ton bible, *Harper's Bazaar:* "Taste and exquisite reticence have become one of the fine arts. Eccentricity is thought a crime and is actually the most 'démodé' and unfashionable thing a woman can indulge in nowadays!"[57] Such new trends in fashion as the streamlined couture of Chanel and Patou and the vogue for stark and blatantly faux jewelry appealed little to Luisa. As symbolized by its gleaming automobiles and airplanes, the modern world was gaining ever more speed while the society of the Marchesa and her comrades was beginning to waver.

D'Annunzio expressed this himself in a melancholic telegram forwarded to Luisa in December 1924: "The tortoise has fallen into hibernation and will awaken in spring. . . . At ten this morning, I became very old." This bittersweet note was the very last of its kind sent to Casati. Despite attempts to conquer time through years of wild schemes and actions, its passage was being sensed within the walls of D'Annunzio's fortress. The grand sorcerer of Lake Garda had become too tired and exasperated to continually track the wanderings of his eccentric muse. As Luisa followed her own pursuits, D'Annunzio slipped more and more into a dreamworld. This fantasy existence was regulated between periods of monastic abstinence and excesses of an inordinate sexual nature. The poet boasted that these acts of abandon contributed to a revitalization of his creativity.

Time also trapped the Marchesa's boa constrictor, Anaxagarus, in its crystal enclosure at the Palais Rose. The snake had been stricken with pneumonia and the best veterinarians in Paris could not help. Not every member of the palace's household shared in the grief of its mistress, for now the task of slaughtering the multitude of chickens and rabbits required for the snake's diet had come to an end. Alberto Martini was equally unsympathetic when Luisa made a special request of him: "When the frightening reptile died, the Marchesa asked me sweetly to bring the creature's silver-gray, ten-meter-long skin to Venice to spread it out like a tapestry in her black gondola. But when I left, I also left behind the skin of that monster out of an invincible disgust."[58]

After the boa's death, Casati immediately notified the Reptile House at the Zoological Gardens in London to order a replacement. A yellow and black Asian python from Taïpang was ordered. But following its transcontinental flight, the new serpent was left for hours in its cage on the Le Bourget airfield in the frigid January weather. As a result, it expired about two weeks later. Disillusioned by this additional loss, Luisa requested no other. The great glass cube remained vacant during the weeks of mourning. As it was displayed to visitors, the Marchesa would announce: "I leave it there as a monument to an unknown python."

Deciding to find a method of preserving the unfortunate snake, Casati called on the Jardin des Plantes of Paris. Taxidermy expert Dr. Marie Phisalix found the creature to be a specimen of such apparent perfection that she brought it before the attentions of the esteemed Académie des Sciences. There it was analyzed with minute precision for an article that appeared in the institution's journal.[59]

While the outer skin of the massive python was being preserved, Luisa had the idea of reconstructing its intricate skeleton as a gift for D'Annunzio—although its ultimate destination remains unknown. Casati kept him proudly abreast of the snake's growing fame in a letter that also requested some curious advice:

> Dear Ariel,
> I have been to the Jardin des Plantes and have seen the skeleton of the serpent. Madame Phisalix assures me that it will be finished on the 20th of February. You will see, it seems like lace. . . . I am sending you an article that the Académie des Sciences published in a journal about my python. Friday there will be a *bal masque* given by the Comte de Beaumont—*Les types et les prévisions de 1925–1935.* I will go as the ambassador to Mars. Please send a telegram soon describing the nature of Martians to me. You must know! With me, I will have a magnificent dwarf of the "Nouveau Cirque." He walks on his head. . . .
> Coré[60]

Upon its return to the Palais Rose, the stuffed python was curled realistically about a large tree branch in the glass cage. But even in this harmless state, the creature exuded precisely the unsettling aura its owner had hoped it might. In her memoirs, Mrs. Hwfa Williams described her encounter with the palace's reptilian sentinel:

> One day when I went to see [Casati] she said she wanted to show me her pet python. I was by no means eager for the privilege as . . . I am not a lover of snakes. However, I could not very gracefully refuse, so off we went to the python's lair. Repressing my emotion as best I could, I gazed at the lustrous black-and-yellow coils, only half-reassured by the Marchesa's information that the python was not a venomous snake, but merely crushes its victims to death.

I looked with some apprehension at the motionless knot. Was it waiting to spring? Did pythons spring? Did they give one long squeeze or a sharp jerk?

"He is very still," I said after a minute.

"Yes, he is, isn't he? He's been dead quite a long time now."[61]

Luisa's obsession with her own representation resurfaced again in 1925 when she summoned Alberto Martini to Le Vésinet. Martini wrote of his arrival at the Palais Rose:

> One autumn night, I arrived from Italy, urgently called by the great artist. She was covered in gold and armed with an authentic dagger from the Borgias. A tragic portrait.
>
> Far from the noise of Paris, her precious abode of red marble, filled with gold and works of art, was called "*Le palais du rêve.*" The starlight made it seem magically phosphorescent. When I arrived, the windows were lit up by a mysterious violet-red light. A gorgeous garden crowned the artist's nest. Behind the palace, sullen, strange trees were sticking up, like giants in waiting.
>
> A black man, like those in the fairy tales, opened the golden gates and escorted me into a grand waiting room. It was a perfumed temple of Persian amber, filled with luminous Egyptian funereal chimeras, a frowning assembly of Roman emperors, and a gigantic stuffed python, in a great glass case, twisted about the trunk of a sycamore.[62]

During this renewed phase as the Marchesa's court painter, Martini was required to work more often at the Palais Rose than at his studio in Montparnasse. In addition to various profiles and portraits, their association produced a harvest of oversized images rendered in oil, ink, pencil, and pastel. Casati also purchased from the artist a painting entitled *Hamlet,* which depicted the tragic Shakespearean hero clutching the drowned body of his lifeless Ophelia.

During the winter of 1925, the Marchesa began an extensive sojourn in America, beginning with an ocean crossing via the luxury liner the *S.S. Leviathan.* Among the international passengers were Luisa's friend and portrait painter Guiglio de Blaas and her society rival the Princesse de Polignac, as well as Cuban chess master José Raúl Capablanca and Count Byron Khun de Prorok, the colorful adventurer and African explorer, who was transporting jewels and other tomb treasures. The first portion of the journey included a contretemps with a recently acquired boa constrictor she had chosen as traveling partner. Chaos broke out aboard ship when the snake escaped its confines. It was reported that the emigrant passengers panicked, believing their children were in danger of being eaten by the errant serpent—claims were made that one child had already been swallowed whole in third class. The snake was never recovered, and Luisa was found consoling herself tearfully at the ship's Ritz bar.[63]

An appropriate finale to this bizarre voyage occurred when the *Leviathan* crashed into its pier upon arriving in New York on December 21, 1925. There were no injuries. From the Marchesa's landing, and throughout her entire stay in the United States, she became more a newsworthy celebrity than leisurely visitor. Reporters from coast to coast scrambled to deliver the latest scoop on this continental bird of paradise that had alighted on their Yankee shores. Rather than fact, the embellished accounts printed in several newspapers bore the flavor of a nation enthralled by such exotics of the silent screen as Theda Bara and Valentino.

Upon disembarkation in New York City, attired in a very décolleté gown of gold cloth with matching hose, Luisa registered at the plush Ritz-Carlton Hotel on Madison Avenue and immediately made two demands from an American friend—a decent red wine for her dinner and a replacement serpent no less than thirty feet in length. As the latter request was left unfilled, and the city's boutiques proved unsatisfactory, this stop was somewhat of a disappointment except for a visit to the atelier of Guiglio de Blaas. There, the artist rendered yet another full-length portrait of Casati, this one depicting her in a sweeping gold lamé gown and plumed headdress. After celebrating the Christmas and New Year's holidays in Manhattan, which included attending a charity dance at the Madison to aid St. Mark's Hospital, Luisa headed southward during the latter part of January 1926.

When exiting a train for a brief call in Palm Beach, Florida, one of the Marchesa's couture coats prompted a reporter to note that it was "so gaily splotched with color that it would have made Joseph's proud garment look like the garb of a Quaker."[64] During a season marred by unusually cold and rainy weather, she first checked into the Royal Poinciana Hotel, a massive resort on the shores of Lake Worth, followed by a stay at the exclusive Everglades Club, noted for its Mediterranean Revival style architecture. Another of Luisa's ensembles, worn to a dinner there, became fashion news when the March 15, 1926, edition of American *Vogue* noted, "One Sunday night—the smartest night at the Everglades—, the Marchesa Casati caused a sensation by her 'robe de style' of cloth of gold worn with a gold helmet tipped with black plumes, a striking costume that seemed oddly suited to the dramatic setting in the tropical moonlight."

Next, Luisa traveled on to California, where the *San Francisco Chronicle* provided an especially breathless description:

La Casati, as she is known, is famous not only for her extraordinary good looks but for her taste for the exotic, the bizarre, the spectacular. . . . She is always surrounded by the glamour of mystery and romance and she is continually doing something to amaze and amuse the world. . . . Those who have seen La Casati's portrait would scarcely expect to see her appear that way in the flesh, but it is a fact that she does.[65]

After such a provocative introduction, readers hungered to hear the Marchesa speak for herself. The same newspaper did not disappoint them with La Casati's reputed comments worthy of Greta Garbo: "To be different is to be alone. I do not like what is average. So I am alone." For her interview, the reporter noted, Luisa wore a wide-brimmed black sombrero atop waved blonde hair cut quite short, while a fur cloak just covered a dress of glistening green fabric. Outrageous explanations as to the Marchesa's penchant for wearing veils were provided as well. One report divulged this habit necessary so that she might hide the scars incurred at the claws of her exotic pets; another related a grisly story involving an Italian count, who, after being jilted by Luisa, branded his initials into her forehead before shooting himself dead.[66]

During her time in California, the Marchesa stayed at San Francisco's Hotel St. Francis, was a guest of the William Randolph Hearsts, and even met actor John Barrymore in Hollywood. In addition, she made several visits accompanied by Lady Pamela Paget, the London socialite and niece of Lady Diana Cooper. One of these was to Uplands, the enormous Hillsborough mansion of the multimillionaire art patron Charles Templeton Crocker. Beforehand, the stylish pair spent the afternoon in Berkeley at the home of Mrs. Arthur Fredericks and her son Joseph Paget-Fredericks, a young artist and ballet enthusiast.

Prior to leaving the state, Casati attended a baseball game in Los Angeles at the invitation of a friend. In response to her query as to proper attire for the event, she was told to "come as you are." Luisa arrived in a floor-length fur over a simple silk nightgown. Her enthusiastic cheers and leaps at each home run drew the crowd's attention more than the game itself.[67]

Before returning to New York, Casati again met Sir Francis Rose in the most unlikely of locales:

I went to overlook the Grand Canyon. It was covered by a thick mist when I arrived, and only the Marchesa di Casati [sic] stood waiting to be gazed upon. She was the spirit of the golden sunsets and turned the gorges into blood and flame. Veils hid her ruby eyes and leopard-skin pants covered her legs. A vast gold straw sombrero crowned her head, and her feet, stained purple, were slipped into lemon-yellow Arab *babouches.* The mist seemed to ooze out of the violent magenta dye on her wild locks, and she clutched beaded belts, souvenirs, and woven straw toy horsemen on toy mules to her chest as though they were the countless breasts of Aphrodite.[68]

Inspired by her visit to this natural wonder, Luisa would later have Martini depict her as an American Indian, a figure of romantic exoticism for early twentieth-century Europe, standing defiantly at the edge of the Grand Canyon and holding a bow and pistol. Finally, on March 12, 1926, Casati sailed from New York for Europe aboard the R.M.S. *Majestic,* the luxurious flagship of the White Star line. Also on the passenger list were British M.P. Sir Oswald Mosley and his wife and George Eastman, the American industrialist.

Once more at the Palais Rose, Luisa's private life again became a notorious topic of conversation. The staid community of Le Vésinet had never been pleased with their most unconventional neighbor. Casati's fondness for nudity fueled rumors; tales were told of leisurely baths taken alfresco in the gargantuan Montespan basin of pink marble. During these soakings, Luisa was supposed to have delivered the daily orders to her servants, who stood at attention all the while. In very little time, local gossip focused on the relationship between the divorced mistress of the strange mansion and Yamina, her muscular black chauffeur, forever attired in an immodestly tight uniform.

Just as she had done during her years at the Palazzo dei Leoni, Luisa wanted to transform her current residence and its gardens into a carnival wonderland. With renewed gusto, she planned a string of fêtes and showered invitations on the international haut monde. Once again, Casati's fantastic evenings became the coveted diversions for the fashionable set—although some attended out of pity or perverse curiosity since now many of the masquerades tended toward the ludicrous.

One report claimed that at a particular event she flitted nude through the gardens, holding a lighted candle while declaring, "I am the Truth!" When the Bal du Noir was held, many believed that the affair's genuine tribute was to Yamina's prowess in his mistress's boudoir. This rumor was exacerbated by Casati's own strict instructions for guests to appear in blackface. The evening came to an abrupt close when a thunderstorm sent revelers scrambling from the gardens and into the palace, dripping ebony cosmetics onto the marble floors. It was reported that Kees van Dongen remained behind to console Luisa after the flight of her guests. A subsequent celebration also came to a hasty end when a throng of onlookers, who had heard tales of the Marchesa's entertainments, perched on the garden's walls. While the crowd jeered at the costumed party-goers, an infuriated Casati, who was to have made her appearance masked as a jeweled serpent flanked by two nude attendants portraying Adam and Eve, refused to leave her room. At another soirée, this time with an Oriental theme, an abundance of champagne and more powerful stimulants spurred its merrymakers toward rowdy abandon. Neighbors were far from amused. Complaints were made directly to the mayor of Le Vésinet, who appealed to the Italian ambassador. But neither man could change the Marchesa's ways.[69]

Luisa gave the Bal de la rose d'or in May 1927. Among the many invitees were Isadora Duncan and her traveling companion, Mary Desti. *The Untold Story*, Desti's chronicle of the dancer's last years, gives a firsthand account of the event:

> We arrived around midnight in a terrible rainstorm. . . . As we approached [the Palais Rose] we thought we were viewing a scene from a very up-to-date musical comedy or something from fairyland. The house was all outlined with a row of tiny electric bulbs. The garden paths that wind in and out among thousands and thousands of roses were also lined with alternate pink and yellow light bulbs. The entire scene was a blaze of glory veiled in this torrential downpour. Countless footmen were running about in the most attractive coats gaily embroidered in gold, satin trousers, and silk stockings. . . .
>
> Many of the brilliant stars from the Comédie Française were there, [as well as] all the famous poets and writers of the present day. . . .
>
> This ball was intended to be a sort of magic affair. Many were dressed as seers and in one of the salons a very famous lady was telling fortunes, but nowhere could we find the hostess.[70]

It is explained that the Marchesa had been taken ill earlier in the evening. When she finally made her appearance at the party, Desti begins her description of Casati by noting, "Never have I seen so magnificent and terrifying a sight." The writer continues:

> This very slender lady seemed to be about six feet tall and to augment this she wore on her head a very high black cap covered with glittering stars. The middle third of her face was covered with a black mask from which two great amorous eyes flashed. The rest of her costume was that of a seer, heightened by countless jewels covering her arms, neck, and shoulders. . . . She passed around her rooms like one in a dream, greeting one here and there as though she were also one of the invited. . . .

As a memento of this famous event I still have a golden rose, the heart of which held a tiny vial of rose perfume. Each guest was presented with one of these on leaving.[71]

In June 1927, Casati contrived to astound Paris with a spectacle to exceed every one of its predecessors. The theme was to honor the most legendary occultist in Italian history, Joseph Balsamo, known more infamously as the Comte de Cagliostro.[72] Invitations were designed especially to reflect the supernatural atmosphere of the evening. Printed on gilded paper, they prominently featured a reproduction of Casati's Medusa portrait by Martini.[73] The party was already set to begin at eleven in the evening when the Marchesa began to have some doubts about the lateness of the hour, specifically, whether her guests would be capable of finding the Palais Rose in the dark. Her eventual solution required the assistance of her intimidating chauffeur. In full uniform, Yamina arrived at the office of the mayor and presented Luisa's plan, to which the exasperated official reluctantly agreed. A series of road signs, painted to reflect automobile headlights, were then installed along the route from Paris to Le Vésinet. These *tableaux lumineux* started from a bridge over the Seine and led directly to the rue Diderot.[74]

Preparations were begun to glorify the marble palace. Since the Marchesa forbade the use of electricity during the event, the Palais Rose's rooms, gardens, and fountains were illuminated by torches of Lalique crystal, as was the Montespan bath, now filled with water lilies. The mansion's great lawn was hidden beneath a priceless Savonnerie carpet. Supper was served in a small pavilion on long mirrored tables. Surrounded by ice sculptures, the entire repast and towers of pastries were set aglow by multitudes of black candles. A battalion of footmen, in white livery embellished with silver braid and powdered wigs appropriate to the period, bordered the pathways and front steps, each holding aloft a burning candelabra. Bartenders were masked as devils in outfits of black velvet set with jet beads.

Many guests wore the guise of courtiers who had actually been associated with Cagliostro during his lifetime. Mrs. William Randolph Hearst arrived as Madame du Barry, and others attended as Cardinal de Rohan, Maurice Rostand, and Voltaire. Polish chanteuse Ganna Walska, famous for her taste for the most expensive jewels and handsomest men in Paris, made her entrance in a burst of multicolored feathers. The most commented on costumes were those of women masquerading as men. The Honorable Mrs. Reginald Fellowes appeared as Casanova, and the imposing Lady Colebrooke was in the guise of Pierre Le Grand, complete with sword and moustache. Maria Ruspoli, the Duchesse de Gramont, made an amazing entrance as a black serpent; she was brought in on a sarcophagus carried by four pages dressed as Egyptian slaves.

But the Marchesa dominated the scene. As Cagliostro, Luisa's costume was a re-creation of eighteenth-century male attire of breeches, waistcoat, gloves, and a plumed tricorn hat—all rendered in cloth of gold and silver, sparkling with diamonds. She further enhanced the ensemble with high-heeled boots, a gold half-mask, and a specially made "magic" crystal sword. The Bal de Cagliostro was planned to be the most lavish party to be seen in years by *Tout-Paris,* and for a while this was the case. But when the event's meticulous plans were disrupted, it was in a way so disastrous that it seemed the result of some malevolent spell.

The directions to the party required guests to pass through a slum area on the outskirts of the French capital before reaching Le Vésinet. As the Rolls-Royces and limousines passed through this district, inhabitants shouted insults and profanities while pelting the vehicles with tomatoes. Winds began to whip up a mass of storm clouds across the previously clear skies. This occurred at the beginning of a costumed march of the entire assembly through the gardens. Ominously, the start of the procession was signaled by the appearance of a rigged skeleton, which emerged in a halo of light from within a shadowy cave. To conclude the march, an ornate coach drawn by four white horses was to appear carrying the Comtesse de Segonzac and her young escort, Parisian review star Pierre Meyer, outfitted as Marie Antoinette and the Comte d'Artois. As the parade progressed, the team of horses became terrorized by sudden thunder, heralding the approaching storm. The animals bolted at a wild pace back into the safety of their stables. As the carriage sped into the shelter, the doors slammed shut and locked. The mock-royals within found themselves trapped, because the stable was too narrow to allow the opening of the coach doors. A fellow guest, Gabriel-Louis Pringué, described what followed:

> It happened that the key was lost. Everyone tried to break through the door.
>
> The horses attached to the carriage got scared at all the noise . . . something very dangerous to the occupants of the coach. Fortunately, someone succeeded in getting the couple out. . . the two were pallid.[75]

Another of the revelers was not so lucky. According to reports, an unnamed lady spent the evening locked in a closet by the Marchesa after it was discovered that she had imitated her hostess's costume.

The threatening storm finally erupted before Luisa had the opportunity to perform a magical display, which was to be the evening's finale. Thunder shook the palace, and lightning eerily illuminated the ensuing scenes of panic. Rain poured in through the open French doors leading out to the gardens. The supper buffet, candelabras, and ice sculptures were all blown across the windswept terrace. Philippe Jullian described the evening's nightmarish crescendo:

> The lights went out: there was a stampede back into the drawing rooms
> of maskers in mud-spattered hoop skirts, valets with powder running
> in rivulets over their livery, ladies whose terror and wrinkles alike were
> exposed by flashes of lightning, chauffeurs seeking their masters. . . .
> La Casati found herself alone in a devastated house and surrounded
> by streaming ostrich plumes, faded flowers, upset candelabra, and
> forgotten fans and hats.[76]

The very last image of the Marchesa Casati at this doomed masquerade was the indelible sight of her gilt costume and plumage being nearly torn from her flailing body by the swirling winds. To no avail, the crystal sword was waved above her head in a vain attempt to restore order. Then she fainted.

Dragonfly in Amber
1927-1957

Eccentricity is tolerable only in its first freshness.
Cherished until it has gone stale, it becomes unbearably
pathetic and at the same time alarming.
   —*Maurice Druon,* La Volupté d'être

It is possible to argue that the Marchesa's life was
worthlessly profligate, but we take nothing out of the
world and while she was in it she shone like a resplendent
dragonfly. That is worth much in a generally dull world.
   —*Woodrow Wyatt,* Confessions of an Optimist

1

After the debacle of the Bal de Cagliostro, the exaggerated and sometimes cruel gossip that now surrounded Luisa Casati was not surprising. It is not known whether she was aware of the extent of its proliferation or viciousness. Some believed that the disastrous fête was a fitting retribution for her years of excess. Nevertheless, the readers of the September 1927 issue of French *Vogue* were told nothing of the party's unfavorable events. The magazine featured a rose-colored account of the event, accompanied by photographs of selected guests taken by Scaïoni and Hoyningen-Huene and a drawing by Drian of the ball's costumed hostess.

One particular rumor about Luisa's indirect involvement in the death of a holy man was the most provocative of the period. Supposedly, Casati was to have gone through a sort of spiritual atonement for her past. The genuineness of such a conversion seems unlikely, but she proved herself capable of exhibiting eccentric flair even on this sacred crusade. The memoirs of Principessa Jane di San Faustino describe the strange expression of Luisa's implausible change of heart:

> It was in Paris that [Casati's] bizarreness joined with tragedy. The entire city was talking about the Archbishop [Dubois] who preached against the follies of the elegant world. Luisa immediately wanted to meet him and invite him to her house to calm him down, but the Archbishop refused every invitation. Then Luisa's friends no longer saw her. They knew that she had given up every amusement, that she went to Mass every day, that she visited the poor and the sick. This period of virtue lasted only one month. Luisa then announced that she was possessed by a demon and sent for the Archbishop to come and exorcise her.
>
> The Archbishop responded that he was in bed with bronchitis. Luisa replied then, that it was not permissible to refuse to save a soul in danger. The Archbishop communicated to her that as soon as he was well, he would go to save her. To this, Luisa, being too impatient to allow delay, sent someone in the middle of the night, to knock on the door of the Archbishop and inform him that she was dying from a terrible automobile accident and to beg him to give her her Sacraments. It was almost midnight. The Archbishop, though he was feverish, ran to Luisa's house. He found her ready to receive him, just covered by white veils, with a candle in her right hand and a lily in her left. The blessing lasted five minutes at the most. No one knew how it ever could have happened, but Luisa's servants found her face down on the floor in tears. Two days later, the Archbishop was dying of pulmonitis.[1]

Colorful as they may be, the events described in these reminiscences are difficult to substantiate, although it does seem unduly harsh to blame Luisa for the death of a seventy-three-year-old man already in failing health. The Principessa may have presented Casati negatively in retaliation for her insensitive treatment of the smitten Marquis Don Ranieri Bourbon del Monte, the noblewoman's only grandchild. The tale was embellished while circulating through the salons of Paris. According to the enhanced version, Casati presented herself to His Eminence Louis Ernest Dubois clad in white on a settee borne aloft by four naked valets. She supposedly held a white gladiolus in her lap, while a white parrot, representing the Holy Ghost, perched near her feet. With a transfixed stare, the Marchesa repeated continually, "Je suis la Vierge immaculée!" The shocked Archbishop almost had her excommunicated. Soon this hearsay metamorphosed even further. Word spread that Dubois had not gone to see Casati himself but instead sent another priest on his behalf. The cleric arrived at the Palais Rose near midnight and was led through the gardens toward the house. He was only halfway there when Luisa emerged from the darkness, stark naked and holding a lighted candelabrum in each hand, reciting a litany. Horrified, the priest turned and fled. The next day the Archbishop was said to have filed a complaint with the police, accusing the Marchesa of an "attentat à la pudeur" and blasphemy. The anecdote now concluded not with the Archbishop's demise, but with the fallacious report of Casati's commitment for six months to a mental nursing home.

Much closer to reality was the way in which decline and death began to cast their shadows over Luisa's intimate circle. By 1924, her friend and personal designer Léon Bakst had already passed away,[2] and Nijinsky, the celebrated faun of the Ballets Russes, was confined to an insane asylum. Isadora Duncan met her demise in Nice in 1927. A little over a year later, Diaghilev, too, would die. Giovanni Boldini had returned from a wartime exile on the French Riviera to his Parisian studio. Now nearly deaf and blind, the irascible artist countered the obituaries of old friends with angry shouts: "They are all dying just to spite me!" In 1929, Boldini stunned his remaining acquaintances by marrying his thirty-year-old secretary. Less than two years later, he was dead at the age of eighty-nine.

When death touched the Vittoriale in a smaller way, its owner romanticized the misfortune in typical D'Annunzian style. In 1929, Casati traveled once more to Milan to review her finances. She stayed at the Hotel Cavour while meeting with attorneys and Lorenzo Saracchi, her personal accountant. Prized for his patience and chivalrous demeanor, this advisor had handled the monetary affairs of Camillo[3] and Luisa during their marriage and was now continuing to do so for each separately after their divorce.

At this session, he was required to deliver a grim forecast to his client, for although the Marchesa's accounts were solvent at that time, her chronic spending would soon dwindle these reserves to dangerously low levels. A lecture on the value of prudence and compromise would prove futile, as Saracchi knew all too well from his past experiences with Luisa. One can imagine his dismay while reviewing the still unpaid receipts for the Bal de Cagliostro, the cost of which exceeded five hundred thousand gold francs, including a lighting bill alone of one hundred twenty thousand. He could do nothing more than offer a warning. But Casati was more concerned with visiting the Vittoriale.

The now elderly D'Annunzio was thrilled to welcome Luisa back into his kingdom, but the Marchesa was distracted by the growing realization of her precarious financial situation. D'Annunzio did his best to mollify her with humorous epigrams and tales of his peasant youth in the Abruzzi, although an unpleasant moment arrived when Casati was informed of the death of her gift from the Hagenbeck Zoo. The large tortoise had suffered a whimsical demise after gorging itself on too many tuberoses from the Vittoriale's gardens. D'Annunzio was quick to console his guest by proving that the creature had been immortalized in as grand a manner as the python of the Palais Rose.

Leading Luisa into the dining room, D'Annunzio unveiled the chamber's newest ornament. At the head of the table, on a cushion of scarlet satin, rested the deceased tortoise in gilded splendor. Once the creature had met its perfumed fate, it had been sent to the poet's private goldsmith, who promptly saw to the gold plating of its shell. Then the craftsman made castings of the animal's head and feet in bronze. When fused together, the statue seemed truly alive. D'Annunzio honored the now almost mythical beast by christening the dining room with its name. From the day of the Marchesa's visit onward, it would be known as "Cheli's Room."[4] The sly poet may have also relished displaying this symbolic warning against overindulgence. D'Annunzio then presented Luisa with a very special token of his affection. In his directives when commissioning the gift from his favorite jeweler, Mario Buccellati, he called it a "strange jewel." D'Annunzio confided to the artisan, "because you understand the strange, I tell you with discretion that I am to give it to the Marchesa Luisa Casati, noted for her uniquely singular elegance."[5] Unfortunately, the specifics of the baroque bauble remain a mystery. This would be the last meeting, face to face, between Coré and her Ariel.

Luisa returned to Le Vésinet, although soon enough she realized that even this marble fortress could no longer offer protection from the mortality that was seemingly enshrouding her. A groundskeeper had been found dead in the palace's gardens. By the time of his body's discovery, his eyes had already been pecked out by one of the resident parrots. Triggered by this grisly event, rumors abounded, including those that claimed Casati's python as the murderer. Of course, it is unlikely that the deceased and mounted serpent could have managed such a feat. Equally malicious gossip stated that Luisa's only concern in the incident was for the parrot's well being. This tragedy, coupled with monetary woes, dampened her spirits. She had even found no pleasure at her recent appointment to the Comitato d'Onore degli Amatori d'Arte of the Raccolta internazionale d'arte in Milan, a group organizing a tribute to Vittorio Pica, the noted art scholar and close associate of Alberto Martini.[6]

In a sardonic twist, a novel appeared at this moment featuring a central character whose lavish Venetian exploits were inspired by Luisa's more prosperous times. Published in 1929 by the prolific French author Maurice Dekobra, *La Gondole aux chimères* was the second in a series of novels, initiated three years earlier with the international bestseller *La Madone des sleepings*, to follow the adventures of Lady Diana Wynham. The writer imbued his fictional Scottish femme fatale with a flair for the extravagant that was undoubtedly the result of his own fascination with Casati begun during their brief acquaintanceship.

Luisa's debts continued to mount, as did her anxiety at the possibility of being burglarized again after a robbery at the Palais Rose in December 1925. According to *Aux Ecoutes* of January 1926, while Casati was away the concierge left in charge of the palace was bitten severely by one of her parrots and taken to the hospital. During his absence, thieves absconded with many of Luisa's bibelots and pieces of silver.[7] As a precaution, workmen were hired to improve the functioning of the mechanical panther, standing guard in the mansion's front hall. Specifically, its roars were made more ferocious. Casati never knew that the obliging technicians derided her in secret. By this time, the Palais Rose had also become a profitable destination for bands of gypsies, who were aware of its mistress's fascination with the occult and unusual animals. These swindlers would throng the gates, selling spells and incantations, as well as an assortment of talking parrots and trained monkeys. The imposing Yamina was required to drive them off.

Parties at the Palais Rose were held less frequently and then ceased entirely. Unpalatable memories of the Bal de Cagliostro were still too recent to be forgotten by potential revelers, not to mention the fact that Luisa's bank accounts could no longer finance such lavish amusements. But Casati was still a guest at the many galas held throughout the season in Paris. She attended the Bal Blanc organized by high-society coiffeur Antoine to celebrate the opening of his unusual atelier and residence, constructed largely of glass, on the Rue St. Didier. The Marchesa caused a sensation there as a re-creation of a figure from a Salvador Dalí painting. More than one newspaper commented on her latest fashion statement and the living ornament that completed the ensemble. At several aristocratic tea parties and in the finest restaurants, Luisa was seen in the scarlet uniform balloon-pants and leather boots of a Zouave, a particular infantry regiment of the French army, while perched on her chair was a black youth whom she fed from her own fork.[8]

At another affair, given by the Honorable Mrs. Reginald Fellowes, participants were required to disguise themselves in the mode of a fellow member of the aristocracy. As recalled in her memoirs, the Duchesse de Sermoneta chose Luisa as her model:

> I motored to Le Vésinet where the Marchesa Luisa Casati lived . . . and asked if she would let me pretend to be her. She was amused at the idea and lent me some of her wonderful clothes for which she was famous, showing me how to put them on. There were trousers and trailing cloak all in cloth of gold, a hat of gold lace shaped like an inverted waste-paper basket, also many strings of enormous pearls, all things that no one else would dare wear, but which were her everyday attire. It was quite easy to look like her in this get-up, I only had to fasten bunches of bright red curls on either side of my face and paint wide black rings round my eyes.
>
> When I arrived at the party it was reassuring to hear the chauffeurs watching near the door say to each other, "Tins, c'est la Marquise Casati," and when I entered the ballroom solemnly announced as her by a master of ceremonies I received a round of applause. In the small hours of the morning the real Marquise Casati arrived arrayed in cloth of silver, and we walked about together arm in arm.[9]

Luisa's clique of admirers and confidants was growing ever smaller as she tried to maintain a connection with a society that was quickly edging away. She even formed a tentative friendship with her previous antagonist, the Princesse de Polignac. At one masquerade in 1928, the author Colette appeared as herself and was escorted by composer Francis Poulenc, representing her fictional seducer, Cheri. The lesbian Princesse then emerged in men's clothing as the French dramatist Tristan Bernard. On her arm was the still eye-catching Luisa, dressed expensively as the playwright's wife, Argentina.[10]

From his offices in Milan, Saracchi made repeated pleas for his client to halt her spending. Desperately, he forbade any new purchases until her bills had been settled. For a while, the Marchesa was able to fend off creditors by exchanging jewelry and other costly items for some of her outstanding debts. Then she had to relinquish the Villa San Michele after nearly a dozen years when her concocted rental arrangement with Axel Munthe finally expired, leaving fifty thousand lire in arrears. By letter, Luisa implored D'Annunzio to join her in creating a new lease on the property by which both would share the expenses and accommodations. The scheme failed.

Casati handled these infrequent and futile attempts toward solvency in a characteristically careless and ultimately damaging way. The payment of a single small loan was bartered for with an ivory statuette of Christ, once belonging to Pope Alexander II, the value of which far exceeded the liability.[11] Then Luisa resorted to personally liquidating several cherished possessions, again for sums less than their value—her 1908 portrait by Boldini was sold to the Baron Maurice de Rothschild; the Egyptian statue that so impressed Catherine Barjansky in Casati's Roman villa was acquired by the Marquis Georges de Cuevas and his wife, Margaret Rockefeller;[12] and the bronze deer mascots that had already traveled with their owner to Rome and Capri were purchased by Coco Chanel.[13]

That Luisa became prey for unscrupulous moneylenders and pawnbrokers is not astonishing. Taxi drivers, merchants, and grocers were handed diamond bracelets, emerald rings, and pearls for their services. Such behavior caused Augustus John to comment, "[Casati was] credulous as a savage, [and] was ever at the mercy of the first imposter."[14] Even her granddaughter, Moorea, was astounded: "If she saw something—anything—she wanted, she had to have it. So, if she wanted something you had, she would take off one of her jewels and give it to you, even if what you had was worthless. Of course, you could not keep a fortune that way."[15] And that is just what occurred.

Almost the entire sum of monies obtained recently from the sale of Casati's holdings and properties had been squandered on costume balls, travel, and quickly forgotten absurdities. Very soon, tax collectors entered the ranks of those demanding payment. Invoices, grossly past due, arrived at the Palais Rose daily. Some decision to satisfy them had to be made, but instead Luisa went to Rome. While in the Italian capital, she paid an unannounced visit to her late sister's family. Cards bearing reproductions of her portraits by Martini were bestowed here and there before the end of this brief, whirlwind visit.

Returning to Le Vésinet, the Marchesa was confronted by creditors, demanding immediate satisfaction. By her fiftieth birthday in January 1931, Luisa owed more than three hundred thousand francs in France and close to twenty billion lire in Italy, a total debt with the modern equivalent of approximately twenty-five million U.S. dollars. Fearing a scandal, Saracchi requested the intervention of the Italian Embassy in Paris, which refused. But the final devastation was yet to come.

To cash a check in the amount of twenty-nine thousand francs with a Parisian coal seller, Luisa offered the following for collateral, as stated in *The American Weekly:* "two pictures of the Boucher school, an onyx statuette set with semi-precious stones, an eagle adorned with diamonds and two pawn tickets."[16] When the check proved worthless, the merchant had Casati arrested. A court date led to a sentencing of two years' imprisonment, later reduced to a suspended sentence of two months. Then the court set a date for the sale of the Marchesa's remaining property.

In utter despair, one last telegram was sent to the Vittoriale on December 14, 1932:

I am offensively desperate—Palais Rose art sale Saturday—wire me ten thousand lire—send someone to choose the art you would like— gratitude and recognition—Luisa Casati

The plea was signed with neither Luisa's title nor the affectionate name chosen for her by D'Annunzio. The years of magical poetry and sublime excess between the lovers were over. The telegram remained unanswered.

2

On the morning of Saturday, December 17, 1932, an auction of the Marchesa Luisa Casati's personal possessions was organized at the Palais Rose to satisfy countless creditors. The list of items confiscated by the French authorities reveals a partial glimpse of the privileged and decadent heights from which their owner had now fallen. This surviving record includes a variety of gilded Louis XVI furnishings, such as bookcases, consoles, chairs, and footstools; two dozen porcelain dinner plates embossed with the Casati family crest in gold; a Louis XIV Sèvres tea set for twelve with matching coffee service; two hundred books bound in Moroccan leather, also bearing the family crest in gold; four vermeil candelabra; a set of Lalique crystal torches; a pair of Chinese chests of tortoiseshell and mother of pearl; and a brass unicorn and marble phoenix. Even more personal items such as her photograph albums and her bed linens, including four pairs of sheets embroidered with her coat of arms, and a satin bedcover with tigers, stags, and gazelles stitched on it in gold went to the highest bidder.

Among the items sold from the Marchesa's wardrobe was a dress of Persian brocade by Worth; six pairs of gold and silver handmade shoes by

Hellstern in the place Vendôme; a panther-skin coat; six evening dresses with trains; two pairs of silver fox gloves and a pair of tiger-skin gloves; a pair of slippers with diamond buckles; a silk, wine-colored coat by Réville of Paris with sterling buttons of the Casati crest; a pink ostrich feather cloak and fan; twelve sets of satin and lace underwear; and fifteen fancy dress costumes, including one constructed of brocade and diamonds. Also noted was the odd inclusion of two men's suits, one gray and one brown. Luisa's entire collection of mementos once belonging to the Comtesse de Castiglione was for purchase as well.

The majority of the "Casati Gallery" was also auctioned off. The pavilion that housed the Marchesa's shrine to self-glorification was stripped to the bare walls. Among the irreplaceable works sold were drawings of Luisa by Boldini and John, the oils by Beltrán y Masses and de Blaas, the gouache by Brunelleschi, Montesquiou's watercolor, the Troubetzkoy bronze, Corcos's canvases, and a large selection of portraits by Drian and Martini.[17]

Within a few months of the auction, the Palais Rose itself was mortgaged to alleviate the tax debt and eventually awarded to Auguste-Eustache Leprévost, one of Casati's creditors. Then, with its considerable staff of chauffeur, cook, valet, maids, and gardeners dismissed, the residence was abandoned and left to the elements. The eventual pathetic condition of the Marchesa's red marble palace was described in a 1935 report: "It is now almost a ruin, with high grass growing in its lovely gardens and many broken windows."[18] With bittersweet praise, Jean Cocteau later recalled the splendor of Luisa's final fairy-tale castle and the woman who made it so in two separate volumes of memoirs, *The Difficulty of Being* and *Souvenir Portraits*.[19] The poetical quality of his reminiscences transforms them into a laudatory eulogy to both:

> The Marquise Casati owned a haunted house. It was not so before it was hers. . . .
>
> Luisa Casati was originally a brunette. Tall, bony, her gait, her great eyes, her teeth of a racehorse and her shyness did not accord with the conventional type of Italian beauties of the period. She astonished. She did not please.
>
> One day she decided to exploit her type to the full. It was no longer a matter of pleasing, displeasing, or astonishing. It was a matter of dumbfounding. She came out of her boudoir as from the dressing-room of an actress. She was red-haired. Her locks stood on end and writhed about a Gorgon's head, so painted that her eyes, that her mouth with its great teeth, daubed black and red, instantly turned men's glances from other mouths and other eyes. [Men] no longer

said: "She is nothing to write home about." They said to themselves: "What a pity that such a beautiful woman should daub herself in this way!"

As soon as she came out of her dressing-room, the Marquise Casati received the applause usually given to a famous tragedian at her entry on to the stage. It remained to act the play. There was none. This was her tragedy and why her house became haunted. The emptiness had to be filled whatever the cost; never for a moment could one stop bringing down the curtain and raising it again on some surprise: a unicorn's horn, dressed-up monkeys, a mechanical tiger, a boa constrictor. The monkeys developed tuberculosis. The unicorn's horn became coated in dust. The mechanical tiger was eaten by moths, the boa constrictor died. This sinister bric-à-brac defied ridicule. It left no room for it. . . .

I came to know the Marquise Casati's bric-à-brac. I prefer her unicorn's horn, her stuffed boas, her bronze deer, her mechanical tigers, to the genteel audacity of fashion, the good taste that sets yesterday's bad taste on a pedestal and exudes no sense of enigma, of meaningfulness.

With the greater part of her creditors satisfied by the auction, Luisa salvaged the remains of her fortune and confronted the difficulty of finding another home. For a monthly fee of two thousand francs, she moved into an apartment owned by Rumanian novelist the Princess Marthe Bibesco, at 45 quai de Bourbon near the tip of the Ile Saint-Louis in Paris.[20]

Even with greatly reduced means, Luisa's eye for decoration prevailed. Friend and frequent visitor André Germain approved of her efforts, declaring the apartment "très poétique." Remembering the Marchesa during this period, he wrote, "She sometimes crossed the Seine to see me. And, when she arrived in advance, nothing was more impressive than to see her standing on the landing of the small staircase which rose in the courtyard, like . . . a Gorgon."[21]

Bizarrely enough, the eventual sale of the Palais Rose to Olivier Scrive in 1936 did nothing to stop the rumors concerning its notorious former occupant. Erté's memoirs reveal an unfortunate incident involving two painters hired by the new owners. It seems that while one was perched on a tall ladder, the other inadvertently activated the Marchesa's mechanical panther, apparently left unsold or unclaimed. The automaton's unexpected movements and savage growls frightened the workmen, causing the one on the ladder to fall to his death on the marble floor. Even stuffed the beast was still a man killer.

Casati remained in the Bibesco apartment for only six months. During this time she met the celebrated dancer Elise Jouhandeau, who performed under the name Caryathis. During a luncheon together, Luisa suggested she rent Jouhandeau's house on the rue du Commandant-Marchand as the latter was about to embark on an extensive tour. The dancer quickly declined the proposal when she discovered the Marchesa's renovation plans included painting all of the trees in the garden gold and converting the interior into a series of cell-like chambers. The escape of some of Casati's pet snakes from a Renaissance chest during the luncheon may also have influenced Jouhandeau's final decision.[22]

From that point onward, Luisa would have no permanent address in the French capital. For a time, she resided at the Hôtel Laucas on the rue de Berri, surviving on the generosity of such old friends as Filippo Marinetti. Later, she accepted the hospitality of artist and bon vivant the Marchese Giuseppe Nobili Vitelleschi, whom she had known since her glory days in Rome, occupying his suites at the Hôtel Regina.[23] During their association, Vitelleschi painted a portrait of a sleekly fashionable Casati in a strapless gown. Her tilted head and brazen stare capture the viewer while an Egyptian statue stands guard behind her.[24]

Thirteen months after the enforced sale at the Palais Rose, Luisa made an attempt to retrieve some of her seized items. Papers were filed with the French courts on January 27, 1934, including a complete report of all that had been confiscated. Whether the request was dismissed or denied is not known, but none of the property was ever returned. According to Erté, this was not the only endeavor made by Casati to retain her moneyed status:

The opera singer Lucrezia Bori told me an extraordinary story many years later, when I was designing her costumes for the Metropolitan Opera. According to Bori, after the Marchesa Casati had spent all her money on extravagant living, she decided to marry again, setting her sights on one of the richest men in the United States. She wrote to Lucrezia Bori in New York, saying that she was coming over to visit her by the next boat, and asking her to arrange lunch with the man she had chosen as her future husband, for the day after her arrival. Lucrezia Bori cabled back saying this was impossible, for the gentleman in question was already married. The Marchesa cabled by return, "No matter. He will divorce. I am coming." Lucrezia Bori arranged the luncheon-party, and La Casati arrived. She had barely unpacked, when she exclaimed, "I've forgotten my snake." Over Lucrezia Bori's vigorous protests, she telephoned the zoo and asked them to lend her one. After much discussion, the directors of the zoo agreed to do so, for a very high price. The snake was delivered and, next day, when her intended fiancé had arrived for lunch, the Marchesa made a regal entrance with the snake twined round her arm. The gentleman was so terrified that he fled without saying either "how do you do" or "goodbye."[25]

If Erté's report is to be believed, Casati's failed strategy was an ironic one. For more than three decades, she had led a highly independent lifestyle made possible by her own fortune and the divestment of her roles as both wife and mother. Now that the financial means to that freedom were about to collapse, she may have contemplated a more conventional albeit deceptive solution.

In 1934, Luisa met Alberto Martini for the last time. During the past several years, the painter had prospered by creating sets for Italian and French theatrical productions. Martini had continued to fulfill the Marchesa's commissions, regardless of her inability to pay him. One of his later portraits depicts her as Euterpe, the Greek muse of music. Playing a stringed instrument of fanciful design, she is shown with sets of multiple eyes, in obvious homage to Man Ray's famous photograph. Martini's last painting of Casati was an oval portrait, completed in Paris and said to have been destined for the collection of a foreign prince. In his memoirs, Martini recalled their final encounter:

> One day . . . in my Montparnasse studio, I showed her one of my theatrical inventions. A multifaceted theatre project. It performed magic tricks using large mirrors and mechanical platforms and I had baptized it "The Diamond." She was frantic to see it work. There were infinite reflections—enlarged, the object seemed to be suspended in mid-air, and then to vanish. But she just suddenly disappeared. And I never heard of her again.[26]

The Polish artist Sarah Lipska also had an atelier in Montparnasse. By this time, she had carved a bust of Luisa in wood, using an upturned tree trunk so that the roots served as Medusan tresses. Lipska successfully rendered her subject's riveting gaze by the use of deeply hollowed sockets for eyes in the angular countenance. Another woman, Dutch artist Antonia Fokker Cottrau, created a silver mask of Casati's face in the art deco style. Upon the forehead rests a coiled serpent.

In July 1935, the Marchesa accepted her final invitation to the annual masquerade given by the Comte and Comtesse de Beaumont. The theme for that year was Le Bal des Tableaux Célèbres, requiring guests to come attired as famous painted figures, either real or fictional. Luisa arrived as her own interpretation of Franz Xaver Winterhalter's portrait of Empress Elisabeth of Austria. Whereas the Empress had been painted in cascades of white satin and tulle, Casati was dressed in a black skirt and jacket with train, collar, and cuffs of black and white ostrich plumes. She wore a carrot-colored wig of lengthy curls adorned with pins in the shape of stars. When presented to the assembled guests, Luisa posed before a backdrop painted by Christian Bérard of the Empress's rearing white stallions, Flick and Flock, holding a riding crop in her black-gloved hand. According to reports, the entire ensemble was a great success. Indeed, Luisa's final re-creation of one of her childhood inspirations was so captivating that Man Ray commemorated the event by shooting a portrait. The subsequent image of the Marchesa became one of the most famous and most often reproduced. Only a few months later, a full page was devoted to this photograph in the October 2, 1935, edition of the British magazine *Tatler*.

A less flamboyant picture of Casati was presented only a year later in Venice. In December 1936, Luisa was the guest of Prince Louis Ferdinand d'Orleans Borbone. The Prince required his intimates to address him as "Monsignor." Both Borbone and his lover, Antonio Vasconcelos, had acted as part of the Marchesa's costumed entourage when she appeared as the Comtesse de Castiglione at the Bal du Grand Prix more than a decade earlier. Along with their Pekinese dogs and pet monkey, the pair resided at the Prince's villa on the Venetian island of Giudecca. The name given to this home, the Ca'Leone, was coincidentally similar to that of Luisa's former residence on the Grand Canal. Also by chance, the caretakers of Borbone's villa were Emilio and Italia Basaldella. In his youth, Emilio was the loyal gondolier employed by Casati whom she had encouraged to marry, even though his intended's family was opposed. The union proved to be a happy one, and the Marchesa's support was never forgotten.

Although Italia was more than occupied in managing both the household and the couple's six children, she devoted herself to Luisa during her stay. The Basaldellas felt an almost parental concern over their once extravagant benefactress, who had now fallen on hard times. Italia despaired at the spectacle the Marchesa made of herself. Her youngest son, Francesco, would later become an author, and in his book *Giudecca* he recalled their guest:

> The stay of the celebrated Marchesa at the Ca'Leone was never tranquil
> because lawsuits, whims, and piques always followed her. As did long
> waits to know which part of Venice she wanted to visit. She would then
> return precipitously along streets swarmed with curious people who
> followed her until she fled into the stores. To save her from such
> persecution, the Monsignor had to put her into his motorboat and take

her home. The cause of all this fuss was the fact that the "Divine Marchesa," an extravagant and unpredictable woman, had adorned herself with veils and peacock feathers, and even with pieces of fur joined together with pins.[27]

Italia kept a watchful eye on Casati. Vigilant efforts were made to isolate Luisa from the Prince's cronies, who were quite fond of cocaine. According to Francesco, his mother's lack of success at times provoked her fury. "So you want to kill yourself?!" Italia would scream. "That bullshit there is suicide!" During quieter moments, the Marchesa could be found reading D'Annunzio's latest book, *Cento e cento e cento e cento pagine del libro segreto di Gabriele D'Annunzio tentato di morire.* After D'Annunzio had ignored her plea from the Palais Rose, one wonders what Luisa thought of this volume, which contained the highly personal tale *La figure de cire,* written during their earlier days as passionate lovers.

In early 1937, the Marchesa continued her stay in Venice when she rented Olga Rudge's small house on the calle Querini. In addition to two lackeys, she arrived accompanied by "a Pekinese and a black cat . . . with her famous leopard skin wrapped around her and carrying a candelabra (unlighted) in each hand. The *fondamenta* was lined with people calling out in Venetian, 'da dove viene questa vecchia strega?' [Where did this old witch come from?]."[28]

D'Annunzio's lifelong fascination with death had increased with the advancing years. His interest in the occult, so mutually shared with Casati, had now become an obsession as both underwent a similar diminishment of their former provocative powers. Evenings at the Vittoriale were spent before a succession of Ouija boards, tarot decks, and other divinatory objects in an attempt to contact the Great Beyond. On a calendar printed with predictions of forthcoming events, D'Annunzio had underlined the one specified for March 1, 1938, which foretold "the death of a famous man." That very evening, alone at his desk, Gabriele D'Annunzio suffered a cerebral hemorrhage and died at the age of seventy-four. Laid out in full-dress military uniform between a pair of the gaudy plaster cast reproductions of Michelangelo's slaves, D'Annunzio's body was subsequently interred in the marble tomb he had prepared for himself on the grounds of his lakeside lair.

D'Annunzio was dead. Casati did not attend the funeral, nor is it known whether any of the thousands of flowers on the poet's grave bore her sympathies. The last link to the fantasy life she had previously enjoyed was now severed.

Shortly after their divorce in 1924, Camillo left Cinisello Balsamo for Rome, where he shared an apartment with Anna Ewing Cockrell, the daughter of American Senator Francis M. Cockrell of Missouri.[29] Anna was the widow of Lambros Coromilas, Greek minister to the United States. It may have been her marriage to Coromilas that led to the erroneous reports concerning Camillo's involvement with a Greek woman. Luisa would neither acknowledge his companion as a replacement nor would she allow Cockrell's name or that of any of her relations to be mentioned in her presence.[30] In 1927, the unmarried couple had a son named after his father. Even though the child was born out of wedlock, Camillo recognized him as his own. Arrangements were made so that upon Camillo's death, his heir would receive the title of Marchese Casati Stampa di Soncino. The Marchesa's ex-husband lived a quiet life, shared between his family and cherished horses and hounds, until his death from cardiac disease on September 18, 1946, at the age of sixty-nine.[31]

Casati's daughter and her husband left England for the South Sea island of Moorea, where Cristina conceived a child. The couple returned to Britain for the birth of their daughter on March 4, 1928, and named her in homage to the paradise they so loved. Soon afterward, Moorea was left in the care of her paternal grandmother as Viscount and Viscountess Hastings departed on an excursion to Mexico and America. The motivation for these treks was Hastings's desire to study under Diego Rivera. A vocal supporter of communism, the Mexican artist's political beliefs were often reflected in the social realism of his work. In San Francisco, the Hastings finally met Rivera and his wife, artist Frida Kahlo. The quartet's complex friendship lasted well into the 1930s. At one phase of their association, it has been suggested that Kahlo and Cristina may have shared a brief romance.[32] This short affair between artist and model curiously echoes the one between Luisa and Romaine Brooks. During this time, Kahlo completed a portrait sketch of Cristina. In *Frida: A Biography of Frida Kahlo*, Hayden Herrera describes not only this drawing but some of its subject's notable personality traits as well. There is more than a passing similarity between Cristina and the Marchesa:

> One careful pencil drawing captures much of the aristocratic hauteur
> and sophistication of Milan-born, Oxford-educated Lady Cristina
> Hastings, whose swings between states of boredom and explosive anger
> or humor Frida found congenial and amusing.[33]

This tendency toward impulsive rage was once graphically exhibited when Cristina was seen with one arm in a sling following her return from a stay in Italy. When questioned as to the cause of the injury, she stated calmly: "I was angry with a servant and hit him so hard that it broke something in my arm."[34]

Cristina made several politically motivated trips to Brazil and Spain on her own. In Rio de Janeiro, she and two associates were deported back to England when they were suspected of communist activities. While in Valencia, she conducted talks with Italian prisoners held in a convent during the Spanish Civil War. It is interesting to note at what odds the noblewoman's energetic leftist efforts were with her mother's earlier profligate spending.

By the late 1930s, Cristina and Hastings were reunited with their daughter. Life was divided between houses on Wellington Street near Regent's Park in London and Blackbridge House, the Hastings's family manse in Hampshire. During the Marchesa's travels to Britain, Hastings completed a portrait of his mother-in-law. Dated 1934, the painting shows a veiled Casati, dressed in black, seated with a crystal ball in one hand. Cristina, too, pursued a successful but brief career in the arts. A collection of her paintings and handmade rag rugs was exhibited at the Lefevre Gallery in Bruton Street. Every piece sold.

Meanwhile, Luisa was at a loss as to what direction to take next. Too many debts were still waiting to be settled in France and Italy for her to find shelter in either country, and her reputation was still too notorious in European high society for her to find generosity among its members. Her reign as the "Divine Marquise" had finally come to an end. She was nearly sixty years old. With nowhere else to turn, Luisa fled to Britain.

3

It is difficult to pinpoint the exact date of Luisa's arrival in England, nor is there accurate documentation of where she first resided. Although the bulk of the Marchesa's fortunes had been exhausted by this juncture, she still had enough to survive. But this would prove a temporary condition as a result of her unalterable lifestyle.

Several sources claim that Luisa first occupied a house in the fashionable Mayfair section of London. Gabriel-Louis Pringué recalled its decoration:

> The last time I saw the Marchesa Casati was in London in 1939. She
> had succeeded in transforming an English house in Mayfair, in the
> suburbs of Piccadilly, into an Italian Renaissance palace with rooms big
> enough for her to move around freely in her costumes of enormous
> black flamingo feathers and furs.[35]

Count Knut Corfitz Bonde also remembered the same property and its inhabitant but in a different way:

> In London [Casati] rented a grand house for five pounds sterling a
> month. . . . The house was so immense that no one wanted it because

of its enormous dimensions. . . . Sick of London she went back to Paris for a while. The owner of the residence thus retook possession of the house and threw out all of her belongings. However, she managed to recover most of them. . . . The last time I met the Marquise . . . she announced to me that she had retired from the social world and only read the Bible [saying], "There is not a more interesting novel in the whole world if studied to its fullest."[36]

In London, Luisa sought out old friends for companionship and much needed funds. She could depend on Augustus John for both. Even though their brief love affair was now some twenty years in the past, enough affection still existed between them to foster a close bond. John welcomed Casati to the city with exuberance. But as the world drew closer to impending war, the artist, with ominous understatement, would inform Luisa: "Londres n'est pas gai en ce moment."[37]

Previous acquaintanceships were renewed, such as those with Tony de Gandarillas, Lord Berners, and Gerald Napier Sturt, Lord Alington. Alington owned Augustus John's first portrait of Casati from 1919. The work was displayed at Crichel, the nobleman's country house in Dorset, where it would later be joined by Alington's purchase of one of the castings of the Casati bust by Jacob Epstein. Luisa also found new friends in the Baroness Violet de Goldschmidt and Evan Morgan, Lord Tredegar, a former chamberlain at the Vatican, who was then known as "the richest peer in the realm."[38] The latter delighted in inviting clashing personalities to his cocktail parties, waiting for fireworks to erupt. At one of these, in Tredegar's London home, Luisa and Aleister Crowley were finally brought together. In front of horrified guests and much to Tredegar's amusement, the two collided and an argument ensued.[39]

For a while, Luisa was still able to maintain a gossamer semblance of her former lifestyle. A devoted Italian, Vittorio Scarpa, joined the Marchesa in London to become her manservant despite her frequent inability to pay him. Also acting as chauffeur, he would transport Casati around the city in a large green car. But both her attendant and automobile soon disappeared as the Marchesa's means dwindled and war approached. With the advent of war in 1940, Scarpa was held, as were so many other Italian immigrants, in an internment camp on the Isle of Man. Luisa herself was at risk of a similar fate since she had dramatically altered her passport age. She went to the local police station to resolve this dangerous situation, accompanied by the Baroness de Goldschmidt for support. Relying on her resourceful panache, the Marchesa returned in triumph—her safety intact, but decidedly many years older.[40]

Prior to this, in April 1939, Luisa took a service flat at 14 Stratton Street, where she befriended an Austrian family relocated to London at the start of the war. Rose Reitlinger and her son Carl became well acquainted with Luisa during this time. Carl Reitlinger later took the Marchesa's final glamorous photo-portraits in 1942—these remain testaments to her undiminished allure as old age neared. Reclaiming her religious faith, Casati accompanied the Reitlingers to Sunday services at the Church of the Immaculate Conception on Farm Street. When a sermon became overlong, she was known to sigh, "Il ne finira jamais." Alternately, Luisa took the Reitlingers along with her to séances with spiritualist Mary Churchill.[41] Casati was also a client of renowned clairvoyant Estelle Roberts, paying for one of her sessions with the final remnants of her famous 1924 Castiglione costume—a gold and silver underskirt and pearl bodice.[42]

By the early 1940s, the Marchesa's financial plight had worsened. With the same heedlessness demonstrated during more stable times, Casati handed out her last few valuables in place of cash to merchants and taxi drivers; with the latter, she displayed a talent to tame even the toughest of them into becoming her personal servants when packages had to be carried.[43] Whatever monetary assets survived were quickly eroded by constant outlays for occult paraphernalia and other such trifles. If human companionship was not to be found, Luisa could be entertained by the troupe of Pekinese dogs she had acquired in London. She owned as many as five at one time. Her favorite, named Spider, was said to have been a gift from Lady Violet Munnings, wife of noted artist Sir Alfred Munnings.[44] The small dog was fond of displaying its amorous inclinations toward the arm of Casati's tattered fur coat and was taken on regular walks by Carl Reitlinger. Luisa denied herself more than once so that her pets received the best of her provisions. A photograph in the family archives shows the dogs around a tiny Christmas tree decorated with sweetmeats and bones for their holiday treat.

Such deprivation mattered little to Luisa. She was more than capable of sustaining herself on champagne, whiskey, and other rumored stimulants. The Marchesa's slim frame was now emaciated and bony; her hands plagued by rheumatism; and her eyes required the assistance of spectacles to see closely, these being vainly concealed until their absolute necessity. Even so, her thinness, height, and robust constitution made her appear younger than her sixty years. This illusion was enhanced by Casati's continued use of a thick veil, lifted only in the presence of those whom she trusted. Often, she would hold court before a retinue of young artists and members of the dance world. To further mask her age during these occasions, Luisa would forbid her adolescent granddaughter, Moorea, from divulging their familial

Bronze bust of Casati by Jacob Epstein, 1918

The Marchesa Casati, *by Augustus John, 1919. Courtesy of the Honorable Mrs. Mary Anna Marten.*

Portrait of Casati by Federico Beltrán y Masses, 1920

Casati with one of her pet snakes at a Beaumont ball, Paris, ca. 1920s

Portrait of Casati from a framed miniature, artist unknown, ca. 1920s. Courtesy of Lady Moorea Black.

Luisa, *by Kees van Dongen, 1921*

Palais Rose, Le Vésinet, ca. 1922

Casati dressed in Bakst's "Queen of the Night" costume, 1922. Courtesy of Lady Moorea Black.

The Marchesa Casati, *by Ignacio Zuloaga, 1922. Courtesy of María Rosa Suárez-Zuloaga and the Museo Zuloaga, Zumaya.*

Sketch of Casati as the Comtesse de Castiglione, by Alberto Martini, 1925

Casati in St. Moritz, ca. 1925

Sketch of Casati at the Everglades Club, Palm Beach, Florida, artist unknown, 1926

Sketch of Casati as Cagliostro,
by Drian, 1927

La Marchesa Luisa Casati, *by Joseph Paget-Fredericks, ca. 1940s. Courtesy of Lady*
Moorea Black.

Casati, by Carl L. T. Reitlinger, 1942. Courtesy of the late Carl L. T. Reitlinger.

Luisa Casati's grave in Brompton Cemetery, London

ties. Her orders were quite simple: "Remember, you are not a relation!" Moorea recalled their first meeting:

> It wasn't until I was eight that I met Grandma Casati, although she would never have allowed me to call her that. When she arrived at my parents' house, dressed from head to toe in black velvet, top hat, veil, long black gauntlets and high-heeled boots, she seemed like a figure out of a fairy tale come to life, magical, terrifying, and to be treated with considerable awe. She undoubtedly came by taxi, but for all I knew the amazing apparition I saw could have flown in on a broomstick.[45]

By 1942, Luisa's funds had nearly vanished entirely. The generosity of family and friends supported her for a while longer until it became evident that none of the money was being used for rent or food. Cristina was all too familiar with her mother's neediness. While visiting her daughter at Oxford, Casati had often required both Cristina and her chaperon to call on pawnbrokers on her behalf. Sometimes their efforts were rewarded with gracious thanks, but if the amount was not what she had anticipated, the intermediaries had to avoid a volley of flying objects.

That some action had to be taken concerning Luisa's worsening financial situation was obvious after an exasperating incident. Hailing a taxi in London, Casati took the three-hour journey to Lord Alington's Dorset estate to ask for money. The small sum finally provided was immediately spent on her return cab fare to the city. Augustus John addressed these circumstances by establishing a bank account for his drowning muse. Records pay witness to his magnanimity toward Luisa for the remainder of her life.[46] Such friends as Lord Berners, Lord Alington, Lord Tredegar, Tony de Gandarillas, and the Duke of Westminster, as well as Cristina and her daughter, all augmented this source of aid. Later added to this list was the Marquis de Cuevas, with whom Casati conducted an ongoing and humorous competition as to who had given the most lavish parties in the past.

Weekly contributions were made to Luisa's bank account in small amounts of one to five pounds, for everyone knew the instantaneous result of supplying more. The intention was to keep her from begging for money. As stated by John's biographer, Michael Holroyd: "Her one asset was absolute helplessness, which threw responsibility for her survival on to everyone else."[47] Count Knut Corfitz Bonde recalled the altruism she received even from Dr. Axel Munthe:

> A long time after having left Capri, the Marquise asked Dr. Munthe for help. At that time she was living in a little hotel on Jermyn Street in

a very modest neighborhood. In her letter to the doctor, she alluded that her situation was almost desperate. We never understood Munthe's generosity; he ran to the hotel where the Marquise was staying, in the most abominable circumstances. But where she seemed to be perfectly at ease just like in the villa.

"Would you care for a whiskey-coke, Doctor?" she said amiably while she rang for the waiter. The waiter brought the drink immediately, but asked the Marquise to pay him before he gave it to her, saying that the hotel did not give credit.

"But I have no money," the Marquise said with no shame whatsoever. Munthe took money out of his pocket and promised the Marquise he would look after her. . . .

When Munthe told me about this incident a few years later, I asked him: "At least did you get the whiskey and coke?"

He replied, "The whiskey evaporated and so did Luisa Casati, from whom I have had no news since."[48]

With increasing frequency, Luisa could be found in Augustus John's studio on Tite Street in Chelsea. She would come to reminisce in tattered outfits of black velvet and leopardskin. As always, a veil hung from a satin coal-scuttle hat, and her hair was still the color of flame. Holroyd writes, "The layers of powder grew thicker; the stories of Italy longer; her clothes more faded and frayed; her leopard-skin gloves spotted with holes."[49] Making the most of his constant visitor, John decided to undertake a new portrait. He made preliminary sketches, including one flattering head study. Another drawing he did around this time was a caricature of Luisa with bright red lips, a tall hat, and eyes encircled with immense lashes. The sitter's dazed expression is clarified by its title, *A Caricature of Marchesa Casati with a Hang-Over.*[50]

Augustus John's 1942 portrait presents a still refined, sixty-one-year-old Casati seated in a high-back, black leather chair. On her lap is a large black cat, whose defiant stare mirrors that of the sitter. John was well aware of Luisa's fascination with the occult, and the inclusion of this witch's familiar may have been in homage to these interests. To further heighten the portrait's otherworldly quality, John borrowed a blue-tinged background of storm clouds from the religious studies of El Greco. Luisa's enigmatic expression must have been a challenge for John. Restoration on the work has determined that her countenance was heavily rubbed and repeatedly repainted.

John remained a faithful friend to Luisa, taking her eccentricities in stride, and often brought her for meals in Soho restaurants. He once commented,

"The loss of her fortune seems only to have confirmed her faith in her Star and the conviction of its eventual ascendancy. She meets all her tribulations with unconcern."[51] Lady Moorea confirms her grandmother's lack of pessimism even when in difficult straits: "I never heard her complain about her situation."[52] Holroyd relates how Luisa could continue to astonish: "Despite the squalor, she played, to the last notes, this ghostly echo of the D'Annunzian heroine. 'Bring in the drinks!' she would call, and a bent Italian servant would shuffle forward with a half-empty bottle of beer."[53]

Casati's residences continued to change as quickly as her financial situation demanded. For a number of years, she resided in a top-floor flat at Hamilton House in Piccadilly, near Hyde Park Corner, in cobwebbed rooms cluttered with "enormous battered cabin trunks, overflowing with faded photographs, tiger skins, parrot cages, false pearls, cosmetics: all the unsaleable paraphernalia and relics from her days of splendor."[54] Luisa was thrilled with this romantically historical address, for it was once home to Lord Nelson's mistress, Lady Emma Hamilton, and later to Byron. The Marchesa was personally familiar with the site's previously opulent salons recently converted into convenience flats. Decades earlier, she had accepted many invitations to the wild parties thrown there by its then owner, the Baroness d'Erlanger. Casati would wait out the desolate years of World War II in this Georgian building, along with several other colorful personalities of foreign origin (including the Egyptian aesthete Félix Rollo) who were more attracted by the low cost of its rooms than by its fabled past. By a twist of fate, Aleister Crowley resided there briefly as well.[55] Many French refugees and American military officers rounded out this diverse society. In the words of author Maurice Druon, then a refugee who had come to London to enlist in the Free French Forces led by Charles de Gaulle: "The apartments at Hamilton House were splendid but in ruin, the service precarious, the furniture unusual, and the bedding strongly used."[56] Throughout the air raids and bombings of the Blitz, Luisa remained steadfast in a gray, poverty-stricken London. None of the chaos seemed to dampen her spirits; even when rationing brought so many to near starvation, her treasured Pekinese never went hungry.

With the Marchesa's constant changes of address came the necessity of storing possessions with friends and acquaintances. Besides several other items, she entrusted the crystal sword from the Bal de Cagliostro to an Italian grocer in Old Compton Street. When the shop was bombed, Casati became frantic since a gypsy had once promised her good fortune as long as she had possession of the weapon. Miraculously, Luisa managed to recover the sword, although her other belongings were lost in the rubble—including what she reputed to be a fist-sized topaz given to her by the descendant

of a Turkish sultan. The grocer angrily dismissed such an obviously dubious claim.[57]

During the 1930s, Luisa became friends with Cecil Beaton. Since enjoying a flamboyant youth in the 1920s, Beaton had attained a reputation as
one of Britain's preeminent photographers and theatrical stage and costume
designers. In his diaries, Beaton recalled vividly her first visit to Ashcombe,
the Georgian estate he rented in the Dorset countryside:

> Once the eccentric and wonderful Marchesa Casati came over for tea
> from Crichel on one of the coldest days of the winter. For her initial
> visit to Ashcombe she selected to wear a huge cowboy hat of straw, a
> gold brocade coatee, white flannel tennis trousers, and her stockingless
> feet were shod in cork-soled sandals. On her way through the icy
> snow to see the signs of snowdrops in the bare woods she made a
> delightfully incongruous picture.[58]

Although their relationship would become severely strained in subsequent
years, Beaton was one of Luisa's most ardent admirers. In his book *The Glass
of Fashion,* he later remembered his friend and her always-worsening living
conditions. On a bleak winter's day during the war, Beaton called on the
Marchesa to invite her to his home for a private luncheon. He found her
seated at a table in the center of her room at Hamilton House, applying
heavy cosmetics to her eyes. According to Beaton, this dusty setting "offered
me a terrifying glimpse of degradation: old artificial flowers, broken clocks,
bottles of methylated spirit." He continued:

> When we arrived at my house, she relaxed in the warmth and became
> enthusiastic and happy as a child. "Now let us enjoy everything. This
> good glass of sherry, it is so rare. This open fire, this scent of rosemary,
> how good it all is." She held forth like an empress, her gestures bold
> and valiant. Somehow the indomitable spirit sublimated the old
> wastepaper basket of black satin that she wore on her head and
> metamorphosed the old cotton rose on her shoulder into a thing of
> beauty. Here was a great woman, someone whose character and pluck
> could overcome all mediocrity and create nobility out of poverty.[59]

Although plausible, reports that Luisa lived at more than fifteen different addresses during her nearly two decades in London have never been
completely substantiated. Adequately documented are her occupancies of
the house in Mayfair, the service flat in Stratton Street, Hamilton House in
Piccadilly, the hotel on Jermyn Street, a flat at 110 Ebury Street, and another
on Moscow Road near the northwest corner of Kensington Gardens. She was
known to have also taken flats in Half Moon Street, at 1 Clarges Street, and

in Cheyne Row. The Marchesa was also a regular guest at the homes of her dedicated supporters and their friends, including Augustus John's studio in Chelsea and his estate in Hampshire, Fryern Court.

It is not surprising to learn that Luisa quickly became infamous for over-staying her welcome. Theatrical designer Oliver Messel noted this bother-some habit to his close friend Carl Toms, who would later recount one such incident as follows:

> [Messel] got to know the Marchesa Casati in Venice who had become a good friend. When she lived in London later on I said how much I would like to meet her. "Can't you ask her to tea?" I implored. "I don't think so, Carly," he replied. "I really don't think I could. Hugh Skillen asked her for tea once and she stayed for three days."[60]

Both Lord Alington and Lord Berners were generous in offering numer-ous invitations for weekends away from the city. Mary Anna Marten, Aling-ton's daughter, recalls Luisa's visits to Crichel with affection:

> People thought I should be frightened of her since I was just nine or ten years old at the time. But on the contrary, I thought she was fabulous. I will never forget those huge eyes, her tall top hat with its veil, or the way she always spoke to me with such kindness. During her stays, she gave me a French nineteenth-century automaton doll and a large album covered in red velvet, both of which I still cherish. It would be untrue to assume Casati a crass woman because of her flamboyance. There was not an ounce of vulgarity in her. Casati was the last of her kind. There has been no one like her since. So you can understand why, in her later life, so many of us wanted to assist in any small way. During the Christmas season, I would send her hampers from Fortnum & Mason. Although I had no real contact with her since my childhood, she had made an unforgettable impression upon me which has stayed with me all of my life.[61]

Like Lord Alington, Lord Berners remained Luisa's unfailing comrade until his death in 1950. Even so, she was not immune to his jests. It is be-lieved that Berners started the cruel rumor that, desperate for money, Casati had accepted employment at a Scottish castle. At midnight, so the story claimed, she was required to make herself seen on a terrace, shrouded in white veils, in the role of the resident ghost.

There is another less dignified picture of the Marchesa during this same period. Allusions have been made to her practice of selling the small gifts of leather-bound books, antique porcelain, and crystals given by close friends. It is not known whether her benefactors were aware of this, but after a time these gifts were no longer given in the same abundance. The memories of Edoardo Amman, son of Luisa's cousin Mario, substantiate these tales. In December 1948, the then twenty-six-year-old Amman visited Luisa in London to see the woman whose exploits in Venice, Capri, and Paris had provided family gossip for years. Expecting to meet a still radiant queen from some decadent fairy tale, Amman found something altogether different:

> She was a friendly, very skinny old woman, sometimes wearing a mangy old leopard skin. She pulled out of her bed a bottle of gin. When we went out to lunch [at the Pheasantry Club], she was dressed in black with her face made up like a clown. . . .
>
> At first appearance, she didn't seem at all desperate. She didn't care about anyone. I talked to her about some old cousins, to whom she had become an idol, but she only made fun of them. She missed only my father. . . .
>
> Several nights later, we went to a restaurant. It was owned by an Italian, her friend, with whom—I understood—she was trafficking old books and antiques. Upon our first meeting, she had talked excitedly of local news and disputes that were absolutely incomprehensible for a stranger like me. That night, too, she spoke very spiritedly, but jumped from one subject to another. She didn't succeed in expressing a single discourse.

Amman summed up his infamous relative as "an old woman who had let everything go and who had closed herself up in a tomb of desperate selfishness."[62]

Even the more sympathetic of Luisa's acquaintances sketch a disturbing portrait, one colored by desolation and drugs. Philippe Jullian claimed to have once seen her rummaging through trash bins for bits of velvet and lace. One rumor claimed that she embellished her costume with discarded monkey fur, obtained from a dresser at the Chelsea Palace Music Hall.[63] Now that the Marchesa had no further funds for taxis, the alternative of public transportation was impossible because of her outlandish appearance. Some of Casati's women friends ordered a more conventional set of clothes for her, but when the seamstress arrived for the first fitting, she was ejected with screams.[64] Instead, with pride, Luisa paraded the streets in ensembles of leopardskin and feathers fastened together with porcelain pins, and highly slit ankle-length skirts revealing remarkably graceful legs. Large rings of Cherry Blossom Boot Polish encircled her eyes after she could no longer afford more expensive cosmetics. All of this was topped off by a tall, crushed coal-scuttle hat with her ever-present black veil.

Author Peter Quennell recalled observing Casati, dressed in "the plumage of a shabby raven," from his office window:

> I worked in an advertising agency near Burlington Gardens, overlooking a street where a procession of highly respectable prostitutes strolled regularly to and fro. . . . One afternoon, a colleague called my attention to a particularly outlandish apparition: "Look at *that* old girl!" he exclaimed. "I shouldn't think that *she'd* get many customers!" It was the Marchesa Casati, I saw, who happened to be passing by, wearing her usual disconsolate uniform.[65]

Under the influence of whatever substances she consumed, reports of which ranged from alcohol to cocaine and opium, Luisa could be an entertainingly jovial if at times incoherent dinner guest. It seemed, though, that when such mood enhancers lost their effect, she became ill and unpredictably angry.[66]

In addition to the difficulties of attending to her mother, Cristina was also struggling with a failing marriage. By the early 1940s, both she and Hastings were considering divorce. During this time, their daughter had been enrolled in a school in Switzerland. On vacations, Moorea often escorted Luisa to lunches at the Royal Court Restaurant in Sloane Square. Before these outings, Cristina would impart a firm warning: "You must never give your grandmother money. You may take her out, give her presents, and give her food. But never offer money or let her into your house. For from that moment on, it will be *her* house."[67]

Lady Moorea remembers the trepidation she experienced as a schoolgirl when calling on her unpredictable grandmother, affectionately known by the diminutive "Malu" in the family: "You were terrified of her because you never knew what you were going to get! When she would make her entrance at the restaurant, the entire clientele would turn around and look. You can imagine the embarrassment!" But almost always, the two enjoyed each other's company. Abashed but helplessly amused, Moorea more than once watched Luisa playing out one of her most wicked pranks. First, she selected an unknowing patron of the restaurant. Then in a deeply resounding whisper, mingling French, Italian, and heavily accented English, she mimicked the chosen person in an alarmingly precise manner. Next, she speculated about the individual's character and lifestyle. Of course, her sarcastic conjectures were usually not in the victim's favor.[68]

Cristina and John Hastings divorced in 1943, and each remarried the following year. Hastings's new wife was writer Margaret Lane. Cristina married Wogan Philipps, who later succeeded to the title of Lord Milford in 1962. He also earned another appellation of a somewhat more dubious distinction:

because of his standing in the British Communist party, Philipps became known as "The Red Peer." Before the couple eventually retired to his estate, Butler's Farm in Colesborne, Gloucester, they founded an agricultural cooperative in Italy. The already tenuous relationship between the Marchesa and her daughter became even more strained when Philipps refused his mother-in-law entry into Butler's Farm. His objections were based on his knowledge of her potential dependence on him and what he considered to be the neglectful treatment of Cristina for so many years. Casati's political views were also at extreme odds with those of Philipps. For the next decade, contact between Luisa and her daughter and son-in-law was limited at best.

In the early 1950s, Cristina was diagnosed with breast cancer. Treatments proved unsuccessful and the disease spread. Cristina Philipps died at Butler's Farm on March 22, 1953, at the age of fifty-one. Casati did not attend the funeral, which was held at the country estate. It was discovered later that, during her illness, Cristina had recorded hours of autobiographical audiotape. Wogan Philipps destroyed these on her death, obliterating the only document that might have elucidated Cristina's complex relationship with her self-devoted parent.

Several years before, an American society columnist reported on her attendance at a masquerade ball with Cristina. The latter's rare remark may reveal at least some level of admiration for her mother's achievements as a concocter of spectacles:

> As we walked up the long hallway of the house, we noticed at regular intervals gentlemen who, though they had been hired for the occasion and would later return to suburban apartments, were at the moment giving a rather reasonable facsimile of being Nubian slaves. They were all dressed in loincloths. . . . The effect was strictly grade A. All of the guests were impressed with the Nubian slave touch to the party, with the exception of Lady Hastings. She had only a single comment to make: "Mother would have had the real thing."[69]

By the time of her daughter's death, Luisa was living at the last address she would occupy, 32 Beaufort Gardens, a block of flats in London's Knightsbridge district near Harrods department store. She rented a single room on the second floor, with a balcony shared by those flats overlooking the street. One of these was home to Prince Monolulu, the self-proclaimed African nobleman illustrious for his feathered native costumes and horse racing tips who had also known more affluent days. Here, Casati took up a quieter but no less eccentric life. It was an existence far removed from her days as one of the world's foremost artistic muses. But that very same year in Italy, and then soon in America and France, Luisa would provide inspiration once again.

4

"How does it feel, Mrs. Goforth, to be a legend in your own lifetime?" Goforth is the central character of Tennessee Williams's 1953 short story "Man Bring This Up Road." Analysis of the piece reveals that aspects of Luisa Casati's extraordinary life were influential in its writing. The allegorical tale concerns Flora Goforth, a wealthy art patron living with a menagerie of animals in a villa off the Amalfi coast, and her apocalyptic meeting with a wandering poet who may, in fact, be the Angel of Death. At the time of its conception, Williams was in Venice collaborating with director Luchino Visconti on the film *Senso*. In all probability, Williams learned of the Marchesa through Visconti, who, as a boy, had met her on a train to Cortina.[70] Additional information was most likely provided by Sir Harold Acton, Casati's ally, with whom Williams became friendly while living in Rome.[71]

The story later became the basis for Williams's play *The Milk Train Doesn't Stop Here Anymore*, which opened on Broadway in 1964 starring Tallulah Bankhead in the lead role.[72] Here, Goforth's connection to Casati was expanded to comprise her associations with the Ballets Russes, her ownership of a distinctive house outside Paris, and comments on her spectacular entrances at costume balls in the 1920s—including one as a gilded Lady Godiva astride a horse led by a Nubian slave.[73] Apparently, Casati also inspired another of the play's characters, the Marchesa Condotti—known as the Witch of Capri. Her costume and arrival via funicular mirror Luisa's initial appearance on Capri in 1920. With her elaborate dress, bejeweled hands, and veiled conical hat adorned with pearls, Williams describes Condotti as "a creature out of a sophisticated fairy tale." In 1968, Williams adapted his play for the film *Boom* starring Elizabeth Taylor, Richard Burton, and, in a bizarre gender twist, Noël Coward as the Witch of Capri.

With the appearance of *On the Road* in 1957, Jack Kerouac achieved notoriety as the premiere iconoclastic voice of the Beat generation. Before the publication of that literary land mine, the American writer had spent many years gaining inspiration from an itinerant and ultimately self-destructive lifestyle. Three years earlier, in March 1954, Kerouac was living at the Cameo Hotel in San Francisco's Skid Row district. There he wrote *San Francisco Blues*, a series of eighty brief poems. Kerouac labeled each of these numbered pieces a "chorus" to recognize the jazz form that influenced them.[74] By chance, one wall of his room at the Cameo was adorned with a stained and torn reproduction of Augustus John's 1919 portrait of Casati.[75] Kerouac knew little of the sitter's history, or anything of her coincidental 1926 stay in San Francisco. Instead, it was Luisa's unique aura, as well as John's skill at capturing its complexity, that inspired him to devote three poems in the collection to her. Kerouac's "74th Chorus" not only reveals the writer's sensual fascination with this muse but also makes several startlingly similar D'Annunzian references:

Marchesa Casati
Is a living doll
Pinned on my Frisco
Skid row wall

Her eyes are vast
Her skin is shiny
Blue veins
And wild red hair
Shoulders sweet and tiny

Love her
Love her
   Sings the sea
   Bluely
Moaning
In the Augustus John
   de John
   back ground

By the early 1950s, Maurice Druon was a prolific and well-respected French author. His novel *La Volupté d'être,* published in May 1954, details the final days of the Contessa Lucrezia Sanziani, a courtesan from the golden days of the Belle Époque. Her past lovers included kings, warriors, literati, and artistic geniuses. Once immortalized on both canvas and page, La Sanziani now occupies rooms in a decrepit Roman hotel, where her days are lost in reverie. There, she relives her dazzling youth in Parisian palaces and Venetian palazzi through the tales she tells an awestruck chambermaid. In interviews after the book's release, Druon stated that the fictional character of the Contessa Sanziani was three-quarters based on the Marchesa Casati. Inspiration for the remaining portion was taken from the life of the Italian beauty and mistress to Kaiser Wilhelm II, the Contessa Anna Morosini.[76]

More than a decade before the publication of the novel, the author had befriended Casati while both resided at Hamilton House during World War II. His firsthand account reveals the lasting fascination that would later inspire him:

When Luisa Casati walked along the streets of London, it took all of
the dignity of the English, who were used to not being shocked by

anything, not to just gawk at this phantom dressed as she was in her threadbare ensemble of velvet, leather, and panther trim. At home, she loved to look at herself in a hand mirror while wandering in her memories which were a bit scrambled. These she would recount at length with a tragic, expiring voice as if a sort of elderly *La Dame aux Camélias*. But even though she was penniless, Casati kept her self-esteem and that illusion of charms found in women that have often seduced and been seduced.[77]

La Volupté d'être was praised in France, where it has remained continually in print. It was translated into several languages, the title of the English edition being *The Film of Memory*.[78] The novel's English title has a double connotation: it refers not only to the liberated chambermaid's possible subsequent movie stardom but also to the specific workings of the Contessa's memories, which rewind from her later years back to her childhood. Druon's work was a notable enough success to warrant his decision to rewrite it as a play. Eight years later, in 1962, *La Contessa* premiered at the Théâtre de Paris. In the leading role of the Italian noblewoman was Rumanian actress Elvire Popesco. In France and later in Italy, Greece, and Russia, the production was received with numerous accolades.

Not long after its popular run in Paris, American producer Leland Hayward prepared *La Contessa* for the London stage. Playwright Paul Osborn was hired to undertake the work's adaptation into English. The main difficulty was casting an actress capable of embodying the poignant yet powerful La Sanziani; as the producer stated, "Unless the audience is absolutely convinced at once that this old woman was the most exciting and glamorous woman of her time, the play makes no sense. It all depends on that."[79] Hayward believed he had found the most appropriate choice in Vivien Leigh.

Tryouts for *La Contessa* began at the Theatre Royal in Newcastle-upon-Tyne on April 6, 1965, under the direction of Sir Robert Helpmann. The opening-night notices were disastrous. Almost every element of the production was lambasted by the press, from the staid direction and overwrought dialogue to the bleakness of its sets. Stunned by the negative response, the company did its best in staying with the production, but such abysmal reviews ruined any hope of filling the theater. A month later, during a run in Manchester, *La Contessa* was canceled, dashing any hopes for a future West End or Broadway opening.

This theatrical miscarriage did not prevent Hollywood director Vincente Minnelli from sensing the possibilities of presenting Druon's story in yet another form a decade later. He believed that the book could provide material for both a new film and a stellar role for his daughter, Liza. Leaving Druon's own 1972 screen adaptation of the novel unrealized, British author John Gay was hired to provide the script. Minnelli envisioned his daughter in the part of Carmela, the timid chambermaid befriended by the Contessa. The character's name was the film's actual working title before the final change was made to *A Matter of Time*.[80] What remained unchanged was the age of the novel's seventeen-year-old waif, to be played by the nearly thirty-year-old singer-actress. A search was now undertaken for the all-important La Sanziani. Ingrid Bergman would accept. In October 1976, *A Matter of Time* premiered at New York City's Radio City Music Hall. Much like its British stage predecessor, it received catastrophic reviews and was soon pulled from general release as a financial disaster.[81]

Nevertheless, more than a half-century after their first meeting, Maurice Druon continued to remember the remarkable woman who acted as muse to one of his most famous works:

> Luisa Casati remains a unique character in my gallery of humankind, a woman filled with self-contemplation, of the romantic construction of her living dream, and an obsession with seeing herself disappear.[82]

5

The once extravagant life of the Marchesa Luisa Casati had begun in vast villas and luxury suites. Marriage had afforded her more of the same in a world of privilege. Still later, there were the Venetian palazzo along the Grand Canal and the palace of red marble on the outskirts of Paris. Serge Diaghilev, Vaslav Nijinsky, Isadora Duncan, Robert de Montesquiou, Giovanni Boldini, Arthur Rubinstein, and Jean Cocteau had shared all of this opulence. Casati had been loved by Gabriele D'Annunzio, Kees van Dongen, and Augustus John. Immense fortunes were spent on creating a nocturnal universe of endless masquerades, Bakst costumes, and Fortuny gowns—on commissioning her own immortality. But now, Casati was bound by the four walls of a small rented room at 32 Beaufort Gardens.

A secondhand dealer in Portobello Road would have hardly coveted the Marchesa's remaining possessions—a horsehair sofa and an old-fashioned bathtub, a broken cuckoo clock, and bouquets of dusty artificial flowers. But there was also an assortment of oddities, including a stuffed lion's head, a mask of Pericles displayed on the mantelpiece,[83] and a crystal reliquary enshrining what Casati reputed to be a genuine fragment of St. Peter's finger, flung at her during a séance. The remaining books in her collection were displayed with their gilt-edged pages facing outward. In this way, what would have been an otherwise standard-looking row of volumes was transformed into a glittering block of gold.[84] Padding through this curious setting was Luisa's pack of aging Pekinese dogs.

Even living under such reduced conditions Luisa maintained an infectious zest for life. Fred Rainer, one of her later London acquaintances, recalled how the Marchesa invited him for dinners of tinned food at Beaufort Gardens. Also remembered was Luisa's habit of telephoning him to ask with adventurous enthusiasm: "I have ten shillings. Shall we have a bottle of cheap wine or go for a taxi ride?"[85]

Although bereft of her material wealth, Casati still possessed a rich imagination. This fact is no better exhibited than by an unexpected pastime that helped wile away her later years. The Marchesa spent hours clipping photographs, captions, and any other bits of ephemera that struck her fancy from newspapers and magazines. This assortment of scraps, chosen for their beauty or bizarreness, were then assembled into collages, which would ultimately fill every page of three oversized, leather-bound albums.[86] She was also fond of devising satirical caricatures of her friends and enemies.[87] These hobbies were strikingly similar in spirit to those first solitary artistic endeavors Luisa had made in her childhood.

The collages demonstrate that Casati had an unerring eye for composing images both wryly humorous and attractively designed. What is most impressive is the total unity in expressing a particular theme or idea in so many disparate pieces. The evident care with which they were constructed shows that this was no random amusement. On a page that is dominated by a cutout of King Henry VIII, a surrealistically large straightedge razor is floating ominously. The notorious monarch presides over a chorus line of much smaller department-store mannequins, each with its head neatly snipped off. Another collage features a romantically windblown Lord Byron beside a winged medieval angel, clad in black armor, whose face has been obscured by a multifaceted gemstone. The two figures hover over a Venetian palazzo on a sea dotted with gondolas. Other pages contain images of Rasputin, the Duchess of Windsor, Queen Mary, and even Lord Berners. But Casati's hobby came to an abrupt end, as explained by Philippe Jullian:

> The Marchesa seemed to have a genuine horror of money. One day,
> one of her younger friends, Cecil Beaton, admired the collages that she
> amused herself by making out of old engravings. Like everything the
> Marchesa touched, these "scraps" had a strange charm. He proposed
> that she prepare an exhibit of them . . . but the moment she had to
> work toward a lucrative end, inspiration fled, and the Marchesa
> touched her scissors no more.[88]

Strewn about the flat, on tables and in cupboards, was Luisa's collection of magical paraphernalia. Invoices, stained with wax and burnt through by matches, show the purchase of such essentials as crystals and Indian musk incense.[89] No longer able to afford the services of professional psychics, Casati concocted her own methods of contacting the spirit world. In addition to a Ouija board and a wand that she alleged once belonged to a great magician, a large decorative bronze key, topped with the figure of an angel, was used as a divinatory tool.[90]

Whereas her evenings were absorbed by occult passions, the Marchesa spent part of her days writing lists. One was an inventory of the renowned personages she had known. There were others cataloguing the many artists, famous and lesser known, who had represented her. The difficulty of creating a comprehensive index of contributors to the "Casati Gallery" is compounded both by Luisa's incomplete and inaccurate records and by the lack of information concerning the minor portraitists, such as Mrs. Leslie Cotton and Karel de Nerée tot Babberich,[91] and those who were simply wealthy dilettantes. Boldini, John, van Dongen, and Epstein are noted alongside Hohenlohe, Nikolai Riabushinsky, theatrical designer Oliver Messel, and Eduardo Chicharro, director of the Spanish Academy of Fine Art in Rome. For the latter group, no currently documented examples of their Casati portraits survive. Curiously, Luisa's records contain the name of artist Tranquillo Cremona, who had already been deceased for more than three years at the time of her birth.

Yet another list in the Marchesa's hand was of a much darker nature. Its purpose was to enumerate all those persons whom she felt had wronged her in some way. Cecil Beaton held a place of honor on this particular list. Since the mid-1940s, the photographer had maintained a friendship with Luisa, and she enjoyed being a frequent guest at his London home at 8 Pelham Place. Forever low on funds, the Marchesa once tried to sell Beaton one of her last cherished articles—a scrap of material embroidered with hearts from the Queen of Hearts costume worn by the Comtesse de Castiglione during her affair with Napoleon III.[92]

The event that precipitated this schism occurred at a soirée attended by Casati and her Pekinese dogs. Under the pretext of wanting to photograph her pets, Beaton instead shot a series of black and white images of his most eccentric guest. The Marchesa, approximately seventy-three years old, is shown dressed in her worn black velvet and leopardskin. Quickly realizing Beaton's trickery, Casati is caught by the camera either turning away or shielding herself from the lens with a gloved hand. It is ironic that these photographs are the last representations of a woman who once craved the glorification of her own image. But even so, Luisa's fierce defiance was meant to preserve a legend that she had spent a lifetime creating.

To placate Casati's fury, Beaton promised to destroy the film, but instead he committed a further injustice. In 1954 he published *The Glass of Fashion,* a celebration of the world's most fascinating and beautiful women.[93] The Marchesa was, of course, included. To promote the book, window displays were arranged at Harrods. Behind one huge glass expanse, looking onto Brompton Road, was an enlarged print of one of Beaton's illicit photographs of Casati. She was outraged by this betrayal. Matters were made worse by the close proximity of her flat at Beaufort Gardens to the offending site. Luisa believed that it was now impossible for her to walk about in public for fear of suffering the embarrassment of immediate recognition.

But Casati had yet to actually read Beaton's book. One of his recollections concerned her ill-fated appearance as Saint Sebastian at one of the annual balls given by the Comte Étienne de Beaumont. Beaton claimed that during her costume preparations, she had called for continual cups of coffee and tea. The Marchesa thought this defamation worthy of a lawsuit. Never would she have drunk such gauche beverages before a fête of this caliber. Without question, Luisa insisted, it would have been nothing but champagne. Her granddaughter was able to soothe away at least her threat of legal action. Besides its cost, Moorea explained that the courts would not take this aesthetic accusation seriously.

Undaunted by reality, Luisa released her anger by calling upon the occult. Crumpled sheets of paper in the Casati family archives contain the handwritten messages she received from the spirit world: "Pelham Place finished. I have killed Beaton. I am now trying further manner to destroy him. . . . Give you power over horrible person." Despite such maledictions, Beaton would survive for nearly another twenty-five years. Other mystical communications reveal a woman who, although never known to complain, apparently found displeasure in her current existence, additionally strained by the deaths of such financial supporters as Lord Alington, Lord Tredegar, and the Duke of Westminster. The otherworld promised wealth and adulation: "Marvelous will be your joy. Arrive now great present from Cuevas. Westminster has will made for you. . . . I promise you to be a rich Marquise. People will respect you and obey."

Even into old age, Luisa still possessed a commanding personality, capable of fascinating those who met her. But while some appreciated her eccentricity and undeniable camp value as onlookers only, others became close friends.[94] One such was Joseph Paget-Fredericks, then living and teaching in California where she had visited him and his mother in the 1920s.

Establishing contact with the Marchesa once more, and clearly intrigued by her past, he drew several portraits of her. One shows a much younger Casati in a costume of green baubles, entitled *La Marchesa Casati as a Serpent of Jade*. Another presents her in tigerskin, reclining beneath a calligraphied verse by Robert de Montesquiou. In a third, Luisa is dressed in black, white, and gold silk. Bearing a tasseled walking stick taller than herself, she is accompanied by her pet cheetahs, set against a backdrop of gold ink.[95] In addition, the artist completed a series of fantasy costume designs inspired by Casati. Paget-Fredericks was so taken by the Marchesa that he arranged for a portion of an exhibition on the world of dance to be dedicated to her alone. Its success was discussed in a letter written on the reverse of one of the portraits:

> Dearest Marchesa—
> The exhibit is an enormous success and everyone wonders if we can conjure black and white magic and bring you here for a marvelous ball or grand fête, you being the enchanting attraction?
> I shall send you a résumé critique of the exhibit which is *huge!* A wall is devoted to yourself with innumerable portrait reproductions in a very long glass case—everyone is delighted! *Vogue* and several others want photos of the exhibit, and so many recall your magic and beauty.[96]

Paget-Fredericks was correct in stating that many still recalled Luisa and her past extravagances. As her friends and acquaintances advanced in age, a number of them published reminiscences and diaries that included tales of their amazing encounters with this singular woman. Casati's flamboyance and outrageous style were sorely missed in the gloom of postwar Europe. Nostalgia for the glorious days of the Venice Lido and the glittering nights of Paris and St. Moritz was pervasive. Author Beverley Nichols perhaps best captured this sense of melancholy in his memoir *The Unforgiving Minute*, in which his thoughts, too, turned to the once legendary Marchesa, asking:

> Do you remember the Marchesa Casati . . . a monster who might have been created by Beardsley . . . and how she stalked into that fabulous ball accompanied by a page whom she had caused to be encased in gold leaf, and was it true that as a result of this treatment the page had expired from asphyxiation? If so, what had happened to the body? Would we ever learn the answers to such questions, which once had so enthralled us?[97]

Luisa is even mentioned in Evelyn Waugh's novel *Unconditional Surrender*.

From March through June 1954, the Royal Academy of Arts held an exhibition honoring Augustus John. Among many other noted works on display was the first of the two portraits of Casati he completed in 1919. Luisa attended the special event escorted by Bernard Nevill, a friend and art student at the time. Nevill would later recall: "I remember when we went to look at the great John portrait of her on show at the Royal Academy that the crowds literally parted as she went toward her portrait. She was still exquisite." [98]

About a decade earlier, Luisa had become reacquainted with Otto Haas-Heye through a chance meeting at the Shanghai, a Chinese restaurant in Soho. The modest setting of this reunion was in sharp contrast to their original encounter at the glamorous Palace Hotel in St. Moritz more than thirty years before. Similar to the Marchesa, by this time Haas-Heye had squandered a vast inheritance that had afforded him a once luxurious lifestyle. He was currently surviving as an art instructor in the city. During the years of their renewed friendship, Haas-Heye visited Beaufort Gardens on many occasions:

> When I called upon Luisa, I brought along some provisions, including Nescafé, macaroni, dog biscuits, salad, tomatoes, rolls of ham, cake, and a magazine with pictures of San Michele. She was overjoyed and spoke animatedly of her time on Capri so long ago. And with her hair extending upwards, I could not help but be reminded of the famous portrait by Augustus John. Luisa kept the drapes always closed, the bathtub covered, and everything very tidy. Her little Pekinese dog lay on her knees, presumably feeling safe with its exceptional protectress. Its eyes twinkled the colour of smoky quartz, a shade that was reflected in its mistress's dress and culminated in Luisa's inexpressibly deep and large eyes. I told her how beautiful she was today.
>
> I left her then and looked back once again at the large, now almost dark room with one lamp lit on a high column; the big furniture; the great pale cloth spread across the table as though it was a high altar in front of the window; and in the middle, a life-sized portrait of D'Annunzio. His name "Gabriele" had been written in Luisa's handwriting in dark green upon the canvas. Giant white flowers stood on her dressing table, looking every bit like doves. [99]

By 1956, the Marchesa was in her midseventies. The company of her friends and granddaughter eased the seclusion that she so detested. Sydney Farmer, a bon vivant and self-proclaimed spiritualist, shared her obsession with the occult, and many afternoons were livened by his appearance at Beaufort Gardens, bearing bouquets of flowers and other small gifts. Together the two would spend hours before Luisa's Ouija board in a room shrouded by clouds of incense.

In the spring of 1957, Luisa retreated even more into a dreamworld. She no longer sent letters, as she believed herself capable of communicating by telepathy. She claimed further that the birds around her flat were actually spirits, whose language she understood. As each of her Pekinese dogs died, its mistress had it stuffed by a Regent Street taxidermist, the bills being forwarded to her granddaughter. Moorea also arranged for a nurse to make daily calls on a grandmother who still dressed in velvets and furs, still dyed her hair bright red, and still relied on belladonna to add sparkle to those notorious eyes, which were now losing their sight.

On Saturday, June 1, 1957, not long after a spiritualist session with Sydney Farmer, Luisa suffered a cerebral hemorrhage and died in her flat at three in the afternoon.[100] She was seventy-six years old. The chapel at Harrods arranged her funeral. Learning of her death, Farmer made up a new set of false eyelashes for her and collected one of the taxidermed Pekinese. The Marchesa was laid out in the black and leopard finery that had served as her uniform for the past decade. A requiem mass was given at ten o'clock on the morning of June 5 in the Chapel of Our Lady of Sorrows at Brompton Oratory, where Casati's bier was surrounded by white carnations. Mourners at the service included Lady Moorea Black and her then husband, Woodrow Wyatt; Sydney Farmer; Fred Rainer; and Robert Heber Percy, the late Lord Berners's companion. Also in attendance, but remaining anonymous, was Emilio Basaldella, the ever-faithful gondolier of the Palazzo dei Leoni.[101] Neither Augustus John nor Cecil Beaton was present. Before the coffin was sealed, one of Luisa's stuffed Pekinese was slipped inside to rest at her feet. Maybe it was this last element that inspired one mourner's remark that the Marchesa, as she lie in her coffin, resembled some "great Gothic figure."[102]

Luisa Casati was interred in Brompton Cemetery, a sprawling Victorian burial ground in the Kensington district of London. She lies beneath a small monument of a sculpted urn draped with floral garlands inscribed with her name and death date. Chosen by her granddaughter, the headstone's fitting epitaph is taken from Shakespeare's description of the notorious Queen of the Nile in *Antony and Cleopatra*. The single engraved line reads:

Age cannot wither her nor custom stale her infinite variety.

EPILOGUE
Phoenix Rising

Well-behaved women rarely make history.
—*Laurel Thatcher Ulrich*

The marble staircase of the Palais Garnier is glowing with a supernatural blue light. An exotically attired male attendant can be seen, to one side, motionless among the shadows. Suddenly, thunder reverberates overhead as flashes of lightning set the hall ablaze. On the lowest step, a shape begins to make its slow ascent. The figure appears to be that of a woman. Her head crowned by a plumed tricorn hat and lace veil, the specter is concealed within the voluminous folds of a ball gown of black taffeta in the style of an earlier century. The lady pauses for a moment on the stairway, almost draping herself across the marble, as she reaches out to the attendant before continuing to the summit. The applause that surrounds this phantom in fancy dress is as deafening as the thunder, which continues to rumble above. More than four decades after her death, the Marchesa Luisa Casati has been conjured up as the most fashionable of apparitions.

The spring/summer 1998 haute couture collection by John Galliano for Christian Dior proved to be a triumph. In the lengthy notes prepared for the premiere, Galliano dedicated the collection to the singular woman who inspired it. Towering models shimmered in a variety of creations, each evoking a specific outfit, event, or attitude associated with La Casati. One appeared with flame-colored hair and kohl-ringed eyes; another led three greyhounds about before turning their leashes over to a uniformed man-servant; and yet another was dressed in a metallic silver gown, one arm of which mimicked armor reminiscent of Casati's Cesare Borgia costume. It was more than fitting that this extravaganza unfolded on the very steps where Luisa had ascended victorious more than once almost three-quarters of a century earlier.

Attendees were dazzled by more than just the fashions. Members of the

185

international press sat at tables covered in faux zebra-skin, with reproductions of love letters between Coré and Ariel scattered beneath their feet, while the air was spiced with burnt orange. Art director Michael Howells, who designed the event's décor, explained its conception:

> The show begins during the same thunderstorm that brought Casati's infamous Bal de Cagliostro to an end. We first see the Marchesa, completely alone, upon the steps of her marble palace. Then she is joined by what I imagined to be all of the fantastic personages whom she had known throughout her life. . . . Soon, the place is filled with an assembly of very fashionable ghosts with Casati maintaining center stage, as she would, I think, have wanted to be.[1]

Almost all of the publicity for Galliano's award-winning collection, seen in every major fashion publication worldwide, included a reproduction of Boldini's 1914 portrait of the Marchesa adorned with peacock feathers. As a result, she became a source of international intrigue. Summing up his fascination with Luisa, Galliano noted:

> The Marchesa Casati is one of the most amazing women that I have ever come across in my research. She inspired this entire collection. Although no longer with us, her life stays as a beacon and as a constant source of inspiration.[2]

Galliano was not the first couturier to be influenced by Casati following her death. Norman Norell is considered one of the founders of American high fashion. During a career that spanned a half-century, he became renowned for attiring Jacqueline Kennedy during her White House years and for his form-fitting, sequined mermaid dress. After years in the industry, the designer presented the Norell label for the first time in fall 1960. Known as "the Van Dongen Collection," its creation was directly inspired by Norell's ownership of the Dutch artist's portrait of Luisa standing by a nighttime Venetian lagoon. The collection was deemed important enough to become a cover story for *Life* magazine. Included in the article was a photograph of Norell, surrounded by four kohl-eyed models, posing before the van Dongen portrait. The designer's longtime interest in the Marchesa may have begun during business trips to Venice in the early 1920s. During such stays, he very well may have become acquainted with Luisa's notoriety in that city.[3]

Undoubtedly, there will be future couturiers influenced by the Marchesa. In July 2003, she was the inspiration for Italian designer Marco Coretti's autumn/winter 2003/2004 haute couture collection that premiered at the Alta Roma fashion event in Rome. Coretti's creations were presented upon a stage of mirrors. Incorporated into the ensembles of silk, organza, and leather were domino masks of the Venetian Carnivale. One chiffon gown culminated in an exaggerated ruff evoking Luisa's living serpentine adornments. In September 2003, superstar couturier Karl Lagerfeld provided a portfolio of sketches and photographs for an important feature article on the Marchesa for *The New Yorker* magazine. The designer reinvented Luisa in these images by outfitting Carine Roitfeld, editor of *Vogue* Paris, in an exotic assortment of furs and pearls. Explaining the project, Lagerfeld commented, "[Roitfeld] plays a modern Casati, but the drama of Casati was that she was not playing."[4] For his spring/summer 2004 prêt-à-porter collection for Yves Saint Laurent Rive Gauche, American designer Tom Ford revealed how he, too, had looked to Luisa for inspiration: "The Marchesa Casati was the first European dandy of the early twentieth century. And therefore, she is the perfect ideal of a woman for Yves Saint Laurent. I thought it was appropriate to return to her sort of elegance, that kind of chic and eccentricity." At the collection's premiere in Paris, kohl-eyed models glided along a catwalk strewn with zebra-skins in stylishly tailored outfits of the Marchesa's favored black, white, and gold. Many of these were accessorized with Gucci handbags appliquéd with writhing green, purple, and bronze metallic snakes, also designed by Ford. So even if the woman herself is not here to do so, her flamboyant heritage is still acting as muse to formidable talents that have succeeded her. Some remnants of her legendary life have vanished completely, but others continue to exist or survive in some metamorphosed state.

Fortunately, almost a century after Luisa's young imagination and later masquerades filled them with costumed revelers, several of her residences still stand—albeit in altered forms. The Marchesa's childhood home, the Villa Amalia, is now a convention center owned by the Italian government. The villa at Cinisello Balsamo, once the property of Camillo Casati's family, has become a convent. Luisa and Camillo's house in the center of Milan on the via Soncino is presently the offices of art book publishers Skira Editore. In 1923, the villino on the via Piemonte in Rome was sold to the Macchi di Cellere family; forty years later, the building was acquired by Mediocredito Centrale, who has carefully restored its former opulence while maintaining offices there. The Casati estate at Arcore is the current residence of Silvio Berlusconi, elected Il Presidente del Consiglio del Ministri in 2001.

Following the departure of its most infamous inhabitant, the Palazzo Venier dei Leoni on the Grand Canal was transformed by the city of Venice into a somber public museum that sank slowly into disrepair. In 1938, Lady Doris Castlerosse purchased the palazzo. After spending a sizable sum on refurbishing the ruin, she rented it a year later to actor Douglas Fairbanks Jr.

During the war years, the palazzo served as a shelter for occupying German, British, and American troops. Then, in 1949, another eccentric art patron decided the palace could become the ideal setting for her own extravagance. Devotee of modern art and wife of painter Max Ernst, Peggy Guggenheim purchased and restored the palazzo into an exhibition hall for her vast avant-garde and surrealist collection. Also using the building as a home, she was often seen sunbathing on its rooftop. Just as frequently, Guggenheim was glimpsed being rowed about the waterways in a gondola in search of new talent while bedecked in outrageous fashions and wildly designed sunglasses. The Palazzo Venier dei Leoni is today one of the world's most prestigious museums. The Palais Rose in Le Vésinet was damaged during World War II, but the structure of red marble has been returned to its former opulence by a series of subsequent owners, including Emad Khashoggi, nephew of the Saudi Arabian arms dealer and financier Adnan Khashoggi. It remains a private residence and was registered as a historic monument in 1986.

Tourists and admirers of Gabriele D'Annunzio fill the Vittoriale, which has become a museum dedicated to his memory. This shrine, as well as the Biblioteca Nazionale in Rome, preserves the enigmatic telegrams, postcards, and notes shared between the writer and his muse. Neither the Hôtel du Rhin nor the stately Princess Hôtel can be found along the place Vendôme in Paris, but the luxurious Ritz still presides on the same thoroughfare as the epitome of its kind. In London, 22 Jermyn Street, the small hotel that served as the Marchesa's residence for a time, continues as one of a much higher standard. The site once containing flats at 1 Clarges Street has been extended through the adjoining buildings to serve as the present home of The Kennel Club. Luisa's final home at 32 Beaufort Gardens remained a block of flats for several decades. Since the late 1980s, this address and the adjacent building at number 33 have been renovated into a small plush hotel known as The Beaufort.

Of the once proliferating "Casati Gallery," several of its key pieces have survived, whereas numerous others met less deserving fates. Augustus John's three oils of Luisa are kept in diverse locations. The first is in the possession of the Honorable Mrs. Mary Anna Marten, Lord Alington's daughter; the second is on permanent display at the Art Gallery of Ontario, Toronto, where it was the centerpiece of a 1987 exhibition devoted to the Marchesa's artistic legacy; the final canvas is in the National Museum of Wales, at Cardiff. Ignacio Zuloaga's portrait of Casati is displayed in the museum that bears his name in Zumaya, Spain, in his native Basque region.

While the Troubetzkoy bronze is in a private collection, an incomplete wax study can be seen at the Museo del Paesaggio in Verbania Pallanza, Italy.

The Musée de Poitiers, France, owns the wooden bust by Sarah Lipska. Both of Giovanni Boldini's lauded portraits continue to receive admiration. The "anti-Gioconda" image of Luisa, swathed in her elegantly funereal ensemble, was in the collection of the Baron Maurice de Rothschild until well after his death in 1957. Christie's in New York City auctioned it, along with the Baron's other Boldini canvases, in November 1995. The massive, gilt-framed portrait of the Marchesa was sold to theatrical composer Andrew Lloyd Webber for a sum exceeding one and one-half million U.S. dollars, a record price for the artist's work. Boldini's 1914 painting of Luisa is housed in the Galleria Nazionale d'Arte Moderna in Rome. The images by van Dongen and Depero and sketches by Helleu and Balla are in international public and private collections. The original plaster of the Epstein bronze is in the collection of the Ein Harod Museum of Art, Israel. Castings of the bust are displayed at the Art Gallery of Ontario; the Allen Memorial Art Museum at Oberlin College, Oberlin, Ohio; and the Beecroft Art Gallery, Westcliff-on-Sea, England; other castings are owned by Lady Moorea Black and C. Pelham Lee.

The originals by Drian, Beltrán y Masses, de Blaas, Larionov, Gontcharova, Survage, and Mossa, as well as many of the Martinis, are missing. The wax figures by Catherine Barjansky and Lotte Pritzel are considered lost, while Balla's futurist sculpture has been reportedly destroyed. Recently, the long unaccountable portrait by Romaine Brooks, Martini's Cesare Borgia and Grand Canyon pastels, and an important selection of Alastair drawings have all been discovered in a private collection in France.

In 1970, notoriety of a less fashionable kind fell on the still wealthy Casati dynasty of Milan. The events that precipitated the affair concerned Camillo's son, the Marchese Casati Stampa di Soncino. The forty-three-year-old nobleman had been under intense scrutiny by the Italian government for tax evasion. The investigation proved that Casati had paid approximately three hundred twenty U.S. dollars in personal taxes on an estate that had been estimated to be worth nearly six hundred million U.S. dollars. Before further legal proceedings could begin, the nobleman was discovered dead in his Roman penthouse alongside the slain bodies of his wife, Anna Fallarino Casati, and her lover, a twenty-five-year-old student. It seems, as the police later revealed, that the Marchese was fond of procuring young men to amuse his spouse while he photographed their "erotic games." With scrupulous care, Casati noted in his diary the fees paid for the services of numerous hired lovers. But then he learned of Anna's infatuation with one of them in particular, and, armed with a prized hunting rifle, the Marchese shot the illicit couple before turning the gun on himself. Far baser than any of the grand scandals connected to his father's flamboyant ex-wife, the murder-suicide was dubbed by an Italian journalist "a sordid Roman story, vulgar and of the trattoria. It is not chic."[5]

By odd coincidence, this scandal erupted at precisely the same moment as the appearance of a lengthy, well-illustrated article on the exploits of the Marchesa Luisa Casati in the September 1, 1970, issue of American *Vogue*. The piece was written by Philippe Jullian, who had previously authored biographies of Casati intimates D'Annunzio and Robert de Montesquiou. More significantly, it was the only attempt to explore this woman's life up to that time.[6] Another sixteen years would pass before Italian biographer Dario Cecchi would write a romanticized account of the relationship shared between Luisa and D'Annunzio, *Coré: Vita e dannazione della marchesa Casati*. A companion volume, *La divina marchesa: La prima dandy della nostra storia*, was released simultaneously from the same publisher. Edited by Alberto Arbasino, it features a series of essays by various authors on the Marchesa and reviews of Cecchi's book. In 2001, a volume of the Casati–D'Annunzio correspondence was published in Italy under the title *Infiniti auguri alla nomade: Carteggio con Luisa Casati Stampa*, edited and with a preface by Raffaella Castagnola. Later that same year, the Marchesa was celebrated in two French-language surveys of extraordinary personalities— Jean-Noël Liaut's *Les anges du bizarre: Un siècle d'excentriques* and Florence Müller's *Excentriques*.[7]

The haut monde of Europe once again witnessed a re-creation of La Casati at a fête the extravagance of which had not been seen since the muse's own heyday. In December 1971, Baron Guy de Rothschild gave a party to honor the centenary of Marcel Proust's birth. Many of the seven hundred guests were costumed as real or fictitious characters associated with the Belle Époque. Among them were Elizabeth Taylor, dressed as Ballets Russes icon Ida Rubinstein; Sir Cecil Beaton as the photographer Nadar; and fashion model and actress Marisa Berenson as Luisa Casati. Berenson, Elsa Schiaparelli's granddaughter, was faithful to the original in an ensemble of ebony feathers and fur, further adorned by a vivid red wig, a face powdered white, and eyes ringed with kohl.[8]

Artworks of the Marchesa Casati continue to provide provocative centerpieces for important exhibitions worldwide. The 1998/1999 retrospective of Man Ray's oeuvre at the Centre Georges Pompidou, Paris, and the International Center of Photography, New York, featured a group of images from the 1922 photographic series, as well as the original glass plate of the famous triple-eyed portrait—the latter being reproduced on the show's official souvenir T-shirt. The catalog for the in-depth 1999/2000 survey of the life of the Comtesse de Castiglione, held at the Musée d'Orsay, Paris, and the Metropolitan Museum of Art, New York, included Martini's pencil sketch of Casati dressed as the Comtesse. When a retrospective of Romaine Brooks's work, *Amazons in the Drawing Room*, took place at the National Museum for Women in the Arts in Washington, D.C., and at the University of California, Berkeley, in 2000/2001, the artist's intense portrait of the Marchesa, seen publicly for the first time, was selected by the press as the most powerful image in the entire exhibition. In spring/summer 2001, Boldini's 1914 portrait and Man Ray's 1922 and 1935 photo-portraits of Casati were displayed at an important exhibition on D'Annunzio at the Musée d'Orsay.

In winter 2001/2002, the Worcester Art Museum, Massachusetts, held the exhibition *Dressing Up: Photographs of Style and Fashion*, a compilation of those pictures most defining the profound changes in culture and trends during the past one hundred years. Included alongside images of icons Jacqueline Kennedy and Fred Astaire was the glamorous full-length portrait of Luisa taken by de Meyer. From spring 2001 through winter 2001/2002, the ceramic ewer sculpted as the Marchesa's face by Bertelli was on view at a major show on Italian Art Nouveau, *Il Liberty in Italia*, held first at the Chiostro del Bramante, Rome, and then at the Palazzo Zabarella, Padova. During winter 2001/2002, two of Galliano's Casati-inspired gowns for Dior, including the magnificent black ensemble that opened the Palais Garnier premiere, were displayed at the Metropolitan Museum of Art, New York. This exhibition, *Extreme Beauty: The Body Transformed*, and the black taffeta ball gown in particular, received international media coverage. Spring 2002 saw Man Ray's triple-eyed photograph on display once more for *La Révolution surréaliste* at the Centre Georges Pompidou, Paris. The image was utilized prominently by the media as the most potent symbol of this major exhibition. In spring/summer 2003, *Dada a Zurigo, Cabaret-Voltaire, 1916–1920*, was held at the Spazio Culturale Svizzero, Venice. One of the highlights of this show dedicated to dadaist art was the rarely seen oil of Luisa, *Una strana signora*, by Alberto Martini. During fall 2003, London's Royal Academy of Arts held the exhibition *Pre-Raphaelite and Other Masters: The Andrew Lloyd Webber Collection*. On view was Boldini's 1908 painting of the Marchesa with her greyhound—the scandalous portrait that launched her into international society nearly a century before. Christopher Wood, one of England's leading art historians, commented on its importance by stating: "The staggering Boldini portrait of the legendary Marchesa Casati is surely the greatest portrait of the Belle Époque."

During the latter part of the twentieth century and the beginning of the twenty-first, Luisa's influence surfaced in many guises. Not unexpectedly, she continued to influence major artists, such as world-renowned Spanish architect and artist Juan Navarro Baldeweg. His 1980 collage work *Movimento davanti all'occhio, movimento dell'occhio* includes a reproduction of the Marchesa's 1922 triple-eyed photograph by Man Ray. More curious was acclaimed New York–based drag performer and writer Charles Busch's 1979 solo show *Vagabond Vignettes*, which featured a segment titled "La Marquesa." Described by its creator as "complex and impressionistic," Busch starred as Casati recounting her life during a séance.[9] Throughout 2002 and 2003, Canadian dancer and choreographer Paul Ibey presented his solo Butoh work, *La volupté d'être*, in France, Croatia, Lithuania, England, Turkey, Italy, and Portugal. Ibey stated: "My dance piece was not biographical, however—more an exploration of various themes about Casati: illusion, fantasy, dabbling in sorcery, and with the final resolution of one coming to terms with being alone, as one came into the world. It was not a female impersonation either. As with all Butoh dance, I found the themes and associations of Casati to be unisexual and universal."[10] In fall 2003, world-renowned illustrator and fine artist Ted CoConis unveiled the highlight of his one-man exhibition at the Lanning Gallery of Sedona, Arizona: a fantasy oil portrait of the Marchesa Casati caressing two jewel-collared cheetahs before a retinue of ghostly Venetian footmen. The painting sold immediately to a private collector. Nearly thirty years prior, CoConis had been the artist responsible for the movie poster for the Casati-inspired film *A Matter of Time*.

In different forms, Luisa made several cinematic appearances as well. Most notable is the 1974 Italian release *Il Bacio* that features an integral character based on the Marchesa and portrayed by Valentina Cortese. Into this gothic melodrama, set in a fog-enshrouded Venice of the Belle Époque, enters Madame Blixen. This strange high priestess of the city's decadent underworld first appears in gold lamé and crimson gorgon wig leading a leopard through a masquerade. Later, Blixen presides over a black mass. Lit by the glow of flickering candles, Cortese's dark eyes and slender shape sheathed in gold silk present a vision of Casati that would, perhaps, have been approved of by the original.[11] Although the location of Beltrán y Masses's "odalisque" portrait of Luisa is unknown, a reproduction of it is clearly visible during a scene in Ken Russell's 1977 film *Valentino*. In 1982, the set décor for the film of Agatha Christie's *Evil under the Sun* incorporates a replica of Augustus John's famed 1919 painting of the Marchesa, replacing its original subject with actress Maggie Smith.

One can only imagine what the Welsh artist would have thought of such a reconfiguration or of the Augustus John Restaurant, Pub, and Hotel, now located in Hampshire, England. According to its promotional material, the establishment boasts "four beautifully styled rooms named after the four mistresses of the artist and philanderer," including one dedicated to Casati. And since 2001, there has been an official Web site, www.marchesacasati.com, devoted to Luisa's life and artistic legacy,[12] which prompted Bernard Nevill, one of the Marchesa's later London friends, to comment, "If here today, she would be venerated like a pop star."[13] Indeed, Casati continues to be embraced by the Goth community since its wider discovery of her in the late 1990s. In various publications and Web sites, adherents to this sub-culture have recognized Luisa as a significant progenitor of their macabre visual aesthetic and interest in the darker elements. It is only appropriate that the Marchesa, whose influence remains so diverse, should impact upon the culinary arts as well. For fall/winter 2004, renowned chocolatier Katrina Markoff produced for her company Vosges Haut-Chocolat an exclusive truffle inspired by Casati. Combining rare spices and exotic flowers with premium chocolate, this delectable tribute would have been worthy of a grand fête at the Palais Rose.

On the evening of January 24, 2000, the Art Gallery of Ontario's Jack-man Hall became a scene of pandemonium. It would be the world premiere of *Infinite Variety: Portrait of a Muse*. This presentation of the one-woman dramatic work based on the life of Luisa Casati followed its November 1999 invited staged reading in New York City. Chaos ensued when an unantici-pated throng arrived in numbers far exceeding the theater's capacity. This enthusiastic response was incited by the appearance of a major newspaper feature in the *Toronto Star* heralding the one-night-only event.[14] The article was accompanied by an analysis of Augustus John's celebrated 1919 portrait of Casati on view at the gallery. Finally, the doors to the hall had to be bolted as many disappointed hopefuls were turned away. It was a sold-out house with an international television crew in attendance.[15] As the lights of the theater dimmed, a sinuous form clad in a shimmering gown of pavonian blue, with a face obscured by a peacock feather fan, commanded the stage. Then the fan was thrown aside. "*I want to be a living work of art!*" proclaimed British actress Elizabeth Shepherd. She then proceeded to astonish the assem-bly with a kaleidoscopic journey through Casati's life based on firsthand accounts of those artists the Marchesa had inspired. The audience was capti-vated. The show enjoyed an equally sold-out London premiere on January 15, 2001. In this audience were several members who had journeyed from France, Austria, North America, Mexico, and throughout England to be part of this special night. Among them were Carl Reitlinger, Bernard Nevill, and Lady Moorea Black. Following the ovation, Lady Moorea offered praise for both Miss Shepherd's performance and the show that brought her grandmother magnificently back to life. Luisa would have undoubtedly been pleased.

The Marchesa would be similarly contented by her continuing power to inspire artists of all kinds in the twenty-first century. This fact took notable form in spring 2003 with *The Princess of Wax—A Cruel Tale* (or *La Princesse de cire—Un Conte cruel*).[16] A darkly decadent fairy tale, the work fancifully incorporates the most outlandish elements of Luisa's life and eccentric persona. Published and designed by Neil Zukerman and CFM Gallery, the lavishly produced volume features illustrations by noted contemporary French artist Anne Bachelier. In conjunction with the book's release, a successful exhibition of Bachelier's artwork for and inspired by *The Princess of Wax* was mounted at CFM Gallery in SoHo, New York City. On view were nearly forty oils that explored the equally bizarre universe of the tale and the many legends associated with the woman who inspired them. On the evening of April 3, 2003, the gallery held an invitational premiere for the Bachelier exhibition. The highlight of the event was a dramatic reading of *The Princess of Wax* by Yolande Bavan. Garbed in a couture dress provided personally by John Galliano, the celebrated actress and jazz singer mesmerized a capacity audience. Summing up the project, attendee Grazia D'Annunzio, great-grandniece of Gabriele D'Annunzio, noted: "Anne Bachelier's illustrations, so surreal and so wonderfully rich in detail, are the perfect visualization of *The Princess of Wax*, an intriguing, never-ending journey through eccentricity, obsession, love, cruelty, glamour, and destiny."[17]

The year 2003 became a landmark in the continuation of Luisa's legacy through the publication of new editions of this biography, including an Italian-language version titled *Infinita Varietà: Vita e leggenda della Marchesa Casati* and another in French, *La Casati: Les multiples vies de la marquise Luisa Casati*.[18] Both books contained the authors' most current research findings, as well as pictures of its subject never before seen by the public or reproduced for more than a century. Each edition immediately became the subject of major international media attention.[19] This was especially true in Italy. It was with fitting fanfare that Luisa returned to her homeland— once again a celebrity, but now also an artistic and cultural icon of genuine historical merit. In 2005 and 2006 the story will continue when the German and Russian-language editions of *Infinite Variety* will be published.

Augustus John once jested that Casati should have been "shot, stuffed, and displayed in a glass case"[20] in a manner similar to her beloved python. One cannot help but wonder how intrigued she might have been by such an exhibitionistic fate. But the Marchesa Luisa Casati was more than just an eccentric flame from another age. In spite of her many follies, she was a genuine innovator of the arts and an inspiration to creative genius. Casati lived a life of flair and excess in a willful effort to defy convention. Although a century has passed, the need to cultivate a proper public image is as important today as it was in her time. Casati chose to oppose such expectations with the creation of her own individualistic, albeit perhaps extreme, persona. Therefore, in reviewing this exceptional life, one must be aware of its historical context to comprehend its fullest impact.

At the beginning of a new millennium, we greet the outrageous antics of our cultural icons and world leaders with the dubious advantage of having seen it all before. But during Casati's era, the masses and privileged alike were not inundated by the increasingly bizarre images generated by today's media. So, then, simply envision a genteel salon of the Belle Époque, alight with a gathering of Boldiniesque beauties and conservatively dapper gentlemen. Imagine Luisa Casati entering the same room in her characteristic cadaverous makeup and vermilion hair, garbed in one of her outlandish ensembles while leading a leashed cheetah. The aesthetic shock must have been tremendous.

Thus it was with courageous virtuosity that Casati created an existence according to her own ideals, a singular journey pursued to wherever it would ultimately lead her. From among all of life's possibilities, she chose to become a living work of art—and she succeeded. It is undeniable that the Marchesa Luisa Casati challenged the mundane into the fantastic in a way more daringly inventive than any myth.

Acknowledgments

We began this book with an author's sense of solitude and discovered through its creation new friends, kindred souls, and seemingly tireless assistants.

First and foremost, we would like to extend our gratitude and appreciation to Lady Moorea Black, the Marchesa Casati's granddaughter, for her support and generosity in dealing with authors who had so many questions and for her patience in trying to answer them all. The completeness and accuracy of this book would not have been possible if not for her considerable knowledge. Also, much thanks is due Conte Edoardo Amman, the Marchesa's second cousin, for providing invaluable historical information and offering continual encouragement. Additional gratitude must be given to Paola Amman Saffiotti and the late Carl L. T. Reitlinger for giving so freely of their time and memories.

Others who deserve appreciation for their assistance are Philippe Garner, senior director, Sotheby's, London; Edgar Munhall, curator, Frick Collection, New York; Charles Spencer; Hugo Vickers; Lydia Cresswell-Jones, Sotheby's, London; John Fleming; John Richardson; Rebecca John; Adam Munthe; María Rosa Suárez-Zuloaga; Michael Holroyd; Maurice Druon; Barry Humphries; the late Fred Rainer; Paul Busby; Jean-Noël Liaut; Andrew Lloyd Webber; John Galliano; Jelka Music; Anthony Powell; Christina Geiger, Christie's Images, New York; the late Quentin Crisp; the Hon. Mrs. Mary Anna Marten; Lady Selina Hastings; Edward Lucie-Smith; Victor Arwas; Editha Mork; Johannes Haas-Heye; Prof. Bengt Jangfeldt; Gualtiero Nobili Vitelleschi; Marco Coretti; Tom Ford; Shirin von Wulffen; Princess Laure de Beauvau Craon; Etheleen Staley, Staley-Wise Gallery, New York; Camilla McGrath; Charlotte Mosley; Frank Calabrese; Noël Ross; Chiara Barbieri, Guggenheim Collection, Venice; Guillemette Delaporte,

Bibliothèque des Arts Décoratifs, Paris; GiovanBattista Brambilla; Kim Lucas; Xavier Demange; Michael Howells; Lady Antonia Fraser; Marisa Berenson; Annamaria Andreoli, director, Il Vittoriale, Italy; Giandomenico Romanelli, Civici Musei Veneziani d'Arte e di Storia, Venice; C. Pelham Lee; Prof. Bernard Nevill; Dr. Wilhelm Meusburger; Jerry Edward Cornelius; Tristram Cary; Florence Müller; Roger Peters; Richard Manton; Laura Jacobs; Richard Price; Jérôme Kagan; Anne Conover Carson; Mrs. Rosalind Freeman, National Museum of Wales; Sarah Herring, Curatorial Department, National Gallery, London; Salvatore Rubbino, Tate Gallery, London; Dr. Gabriella Cagliari Poli, ministero per i Beni Culturali e Ambientali, Milan; Maurizio Scudiero, Storico dell'arte; Marilyn McCully; Ferdinando M. Amman; Pierre Apraxine; Alexandra Anderson-Spivy; Gina L. B. Minks, Special Collections, McFarlin Library, University of Tulsa; Sara Velas, the Velaslavasay Panorama, Hollywood, California; Luciana De Gemini, Beat Records Co., Rome; Murdo N. Macmillan, Brompton Cemetery, London; Anthony Bliss and J. D. Frank, Bancroft Library, Berkeley, California; Professor Giani Pigoni, Museo del Paesaggio, Verbania Pallanza, Italy; Mireille Bialek, Musée Jacques-Émile Blanche, Offranville; Sarah Davies and Andrew Potter, Royal Academy of Arts, London; Federico Brunetti, Associazione Pro Monza; Anne Raoux, Cabinet Vermeille, Le Vésinet; Prof. Renzo Margonari; Neil Zukerman, CFM Gallery; and Anne Bachelier.

Additional thanks are also due the staffs of the New York Public Library, New York; Frick Art Reference Library, New York; Istituto Italiano di Cultura of New York, Toronto, and London; Metropolitan Museum of Art, New York; International Center of Photography, New York; Christian Dior, New York; Rosenbach Library, Philadelphia; Allen Memorial Art Museum at Oberlin College, Oberlin, Ohio; Archives of American Art, Washington, D.C.; Smithsonian Institution, Washington, D.C.; Library of Congress, Washington, D.C.; Art Gallery of Ontario, Toronto; Metropolitan Toronto Reference Library, Toronto; British Library, London; National Portrait Gallery, London; Heinz Collection, London; Brompton Oratory, London; J. H. Kenyon Funeral Directors, London; Bibliothèque Nationale, Paris; Bibliothèque littéraire Jacques Doucet, Paris; Bibliothèque Margurite Durand, Paris; Bibliothèque Administrative de la Ville de Paris; Man Ray Trust, Paris; Telimage, Paris; Musée de Poitiers; Gallerìa Nazionale d'Arte Modèrna, Rome; Biblioteca Nazionale Centrale V. Emanuele II, Rome; Museo Boldini, Ferrara; Fondazione Axel Munthe, Villa San Michele, Capri; Archivio di Stato, Rome; Archivio di Stato, Milan; Comune di Firenze, Florence; Ritz Hotel, Paris; Carlton Hotel, St. Moritz; Badrutt's Palace Hotel, St. Moritz; Beaufort Hotel, London; *New York Times; Times* of London; *Vogue*, London, Paris, and New York.

Finally, our sincerest gratitude must be expressed to our friends and colleagues at the University of Minnesota Press: to Douglas Armato, for championing the publication of a revised and expanded version of this biography; to Pieter Martin, who helped sort out the myriad changes and additions to this new edition; to Laura Westlund, for refining the text; to Adam Grafa, Catherine Clements, and Ariana Grabec-Dingman, for designing a book as elegant as its subject; and to Alison Aten, whose belief in and passion for this edition are responsible for its creation.

Notes

Introduction

1. Casati was the basis for the characters Isabella Inghirami, from Gabriele D'Annunzio's *Forse che sì forse che no* (Milan, 1910), and La Casinelle, from two novels by Michel Georges-Michel, *Dans la fête de Venise . . .* (Paris, 1922) and *Nouvelle Riviera* (Paris, 1924). At least in part, Casati was the inspiration for the character of the Contessa Adelina Corzio in Eugene MacCown's novel *The Siege of Innocence* (New York, 1950). It has also been stated that Casati was the inspiration for the femme fatale Mme Zalenska of Elinor Glyn's scandalous Edwardian classic *Three Weeks* (London, 1903). This has been proven incorrect; Glyn stated that the character was actually based on a member of the Russian aristocracy.

2. Philippe Jullian, "Extravagant Casati," *Vogue* (New York), September 1, 1970. In the article "Fashion Forward" from the July 2002 issue of *Vogue* (New York), Casati was chosen as the only fashion icon during the years 1900–1920.

3. Dario Cecchi, *Coré: Vita e dannazione della marchesa Casati* (Bologna, 1986).

Dream Child, 1881–1903

1. *International Studio Magazine* 46 (New York, 1912). This portrait of Casati was also selected by Alfred Stieglitz to appear in an issue of his magazine devoted entirely to de Meyer, *Camera Work* 40 (October 1912).

2. For a complete history of the Amman–Wepfer cotton plant, see Walter Bigatton, Maurizio Bordugo, and Guido Lutman, *Storia del Cotonificio Veneziano: L'industria Pordenonese Amman–Wepfer tra ottocento e novecento* (Pordenone, 1994). One of eleven children, Alberto Amman named the Villa Amalia in honor of an elder sister.

3. Authors' interviews with Paola Amman Saffiotti, March 1998–June 2003.

4. Authors' interviews with Lady Moorea Black, the Marchesa Casati's granddaughter, September 1997, and Conte Edoardo Amman, the Marchesa's surviving second cousin, July 1998–December 2001.

5. Authors' interview with Bernard Nevill, January 2001.

6. In addition to becoming guardian of the orphaned Amman sisters, Edoardo Amman (1851–1921) also became counselor to the Associazione Cotoniera Italiana and president of the Banca Lombarda di Milano.

7. Philippe Jullian, *The Triumph of Art Nouveau: Paris Exhibition 1900* (New York, 1974).

8. This portrait of Casati appeared in the exhibit *Signore di Milano, 1900–1950* at the Villa Della Porta-Bozzolo in Casalzuigno, Italy, September 17–November 16, 1997.

9. Cristina Trivulzio (1808–1871) was, during her youth, obsessed with the occult. She preferred to live in windowless rooms decorated in black and lit by candles. In her old age, the spirits she had so willingly summoned decades before now terrified her, and she spent her final years, petrified of the dark, in rooms emblazoned with light.

10. Alessandro Casati (1881–1955) became Italy's minister of war from 1944 to 1945. A Partisan leader, he was called into the cabinet of President Ivanoe Bonomi soon after the liberation of Rome. He was also the president of Italy's national committee for the United Nations Educational, Scientific, and Cultural Organization.

11. Virginia Oldoini (1837–1899) was originally used as a political pawn by Count Cavour of Italy in an attempt to win Napoleon III's support in the war between Piedmont and Austria. The French emperor was immediately smitten, and some historians believe that the Milanese beauty wielded considerable influence at the imperial court.

12. Four hundred thirty-three of these photographs were once owned by the Comte Robert de Montesquiou. They are now preserved at the Metropolitan Museum of Art, New York.

A Slow Awakening, 1903–1910

1. Letter dated February 22, 1922, quoted in Guglielmo Gatti, *Vita di Gabriele D'Annunzio* (Florence, 1956).

2. Michel Georges-Michel, *Dames Étranges* (Montreal, 1944).

3. Gabriele D'Annunzio, *Cento e cento e cento e cento pagine del libro segreto di Gabriele D'Annunzio tentato di morire* (Milan, 1935).

4. Gilbert Adair, "Arts Diary," *The Guardian*, November 14, 1991. In the same article, Adair goes on to describe Casati as resembling a thermometer wearing a cloche hat.

5. Jullian, "Extravagant Casati."

6. Authors' interviews with Fred Rainer, May 2001–March 2002.

7. Tryphosa Bates Batcheller, *Italian Castles and Country Seats* (New York, 1911).

8. D'Annunzio, *Cento e cento*.

9. Philippe Jullian, *D'Annunzio* (New York, 1972).

10. D'Annunzio, *Cento e cento*.

11. Harold Acton, *Memoirs of an Aesthete, 1939–1969* (New York, 1971).

12. Ibid.

13. Gabriele D'Annunzio, *Nocturne and Five Tales of Love and Death* (Marlboro, 1988).

14. Ludovico Pratesi and Giada Lepri, *I Villini* (Rome, 2003).

15. Cecchi, *Coré*.

16. Ibid.

17. A reproduction of this early portrait is preserved in the Bancroft Library, Berkeley, California.

18. Filippo Marinetti, *Poesia* (Milan), February 1905.

19. The Baroness Ernesta Stern was an imposing Jewish grande dame from Trieste. Enormously wealthy, she spent her time among her Byzantine villa in Cap Ferrat, her immense apartments in Paris, and her palace on the Grand Canal, where she wrote privately published books under the pseudonym Maria Star.

20. Dario Cecchi, *Boldini* (Turin, 1962).

21. Bernard Étienne and Marc Galliard, *Great Hotels of Paris* (New York, 1992).

22. Cecchi, *Coré.*

23. Cecil Beaton, *The Glass of Fashion* (New York, 1954).

24. Ève Lavallière (1866–1929) was the undisputed darling of the Théâtre des Varietés of Paris and enjoyed a tremendously successful career until mysteriously disappearing at the height of her fame in 1917. She entered the order of the Carmelite nuns, repenting her former life of extremes. But in incredibly melodramatic circumstances, Lavalliére, a year before her death, became a cocaine-addicted ruin through the machinations of a devious daughter.

25. Arsène Alexandre, *Le Figaro,* April 14, 1909. At the Salon, Boldini's portrait of Casati was catalogue no. 119. The painting's only other public exhibition during the twentieth century was at the Esposizione d'Arte della Secessione, Rome, in 1914, catalogue no. 11.

26. *Femina,* December 1909.

27. Emilia Cardona, *Boldini: Parisien d'Italie* (Milan, 1952).

28. Ibid.

29. Philippe Jullian, *Prince of Aesthetes: Count Robert de Montesquiou, 1855–1921* (New York, 1968).

1001 Nights on the Grand Canal, 1910–1914

1. Alvise Zoizi, *Venetian Palaces* (New York, 1989); Giandomenico Romanelli and Mark E. Smith, *Portrait of Venice* (New York, 1996). The official address of the Palazzo Venier dei Leoni is 701 Dorsoduro.

2. Authors' interviews with Fred Rainer, May 2001–March 2002.

3. Guillermo de Osma, *Fortuny: The Life and Work of Mariano Fortuny* (New York, 1985).

4. Authors' interview with Lady Moorea Black, September 1997.

5. D'Annunzio, *Forse che sì forse che no.*

6. Jullian, *D'Annunzio.*

7. Isadora Duncan, *My Life* (London, 1928).

8. Romola de Pulszky Nijinsky, *Nijinsky* (London, 1933).

9. Mercedes de Acosta, *Here Lies the Heart* (New York, 1975).

10. Authors' interviews with Carl L. T. Reitlinger, June 2000–December 2001.

11. Cecchi, *Coré.*

12. Gabriel-Louis Pringué, *30 ans de diners en ville* (Paris, 1948).

13. Acosta, *Here Lies the Heart.*

14. Charles Spencer, *Léon Bakst and the Ballets Russes* (London, 1995).

15. Letter from Bakst, 1916, written from Antibes.

16. David Wistow, *Augustus John: The Marchesa Casati* (Toronto, 1987).

17. Michael de Cossart, *The Food of Love: Princesse Edmond de Polignac (1865–1943) and Her Salon* (London, 1978).

18. J. B. Priestley, *The Edwardians* (New York, 1970).

19. Cecchi, *Coré.*

20. Mrs. Hwfa Williams, *It Was Such Fun!* (London, 1935).

21. Cossart, *The Food of Love.*

22. Jullian, "Extravagant Casati."

23. Maya Milhou, *Ignacio Zuloaga (1870–1945) et la France* (Paris, 1981).

24. Michel Georges-Michel, "Un bal des mille et une nuits au bord du Grand Canal," *La vie heureuse,* November 20, 1913. This article was highlighted by a full-page illustration by Italian art nouveau master Manuel Orazi of Casati greeting guests on the steps of the Palazzo dei Leoni.

25. "Astonishing Exploits of the Marchesa Casati," *The American Weekly,* December 1, 1935.

26. Charles Castle, *Oliver Messel: A Biography* (London, 1986).

27. "Her Antics Topped Hollywood's Best," *San Francisco Chronicle,* July 30, 1957.

28. Richard Ingleby, *Christopher Wood: An English Painter* (London, 1995).

29. Pringué, *30 ans.*

30. Authors' interviews with Fred Rainer, May 2001–March 2002.

31. Alex Ceslas Rzewuski, *A travers l'invisible cristal: Confessions d'un dominicain* (Paris, 1976).

32. Arthur Rubinstein, *My Young Years* (New York, 1973).

33. Ibid.

34. Ibid.

35. Ibid.

36. Ibid.

37. Anne Ehrenkranz, *A Singular Elegance: The Photographs of Baron Adolph de Meyer* (San Francisco, 1994).

38. Philippe Jullian, *De Meyer* (New York, 1976).

39. Family reports also state that once, while visiting relations, Casati arrived carrying a small box—one that she would not relinquish during her stay. As explanation, she proclaimed, "This box contains the ashes of my Russian prince!" Authors' interviews with Paola Amman Saffiotti, March 1998–June 2003.

40. Ehrenkranz, *Singular Elegance.* This image of Casati was one of the key pieces in a major exhibition of de Meyer's work at New York City's International Center of Photography in 1994.

41. Alberto Martini, *Alberto Martini* (Milan, 1944).

42. Collection of Lady Moorea Black.

43. Martini, *Alberto Martini.*

44. Ibid.

45. Ibid.

46. Ibid.

47. Wistow, *Augustus John.*

48. Marco Lorandi, *Alberto Martini: Mostra Antologica* (Milan, 1985). In her youth, Luisa was associated with the Milanese poet Giuseppe Brunati, whose personal peculiarities, such as sleeping in a coffin, became more celebrated than his work. Their friendship appears to have resulted in no verse inspired by or dedicated to the Marchesa.

49. Authors' interview with Lady Moorea Black, September 1997.

50. It is of interest to note that about 1915, sculptor Enrico Mazzolani completed a bronze catalogued as *Donna con cappello e cane* when it was displayed at the exhibition *Il Liberty in Italia* at the Chiostro del Bramante in Rome in 2001. This work depicts a stylishly dressed woman in a large hat seated next to a borzoi. The subject's resemblance to Casati is considerable. In addition to being a close associate of Troubetzkoy and Carrà, Mazzolani completed sculptures for D'Annunzio's art collection at the Vittoriale.

51. Casati's stationery seemed, much like her appearance, to change with her whims. Other known designs include ivory paper, engraved with either a peacock with an open tail or a seated woman in a marchesa's crown, and black stationery that featured a scarlet skeleton and rose. In contrast, Casati's personal calling cards were of plain white stock, with her name and title simply printed in black.

52. On December 2, 2000, Shapes of Edinburgh, Scotland, held an auction of antiques and fine art, including Lot 287, catalogued as "The Marchesa Luisa Casati, Fantasy Drawing with Female Nude," offered at £3000–5000. Although the unsigned pen and ink work was attributed to Irish illustrator Harry Clarke (1889–1931), the drawing did not bear any genuine resemblance to his work. Furthermore, the auction house could not substantiate its claims regarding either Casati or the Dublin-based Clarke and, to date, there is no evidence that the two were ever acquainted. The drawing sold for £3000.

53. Roberto Montenegro, *Planos en el Tiempo* (Mexico, 1962).

54. Ibid.

55. Georges-Michel, *Dames Étranges.*

56. D'Annunzio wrote only the captions for the film, for which he was paid the enormous sum of fifty thousand lire. *Cabiria* would achieve unprecedented success. During its first presentation, it would run continuously in Paris for six months and for almost a full year in New York in 1914.

57. Authors' interview with Lady Moorea Black, March 1998.

58. Ibid.

59. James Rennell Rodd, *Social and Diplomatic Memoirs, 1902–1919* (London, 1925).

60. Francis Rose, *Saying Life: The Memoirs of Sir Francis Rose* (London, 1961).

61. Authors' interview with Xavier Demange, April 2001.

62. Betty Kirke, *Madeleine Vionnet* (San Francisco, 1998).

63. Jullian, *Prince of Aesthetes.*

64. Among Montesquiou's writings dedicated to Casati is a cycle of satirical poems titled "Casaque" that were to have appeared in the author's unpublished work *Quarante Bergères.*

65. This lost watercolor is listed as being among those items confiscated from the Palais Rose. The legal inventory is in the collection of Lady Moorea Black, London.

66. *Aux Ecoutes* (Paris), November 1, 1925.

67. The ballet premiered at the Théâtre de Châtelet in Paris on May 29, 1911.

68. Cardona, *Boldini: Parisien d'Italie.*

69. Ibid. Boldini's famous 1908 and 1914 canvases were not the only times he depicted Casati. The Marchesa's records state that the artist also captured her in watercolor wearing a large black hat and in an unfinished oil dated 1923 entitled *La marchesa Casati con cappellino giallo seduta con cane in braccio,* in which Luisa is shown in profile seated on a divan, clutching a canine companion.

70. The helmet was from the Italian military division known as the Bersaglieri.

71. Blanche's study of Casati was displayed at the exhibition *Mes Modèles— Images pour L'illustration de Mémoires (1881–1929)* held at the Hôtel Jean Charpentier, Paris, during May 1929.

72. Jean Cocteau, *Lettres à sa Mère: Volume I, 1898–1918* (Paris, 1989).

73. Collection of Lady Moorea Black, London.

74. Nicole Wild and Jean-Michel Nectoux, *Diaghilev: Les Ballets Russes* (Paris, 1979).

75. Williams, *It Was Such Fun!*

76. Comtesse F. d'Orsay, *Ce que je peux écrire* (Paris, 1927).

77. Acton, *Memoirs of an Aesthete.*

78. Vittoria Colonna, *Things Past* (London, 1929).

79. André Germain, *Le fous de 1900* (Paris, 1954).

80. Nino d'Aroma, *L'amoroso Gabriele* (Rome, 1963).

81. Bernard Nevill, "La Marquise Casati," in *The Queen* (London), March 7, 1956.

82. D'Annunzio, *Cento e cento.*

83. Ibid.

84. Ibid.

85. Ibid.

86. Jullian, *D'Annunzio.*

87. Ibid.

88. D'Annunzio, *Cento e cento.*

89. Jullian, *D'Annunzio.*

90. Marie-Louise Ritz, *Cesar Ritz: Host to the World* (New York, 1938).

91. Catherine Barjansky, *Portraits with Backgrounds* (New York, 1947).

92. According to Philippe Jullian's "Extravagant Casati," Barjansky may have designed more than one statuette of Casati, which he described as having "eyes of emerald, flame-colored wigs, a waxen complexion with black and white make-up, dresses studded with cabochons and open in the most unexpected places."

93. Barjansky, *Portraits with Backgrounds.*

94. Ibid.

95. Jullian, "Extravagant Casati."

96. Helen Appleton Read, "Dolls," *The Arts* 3, April 1923.

97. Barjansky, *Portraits with Backgrounds.*

The Basilisk's Stare, 1914–1919

1. The fauves took their movement's name from Louis Vauxcelles, an art critic, who reviewed the group's first exhibition at the Paris Salon d'Automne in 1905. His comments on the show appeared in the October 17 edition of the Parisian periodical *Gil Blas*. Vauxcelles noted how the canvases appeared to have been executed by a pack of "fauves" or "wild beasts."

2. F. Le Targat, "Kees Van Dongen: Le regard fauve," *Beaux Arts* (France), no. 26, July–August 1985.

3. Ibid.

4. Louis Chaumeil, *Van Dongen: l'homme et l'artiste—la vie et l'oeuvre* (Geneva, 1967).

5. Georges Duthuit, *The Fauvist Painters* (New York, 1950).

6. Authors' interview with Bernard Nevill, January 2001.

7. Authors' interview with Lady Moorea Black, September 1997.

8. Jullian, *D'Annunzio.*

9. Ibid.

10. Ibid.

11. Caroline Tisdall and Angelo Bozzolla, *Futurism* (London, 1978).

12. Wistow, *Augustus John.*

13. F. T. Marinetti, *L'alcova d'acciaio: Romanzo vissuto* (Milan, 1921).

14. Giorgio Verzotti, *Boccioni: Catalogo completo dei dipinti* (Florence, 1989).

15. Giovanni Lista, *Balla* (Italy, 1982). Balla's sculpture of Casati later inspired author Carlo Emilio Gadda's satirical work *San Giorgio in casa Brocchi,* in which the piece is referred to as the "Ritratto della marchesa Cavalli."

16. Fortunato Depero, *So I Think, So I Paint: Ideologies of an Italian Self-made Painter* (Trento, 1947).

17. Ibid.

18. Marinetti, *L'alcova d'acciaio.*

19. Authors' interview with Maurizio Scudiero, December 2001.

20. Eugenio Giovannetti, *Satyricon, 1918–1921* (Florence, 1921).

21. Vicente García-Márquez, *Massine: A Biography* (New York, 1995).

22. Authors' interview with John Richardson, March 1997.

23. Duncan, *My Life.*

24. Ibid.

25. Ibid.

26. Authors' interview with Lady Moorea Black, September 1997.

27. Jullian, "Extravagant Casati."

28. Eve Golden, *Vamp: The Rise and Fall of Theda Bara* (New York, 1996).

29. Jullian, *D'Annunzio.*

30. Tommaso Antongini, *Vita segreta di D'Annunzio* (London, 1939).

31. D'Annunzio's right eye had been damaged previously when a snowball struck it in January 1905.

32. D'Annunzio was offered the privacy of the Casetta Rossa by his friend the Austrian Prince Friedrich Hohenlohe.

33. D'Annunzio, *Nocturne.* Brief D'Annunzian musings on Casati are also collected into two works published after the writer's death, *Solus ad Solam* (Milan, 1939) and *Taccuini* (Milan, 1965).

34. Julie Karanagh, *Secret Muses: The Life of Frederick Ashton* (London, 1996).

35. Jacob Epstein, *Let There Be Sculpture* (New York, 1940).

36. Ibid.

37. Stephen Gardiner, *Epstein: Artist against the Establishment* (New York, 1992).

38. Milhou, *Ignacio Zuloaga.*

39. Cecchi, *Coré.* Zuloaga's portrait of Casati was further honored by a full-page reproduction in the March 1925 issue of *Vanity Fair,* which claimed the painting was the artist's "most widely discussed" work. Three years earlier, in the October 1922 issue of the same magazine, Casati was celebrated in a short piece illustrated with her portraits by John, Epstein, Boldini, Bakst, de Blaas, and Man Ray.

40. Jullian, *De Meyer.*

41. Sebastian Faulks, *The Fatal Englishman* (London, 1996).

42. Augustus John, *Chiaroscuro: Fragments of Autobiography* (New York, 1952).

43. Ibid.

44. Authors' interview with the Hon. Mrs. Mary Anna Marten, December 1998.

45. Augustus John, "Fragment of an Autobiography," *Horizon* (London), December 1943.

46. Michael Holroyd, *Augustus John: A Biography* (New York, 1975).

47. Ibid.

48. Osbert Sitwell, *Nobel Essences* (London, 1950).

49. John, *Chiaroscuro.*

50. Ibid.

51. Holroyd, *Augustus John.* Although *The Timetables of History: A Horizontal Linkage of People and Events* (New York, 1975), by Bernard Grun, states that Amedeo Modigliani completed a portrait in 1919 titled *La Marchesa Casati,* no evidence exists to prove this. Authors' interview with Christian Parisot, Archiviste, Archives Legales Amedeo Modigliani (Paris), August 2002. Grun's claim may have been a confusion involving one of John's similarly dated 1919 portraits of Casati.

52. Conservation reports from the Art Gallery of Ontario, October 1986.

53. *Modern and Contemporary, British and Continental Paintings and Sculpture,* Bonhams & Brooks, London, March 22, 2001 (cat. no. 98).

54. John, *Chiaroscuro.*

55. Ibid.

56. From a letter by Lord Duveen to the Art Gallery of Ontario, dated February 26, 1934. In 1987, Casati's portrait was voted the most popular painting in the Canadian gallery.

Tigress on Capri, 1919–1920

1. Nevill, "La Marquise Casati." Luisa must have particularly relished her stay at the Château de Chaumont-sur-Loire, knowing of the occultist practices committed there by these notorious former residents.

2. Pringué, *30 ans.*

3. Mark Amory, *Lord Berners: The Last Eccentric* (London, 1998).

4. Vittoria Colonna, *Sparkle Distant Worlds* (London, 1949).

5. "Her Antics."

6. Authors' interviews with Carl L. T. Reitlinger, June 2000–December 2001.

7. The passport document, nearly six feet in length, is in the collection of Lady Moorea Black, London.

8. Rose, *Saying Life.*

9. Antoine, *Antoine* (New York, 1945).

10. Roger Peyrefitte, *The Exile of Capri* (New York, 1961). In his 1957 book *The Masque of Capri*, the island's former mayor Edwin Cerio recalled what might be either a different version of the same legendary arrival or an entirely separate incident: "[Casati] appeared in the Piazza leading a lion-cub on a chain, wearing a tigerskin and preceded by a Chinese servant carrying on his head a glass bowl containing a sacred fish of Siam." It has been suggested that such ostentatious displays resulted in Casati being the possible inspiration for *Oro e azzurro,* a satirical painting by Italian socialist artist Plinio Nomellini, who frequented Capri during this time. The work's grotesque subject is a full-length nude with flame-colored hair and eyes ringed with heavy cosmetics clutching a bouquet of peacock feathers. Authors' interview with Prof. Renzo Margonari, December 2003.

11. Knut Corfitz Bonde, *A l'ombre de San Michele* (Geneva, 1947).

12. Letter from Axel Munthe to Jessica Brett Young, undated 1920. Courtesy of Prof. Bengt Jangfeldt.

13. Josef Oliv, *Alex Munthe's San Michele: A Guide for Visitors* (Malmö, 1954).

14. Compton Mackenzie, *My Life: Volume V* (London, 1965).

15. Ibid.

16. Depero, *So I Think, So I Paint.*

17. Peyrefitte, *Exile of Capri.*

18. Ibid.

19. Ibid.

20. Ibid.

21. Authors' interview with Lady Moorea Black, September 1997.

22. Peyrefitte, *Exile of Capri.*

23. Meryle Secrest, *Between Me and Life: A Biography of Romaine Brooks* (New York, 1976).

24. Ibid.

25. Françoise Werner, *Romaine Brooks* (Paris, 1990).

26. Ibid.

27. Ibid. Letter from Romaine Brooks to Léonce Bénédite, undated August 1920.

28. Ibid.

29. Ibid.

30. Cecchi, *Coré.*

31. Secrest, *Between Me and Life.*

32. Authors' interview with Adam Munthe, November 1996.

33. Bonde, *A l'ombre de San Michele*.

34. Authors' interview with the Hon. Mrs. Mary Anna Marten, December 1998.

35. In her book *Aventures de l'espirit*, Barney drew a map of all those associated with her salon. The Marchesa's name appears, along with such luminaries as Marcel Proust, Guillaume Apollinaire, Anatole France, and Pierre Loüys.

36. Werner, *Romaine Brooks*.

37. Letter from Romaine Brooks to Natalie Barney, February 1, 1921, Paris, Bibliothèque Littéraire Jacques Doucet, Fonds Natalie Clifford-Barney.

38. "Natalie Barney's 'Isola di Capri,'" *Raritan: A Quarterly Review* (New Brunswick, NJ), Fall 1996.

39. Secrest, *Between Me and Life*.

40. Anne Conover, *Olga Rudge and Ezra Pound* (New Haven, 2001). Authors' interview with Anne Conover, July 2003.

41. Michel Desbruéres, "Romaine Brooks," *Bizarre* (Paris), March 1968.

42. P. G. Konody, "The Art of Federico Beltran-Masses," *Apollo* (London), June 1929.

43. "Une visiteuse nocturne," *Aux Ecoutes* (Paris), March 5, 1922.

44. Ibid.

45. Acton, *Memoirs of an Aesthete*.

46. Now lost, these two paintings are documented in papers in the collection of Lady Moorea Black, London.

47. Barjansky, *Portraits with Backgrounds*.

48. Martin Battersby, *The Decorative Twenties* (London, 1969).

49. Félix Youssoupov, *En exil* (Paris, 1954).

50. "Her Antics."

51. From the unpublished memoirs of Prof. Otto Haas-Heye. Authors' interviews with Johannes Haas-Heye, November 2002–February 2003.

52. John, *Fragment*. In his autobiography, John also described Prince Giraci as an admirer of Casati "whose life she had, by a skilful bluff, saved on the Piave [a river near Venice]."

53. Ibid.

54. Conover, *Olga Rudge and Ezra Pound*. Authors' interview with Anne Conover, July 2003.

55. *Poetry* (Chicago), June, July, and August 1917. The line from D'Annunzio's *Nocturne* that inspired Pound was "In Koré's house there are now only white peacocks."

Medusa in Pearls, 1921–1927

1. For a complete history of the Palais Rose and Le Vésinet, see Georges Poisson, *La curieuse histoire du Vésinet* (Paris, 1975). The Palais Rose at Le Vésinet has often been mistaken for a residence of the same name that once existed in Paris. Located on the avenue de Bois, the palace was built by Boni de Castellane. This building was later requisitioned by Goering during World War II, damaged by bombings, used as offices by NATO in the early 1950s, and finally demolished in 1969.

2. This weighty ornament was originally part of Montesquiou's property at 142 avenue de Paris, Versailles. The Comte had it moved and installed in the gardens of the Palais Rose in 1908. Casati must have been especially fond of the bathing pool since Madame de Montespan (1641–1707) had once been implicated in a royal scandal involving poisonings, debauched ceremonies, and sorcery.

3. Germain, *Les fous.*

4. Roland Toutain, *Mes 400 coups . . .* (Paris, 1951). In a less ferocious display at another party, Casati reportedly released two million butterflies into the air as her guests arrived.

5. Gilberte Gautier, *Rue de la Paix* (Paris, 1980).

6. "Italy's Famous Beauty Who Lives Like a Fairy Princess," *San Francisco Chronicle,* April 18, 1926.

7. Ingleby, *Christopher Wood.*

8. "Astonishing Exploits."

9. Gautier, *Rue de la Paix.*

10. Cécile Sorel, *Les belles heures de ma vie . . .* (Monaco, 1946) and *La confession de Célimène: Souvenirs II* (Paris, 1949).

11. Ibid.

12. Cecchi, *Coré.*

13. Ibid.

14. Authors' interview with GiovanBattista Brambilla, July 1998.

15. Elsa Schiaparelli, *Shocking Life* (New York, 1954).

16. Man Ray, *Self Portrait* (Boston, 1963).

17. Ibid.

18. Ibid.

19. Ibid. Both *Art & Auction* (New York), February 1998, and *American Photo* (New York), July–August 1998, featured articles revealing that Casati's triple-eyed portrait was the most illegally copied piece of Man Ray's oeuvre by art forgers.

20. Jean-Louis de Faucigny-Lucinge, *Legendary Parties* (New York, 1987).

21. Cecchi, *Coré.*

22. Vicomtesse de Sygognes, "Les Surprises de l'Opéra," *Gazette du Bon Genre* (Paris), no. 7, 1922.

23. Beaton, *The Glass of Fashion.*

24. This automobile was a gift to Casati from Lord Alington. Luisa later pawned the car for much-needed funds.

25. Although banned in France in 1914 because of its narcotic effects, absinthe was, and still is, produced in Spain.

26. Authors' interviews with Carl L. T. Reitlinger, June 2000–December 2001.

27. Rose, *Saying Life.*

28. This drawing appeared in the November 1922 edition of *Harper's Bazaar.*

29. Bonde, *A l'ombre de San Michele.*

30. Ibid.

31. Nearly destitute and under the care of a questionable physician who was defrauding her of her remaining meager funds, the Baroness Deslandes spent her

final years in a sanatorium in Madeira, Spain, conversing with trees and lost in hallucinatory reveries.

32. Jullian, *D'Annunzio*.

33. This photograph is preserved in the archives of the Vittoriale.

34. Gabriele D'Annunzio, *Infiniti auguri all nomade* (Milan, 2000).

35. Cecchi, *Coré*.

36. Jullian, *D'Annunzio*.

37. Ibid.

38. Cecchi, *Coré*.

39. Ibid.

40. Ibid.

41. Since its opening in 1907, the Hagenbeck Zoo has earned a reputation as an innovative model of its kind. Carl Hagenbeck, an adventurer and animal preservationist, had become outraged by the deplorable conditions of most international zoos. Thus, he planned what became the first in a series of humane zoos that did away with the cramped, iron-barred enclosures common to their predecessors. In his modern park, wildlife roamed freely through landscapes designed to replicate their particular species' native habitat.

42. Cecchi, *Coré*.

43. Ibid.

44. Nevill, "La Marquise Casati."

45. Cecchi, *Coré*.

46. "Astonishing Exploits."

47. Cecchi, *Coré*.

48. Casati had already purchased a number of these items from the estate of the Comte Robert de Montesquiou.

49. *Comoedia* (Paris), July 1924.

50. "Une fête espagnole chez la Comtesse de Castiglione," *Femina* (Paris), August 1924.

51. André de Fouquières, *Cinquante ans de panache* (Paris, 1951).

52. Erté, *Things I Remember* (New York, 1975).

53. *Aux Ecoutes* (Paris), November 2, 1924.

54. Authors' interviews with Carl L. T. Reitlinger, June 2000–December 2001.

55. A notice in the October 22, 1925, issue of the *New York Times* announced, "Viscount Hastings Secretly Married; Son's wedding to Cristina Casati, Marquis's daughter, surprises Lord Huntingdon."

56. Ibid.

57. Adolph de Meyer, "Paris Gossip by a Mere Man," *Harper's Bazaar* (New York), September 1922.

58. Martini, *Alberto Martini*.

59. The article appeared in the academy's weekly journal, dated February 9, 1925.

60. Cecchi, *Coré*.

61. Williams, *It Was Such Fun!*

62. Martini, *Alberto Martini*.

63. Rose, *Saying Life*.

64. "Italy's Famous Beauty."

65. Ibid.

66. Ibid. An anonymous artist documented Casati's uncharacteristic short, blonde coiffure in a painted miniature from this period now in the collection of Lady Moorea Black. In this painting Casati wears a small gold snake around her neck.

67. "Splendor of Marchesa Casati's Fetes Again Brought to Memory," *San Francisco Examiner*, 1949.

68. Rose, *Saying Life*.

69. "Astonishing Exploits."

70. Mary Desti, *The Untold Story: The Life of Isadora Duncan, 1921–1927* (New York, 1929).

71. Ibid.

72. Joseph Balsamo (1748–1795) was a multitalented swindler who quickly learned the public's gullibility for the supernatural and used it to dupe wealthy clients. He astounded the court of Louis XVI with his trickery before being accused of theft. Balsamo fled to Rome, only to fall into the hands of the Inquisition. Tried for heresy, he was imprisoned for life.

73. Collection of Lady Moorea Black, London. The Bal de Cagliostro took place on June 30, 1927.

74. At another party, Casati was said to have arranged for a series of torchbearers on horseback to illuminate the way between Paris and Le Vésinet. And according to Desti's *The Untold Story*, regarding her attendance at the Bal de la rose d'or, directions to the Palais Rose were provided in yet another manner: "For miles before one arrived at the château there were little electric signs saying 'Château D'Rose' and an electric arrow pointing the way."

75. Pringué, *30 ans*. Another guest at the ball, French actor Roger Gaillard, recalled in his memoirs, *Le "Joueur" et le sapajou* (Paris, 1955), that Casati greeted her guests atop stilts concealed by a long robe decorated with unicorns and later had mechanical snakes let loose across the dance floor.

76. Jullian, "Extravagant Casati."

Dragonfly in Amber, 1927–1957

1. Jane Bourbon del Monte, "The Memoirs of Principessa Jane di San Faustino," *Omnibus* (Rome), April–May 1938.

2. Bakst would die under enigmatic circumstances on December 27, 1924, in a clinic at Reuil-Malmaison outside Paris. During rehearsals for Ida Rubinstein's *Istar*, he suffered a severe mental collapse. Following this breakdown, Bakst was rushed home and never seen again by even his closest friends.

3. Saracchi had also been Camillo Casati's military orderly during World War I.

4. Cheli is still on display in the dining room of the Vittoriale and visited by thousands of tourists each year.

5. Lorandi, *Alberto Martini*.

6. Ibid.

7. Additionally, according to *Social and Diplomatic Memories (Third Series): 1902–1919* (London, 1925), by Sir James Rennell Rodd, a former servant of the author later became employed by Casati in a similar capacity. Rodd reports, "But some months afterwards he robbed her in a very serious manner, and so came to a bad end." This is not surprising since the same servant was suspected of an earlier theft at the British Embassy in Rome. Rodd does not specify at which of Casati's residences the robbery connected with her took place, nor does he give the year of the incident.

8. *Aux Ecoutes* (Paris), February 20, 1932.

9. Colonna, *Sparkle Distant Worlds.*

10. Cossart, *The Food of Love.*

11. "Astonishing Exploits."

12. *Ancient Art,* Sotheby's, New York, December 11, 1980 (cat. no. 306).

13. Authors' interview with Bernard Nevill, January 2001.

14. John, "Fragment of an Autobiography."

15. Authors' interview with Lady Moorea Black, March 1998.

16. "Astonishing Exploits."

17. A complete inventory of all items confiscated from Casati is in the possession of Lady Moorea Black, London. During the early 2000s, furniture pieces attributed to Carlo Bugatti and inlaid with the name "Casati" were offered by several auction houses, including Christie's, New York, and displayed at museums, such as the Cleveland Museum of Art. In each case, the pieces were dated ca. 1895–1900 and described as being commissioned by the Marchesa Luisa Casati. These assertions appear disputable since she did not assume her married surname until 1900. Matters are further complicated by the existence of a little-known cabinetmaker named Casati, who, during this same period, manufactured pieces in the style of Bugatti and Eugenio Quarti.

18. "Astonishing Exploits."

19. Jean Cocteau, *The Difficulty of Being* (New York, 1967), and Jean Cocteau, *Souvenir Portraits* (New York, 1990). In 1958, Cocteau drew a caricature of Casati with four legs, running on the Lido in Venice.

20. Germain, *Les fous.*

21. Ibid.

22. Elise Johandeau, *Le Spleen empanaché* (Paris, 1960).

23. From papers in the collection of Lady Moorea Black.

24. Authors' interview with Gualtiero Nobili Vitelleschi, May 2003. Although adequate proof as to their existence is currently lacking, several documents claim that Vitelleschi also completed a portrait of Casati in oriental garb and another as the Greek sorceress Circe.

25. Erté, *Things I Remember.*

26. Martini, *Alberto Martini.*

27. Francesco Basaldella, *Giudecca (Centro storici)* (Venice, 1983).

28. Conover, *Olga Rudge and Ezra Pound.* Authors' interview with Anne Conover, July 2003.

29. Camillo's apartments were located in the Palazzo Barbarini in Rome, which had been divided into four deluxe flats. D'Annunzio had also lived there for a period of time in the 1890s.

30. Authors' interview with Lady Moorea Black, September 1997.

31. Camillo was denied a Catholic burial because of his relationship with Cockrell and the birth of their illegitimate son. It was only through the intervention of his younger brother, Alessandro, that Camillo's body was allowed interment in the Casati family tomb.

32. Patrick Marnham, *Dreaming with His Eyes Open: A Life of Diego Rivera* (Berkeley, 2000).

33. Hayden Herrera, *Frida: A Biography of Frida Kahlo* (New York, 1983). In addition to Kahlo's portrait, at least three sketches of Cristina are also extant by Augustus John.

34. Woodrow Wyatt, *Confessions of an Optimist* (London, 1985).

35. Pringué, *30 ans.*

36. Bonde, *A l'ombre de San Michele.*

37. Holroyd, *Augustus John.*

38. Jullian, "Extravagant Casati."

39. Authors' interview with Paul Busby, May 2001.

40. Authors' interviews with Carl L. T. Reitlinger, June 2000–December 2001.

41. Ibid.

42. Authors' interview with Bernard Nevill, January 2001.

43. Ibid.

44. Authors' interviews with Fred Rainer, May 2001–March 2002.

45. Authors' interview with Lady Moorea Black, September 1997. Moorea Black, "Spectacular Special Effects," *The Spectator* (London), November 20, 1999.

46. Collection of Lady Moorea Black, London.

47. Holroyd, *Augustus John.*

48. Bonde, *A l'ombre de San Michele.*

49. Holroyd, *Augustus John.*

50. Sotheby's, London.

51. John, *Chiaroscuro.*

52. Authors' interview with Lady Moorea Black, September 1997.

53. Holroyd, *Augustus John.*

54. Michael Wishart, *High Diver* (London, 1977).

55. Authors' interview with Jerry Edward Cornelius, March 2002.

56. Authors' interviews with Maurice Druon, August 1998–December 2001.

57. Authors' interviews with Carl L. T. Reitlinger, June 2000–December 2001.

58. Cecil Beaton, *Self Portrait with Friends: The Selected Diaries of Cecil Beaton, 1926-1974* (New York, 1979).

59. Beaton, *The Glass of Fashion.*

60. Castle, *Oliver Messel.*

61. Authors' interview with the Hon. Mrs. Mary Anna Marten, December 1998. In addition to these visits, Crichel was once the setting for an extravaganza given by Casati at which she had its drive paved in gold dust.

62. Authors' interviews with Conte Edoardo Amman, July 1998–December 2001.

63. Rose, *Saying Life.*

64. Authors' interviews with Carl L. T. Reitlinger, June 2000–December 2001.

65. Peter Quennell, *Customs and Characters: Contemporary Portraits* (Boston, 1982).

66. Authors' interview with John Fleming, March 1997.

67. Authors' interview with Lady Moorea Black, September 1997.

68. Ibid.

69. "Splendor of Marchesa Casati's Fetes Again Brought to Memory," *San Francisco Examiner*, 1949.

70. Laurence Schifano, *Luchino Visconti: Les feux de la passion* (Paris, 1987).

71. Dakin Williams and Shepherd Mead, *Tennessee Williams: An Intimate Biography* (New York, 1983).

72. This was the revised version of the play first presented at the Brooks Atkinson Theatre in New York City on January 1, 1964. It is likely that Bankhead was aware of Casati since the actress had shared an intense relationship with the Marchesa's confidant Lord Alington for many years—an affair that resulted in a terminated pregnancy—and a friendship with Augustus John. An earlier Broadway version of *The Milk Train Doesn't Stop Here Anymore* had been presented at the Morosco Theatre on January 16, 1963, with Hermione Baddeley in the lead role. British actor Rupert Everett played the Goforth role in drag in a critically acclaimed 1994 production of the same play at the Citizens Theatre, Glasgow, and then again in 1997 at the Lyric Theatre Hammersmith, London.

73. A newspaper article ("Splendor of Marchesa Casati's Fetes Again Brought to Memory") reported that Casati had once received guests in Venice dressed only in long tresses of golden hair that nearly reached to the floor, claiming of the Marchesa "even Lady Godiva never had such hair."

74. Jack Kerouac, *Book of Blues* (New York, 1995). Casati was also the subject of the poems "Castration Envy #12 (Collected Portraits of the Marchesa Casati)," from *Outremer: Poems by Bill Knott* (Iowa City, 1989); "Colour Me Blood Red," by Lynn Crosbie, from *Miss Pamela's Mercy* (Toronto, 1992); "What You Should Know before Reading This Poem," by Amanda Pritchard Moore, from *The Salt River Review: Vol. 3* (Mesa, AZ, 2000); and "Painting the Garden Lilac at the Nonfinito," from *Against Paradise: Poems by Shawna Lemay* (Toronto, 2001).

75. It is believed that this reproduction was of John's first portrait of Casati, now in the collection of the Hon. Mrs. Mary Anna Marten, and not the artist's more famous second portrait, now found in the Art Gallery of Ontario.

76. The American artist and author Eugene MacCown also created a fictional character, the Contessa Adelina Cozio, based on both Casati and Morosini for his novel *The Siege of Innocence* (New York, 1950), a romantic comedy of Paris and Venice in the 1920s.

77. Authors' interviews with Maurice Druon, August 1998–December 2001.

78. Maurice Druon, *The Film of Memory* (New York, 1955). The English translation was by Moura Budberg, mistress of author H. G. Wells, herself an acquaintance of Casati.

79. Alexander Walker, *Vivien: The Life of Vivien Leigh* (New York, 1987). Tristram Cary, the composer of the play's incidental electronic music, concurred by

noting: "I believe I saw Casati several times in the early 1950s when I was living in London. She was a striking and well-known sight in the Knightsbridge area, and could often be seen in the smart shops like Harrods." Authors' interview with Tristram Cary, August 2002.

80. The film's original working title was *Carmela*, the name of the novel's chambermaid. This was later changed to *Nina*, the director's term of endearment for his daughter. Just before release, the title became *A Matter of Time*, to match the film's opening song of the same name by John Kander and Fred Ebb, sung by Liza Minnelli.

81. For a complete history of the making of *A Matter of Time*, see Stephen Harvey, *Directed by Vincente Minnelli* (New York, 1989).

82. Authors' interviews with Maurice Druon, August 1998–December 2001.

83. Authors' interviews with Fred Rainer, May 2001–March 2002. Rainer stated that, after Casati's death, this mask was displayed atop a tall column in the gardens of Woodrow Wyatt, Lady Moorea Black's first husband. Pericles was also the name chosen by Wyatt and Black for their only child.

84. Authors' interview with Bernard Nevill, January 2001.

85. Authors' interviews with Fred Rainer, May 2001–March 2002.

86. One of these albums still survives in the collection of Lady Moorea Black, London. The other two were destroyed by water damage.

87. Authors' interviews with Fred Rainer, May 2001–March 2002.

88. Jullian, "Extravagant Casati."

89. Collection of Lady Moorea Black, London.

90. Authors' interview with Bernard Nevill, January 2001.

91. Christophe Henri Karel de Nerée tot Babberich (1880–1909) was a little-known Dutch artist whose pen and ink work is highly reminiscent of Martini and Alastair. Although there is little material documenting Casati's association with or influence on the artist, many of the highly stylized and bizarre female subjects of his drawings share a more than coincidental resemblance to the Marchesa.

92. Jullian, "Extravagant Casati."

93. Beaton, *The Glass of Fashion*.

94. Casati's camp status is explored in two books, Mark Booth's *Camp* (London, 1983) and Philip Core's *Camp: The Lie That Tells the Truth* (London, 1984).

95. Collection of Lady Moorea Black, London. In addition to an education in California, Joseph Paget-Fredericks (1905–1963) claimed to have been the last private pupil of both Léon Bakst and John Singer Sargent, and that at the age of fourteen, to have exhibited his artwork for the first time at the Parisian salon of his godmother the Baroness Deslandes, Casati's friend. If accurate, then Paget-Fredericks would have either met Casati at some point years prior to their later association or, in the least, was acquainted with her reputation. While a detailed account of their relationship remains undocumented, the artist's assertions regarding the more noteworthy aspects of his own career have yet to be substantiated. Paget-Fredericks had once planned to publish a catalogue of the Marchesa's portraits that was never realized.

96. Ibid.

97. Beverley Nichols, *The Unforgiving Minute* (London, 1978).

98. Meredith Etherington-Smith, "Gothic Revival," *Sunday Telegraph Magazine* (London), November 21, 1999. This feature article was illustrated with a fashion layout inspired by Casati shot exclusively for the magazine.

99. From the unpublished memoirs of Prof. Otto Haas-Heye. Authors' interviews with Johannes Haas-Heye, November 2002–February 2003. Haas-Heye was the artist for whom Quentin Crisp was posing as described in his foreword to this book.

100. Some sources claim that Casati spent her final years, and died, in a London nursing home. These reports have been proved erroneous.

101. Authors' interviews with Fred Rainer, May 2001–March 2002. At the time, Basaldella was living in London and the owner of a car hire service in Putney.

102. Authors' interview with Lady Moorea Black, September 1997.

Epilogue

1. Authors' interview with Michael Howells, May 1999. Galliano had also used Casati as partial inspiration for his spring 1996 Couture Collection for Givenchy.

2. Authors' interview with John Galliano, November 2001.

3. Authors' interview with Laura Jacobs, January 2002, and "No One but Norell," *Vanity Fair*, October 1997. The September 26, 1960, issue of *Life* magazine contained the cover story on Norell's Casati-inspired collection. Celebrity photographer Milton H. Greene took the picture of the designer, his models, and the van Dongen painting. Norell originally acquired the van Dongen portrait of Casati at auction for $125 U.S. dollars from Parke-Bernet, New York, in the 1940s.

4. Judith Thurman, "The Divine Marquise," *The New Yorker* (New York), September 22, 2003.

5. *Newsweek*, September 21, 1970.

6. Accompanied by one of de Meyer's photo-portraits of Casati, an essay by Philippe Jullian also discussed the Marchesa's life in the catalog for the 1982 exhibition *La Belle Epoque* at the Metropolitan Museum of Art, New York. This exhibition was conceived and organized by Diana Vreeland, who was editor-in-chief of American *Vogue* during the publication of Jullian's 1970 article on the Marchesa. Vreeland also chose to include another of Casati's portraits by de Meyer in her book *Allure* (New York, 1980).

7. In fall 2000, Florence Müller created an exhibition for the Parisian department store Le Printemps dedicated to eccentric personalities, *Excentrique un manifeste de l'apparence*. This included a large vitrine, its interior designed as a small theater, in which were displayed three nearly life-size images upon a lighted stage: in the center was La Castiglione, on the left was the Comte Robert de Montesquiou, and on the right was Man Ray's 1935 portrait of Casati as Empress Elisabeth of Austria.

8. "Remembrance of Things Proust," *Vogue* (New York), January 15, 1972. In the article, Beaton noted of Berenson's Casati, "I thought it was a beautiful conception

of Marisa's. It was remarkable and very daring of her when everyone else was trying to look beautiful—to be outrageous."

9. Authors' interview with Charles Busch, May 2001. *Vagabond Vignettes* was staged at The Duplex, in New York City in July–August 1979. In a related note, in late October 2002 the Velaslavasay Panorama in Hollywood, California, and the Travelling Wonder Show attempted to contact Casati in a series of séances that were certainly more performance art than sincere occult endeavor. With a boa constrictor wrapped around her, a psychic medium answered questions about the Marchesa's notorious life at the promptings of a spirit facilitator. The final performance took place at midnight on Halloween.

10. Authors' interview with Paul Ibey, April 2003.

11. *Il Bacio* (Euro International Films, 1974), directed by Mario Lanfranchi and starring Maurizio Bonuglia, Martine Beswick, Brian Deacon, and Eleonora Giorgi.

12. The official Marchesa Casati Web site, www.marchesacasati.com, was launched in October 2001 and is designed by Douglas C. Smith, Macsmith designs.

13. Authors' interview with Bernard Nevill, January 2001.

14. *Toronto Star,* January 22, 2000.

15. The world premiere of *Infinite Variety: Portrait of a Muse,* by Scot D. Ryersson and Michael Orlando Yaccarino, was the subject of an edition of the international television entertainment program *Nota Bene* for the TLN Television Network.

16. Scot D. Ryersson and Michael Orlando Yaccarino, *The Princess of Wax—A Cruel Tale* (New York, 2003), illustrated by Anne Bachelier and with a French translation by Guy Leclercq.

17. Authors' interview with Grazia D'Annunzio, April 2003.

18. Both by Scot D. Ryersson and Michael Orlando Yaccarino, *Infinita Varietà: Vita e leggenda della Marchesa Casati* (Milan, 2003) was published by Corbaccio, and *La Casati: Les multiples vies de la marquise Luisa Casati* (Paris, 2003) was published by Éditions Assouline.

19. Major features, announcements, and reviews appeared in *Vanity Fair* (both U.S. and U.K. editions), *AD–Architectural Digest Italia, Casa Vogue, Corriere della Sera, ELLE Italia, La Stampa, Madame Figaro, Vogue* Paris, and *Vogue* Russia, among many others.

20. Holroyd, *Augustus John.*

Select Bibliography

Acosta, Mercedes de. *Here Lies the Heart.* New York: Arno Press, 1975.

Acton, Harold. *Memoirs of an Aesthete.* New York: Viking Press, 1971.

Antoine. *Antoine.* New York: Prentice-Hall, Inc., 1945.

Aroma, Nino d'. *L'amoroso Gabriele.* Rome: Vito Blanco Editore, 1963.

"Astonishing Exploits of the Marchesa Casati," *The American Weekly,* December 1, 1935.

Barjansky, Catherine. *Portraits with Backgrounds.* New York: Macmillan Company, 1947.

Batcheller, Tryphosa Bates. *Italian Castles and Country Seats.* New York: Longmans, Green, 1911.

Beaton, Cecil. *The Glass of Fashion.* New York: Doubleday, 1954.

Bigatton, Walter, Maurizio Bordugo, and Guido Lutman. *Storia del Cotonificio Veneziano: L'industria Pordenonese Amman–Wepfer tra ottocento e novecento.* Pordenone: Edizioni Biblioteca dell'Immagine, 1994.

Bonde, Knut Corfitz. *A l'ombre de San Michele.* Geneva: Edition Jeheber, 1947.

Cardona, Emilia. *Boldini: Parisien d'Italie.* Paris: Gründ, 1952.

Cecchi, Dario. *Boldini.* Turin: Unione Tipografico-Editrice Torinese, 1962.

———. *Coré: Vita e dannazione della marchesa Casati.* Bologna: L'Inchiostroblu/ Ritz Saddler, 1986.

Chaumeil, Louis. *Van Dongen: L'homme et l'artiste—la vie et l'oeuvre.* Geneva: Pierre Callier, 1967.

Cocteau, Jean. *The Difficulty of Being.* New York: Coward-McCann, Inc., 1967.

———. *Lettres à sa Mère: Vol. I, 1898–1918.* Paris: Gallimard, 1989.

———. *Souvenir Portraits.* New York: Paragon House, 1990.

Colonna, Vittoria. *Sparkle Distant Worlds.* London: Hutchinson & Co., 1949.

———. *Things Past.* London: Hutchinson & Co., 1929.

Conover, Anne. *Olga Rudge and Ezra Pound.* New Haven: Yale University Press, 2001.

Cossart, Michael de. *The Food of Love: Princesse Edmond de Polignac (1865–1943) and Her Salon.* London: Hamish Hamilton, 1978.

D'Annunzio, Gabriele. *Cento e cento e cento e cento pagine del libro segreto di Gabriele D'Annunzio tentato di morire.* Milan: A. Mondadori, 1935.

———. *Forse che sì forse che no.* Milan: A. Mondadori, 1952.

———. *Infiniti auguri alla nomade.* Milan: Archinto, 2000.

———. *Nocturne and Five Tales of Love and Death.* Trans. Raymond Rosenthal. Marlboro, VT: Marlboro Press, 1988.

Depero, Fortunato. *So I Think, So I Paint: Ideologies of an Italian Self-made Painter.* Trento: Rovereto (Trentino), 1947.

Desbruéres, Michel. "Romaine Brooks." *Bizarre* (Paris), March 1968.

Desti, Mary. *The Untold Story: The Life of Isadora Duncan, 1921–1927.* New York: Horace Liveright, 1929.

Druon, Maurice. *The Film of Memory.* Trans. Moura Budberg. New York: Scribner, 1955.

Duncan, Isadora. *My Life.* London: Victor Gollancz, 1928.

Ehrenkranz, Anne. *A Singular Elegance: The Photographs of Baron Adolph de Meyer.* San Francisco: Chronicle Books, 1994.

Epstein, Jacob. *Let There Be Sculpture.* New York: G. P. Putnam's Sons, 1940.

Erté. *Things I Remember.* New York: Quadrangle, 1975.

Fouquières, André de. *Cinquante ans de panache.* Paris: Pierre Horay "Flore," 1951.

Gardiner, Stephen. *Epstein: Artist against the Establishment.* New York: Viking Press, 1992.

Gatti, Guglielmo. *Vita di Gabriele D'Annunzio.* Florence: Sansoni, 1956.

Gautier, Gilberte. *Rue de la Paix.* Paris: Julliard, 1980.

Georges-Michel, Michel. *Dames Étranges.* Montreal: Lucien Parizeau, 1944.

———. "Un bal des mille et une nuits au bord du Grand Canal." *La vie heureuse* (Paris), November 20, 1913.

Germain, André. *Les fous de 1900.* Paris: Les Éditions Palantines, 1954.

———. *La vie amoureuse de D'Annunzio.* Paris: Librairie Arthème Fayard, 1954.

Giovannetti, Eugenio. *Satyricon 1918–1921.* Florence: La Voce, 1921.

"Her Antics Topped Hollywood's Best." *San Francisco Chronicle,* July 30, 1957.

Herrera, Hayden. *Frida: A Biography of Frida Kahlo.* New York: Harper & Row, 1983.

Holroyd, Michael. *Augustus John: A Biography.* New York: Holt, Reinhart & Winston, 1975.

Ingleby, Richard. *Christopher Wood: An English Painter.* London: Allison & Busby, 1995.

"Italy's Famous Beauty Who Lives Like a Fairy Princess." *San Francisco Chronicle,* April 18, 1926.

John, Augustus. *Chiaroscuro: Fragments of Autobiography.* New York: Pellegrini & Cudhay, 1952.

———. "Fragment of an Autobiography." *Horizon* (London), December 1943.

Jullian, Philippe. *D'Annunzio.* Trans. Stephen Hardman. New York: Viking Press, 1972.

———. *De Meyer.* New York: Knopf, 1976.

———. "Extravagant Casati." *Vogue* (New York), September 1, 1970.

———. *Prince of Aesthetes: Count Robert de Montesquiou, 1855–1921.* Trans. John Haylock and Francis King. New York: Viking Press, 1968.

Kerouac, Jack. *Book of Blues.* New York: Penguin, 1995.

Konody, P. G. "The Art of Federico Beltran-Masses." *Apollo* (London), June 1929.

Lorandi, Marco. *Alberto Martini: Mostra Antologica.* Milan: Electa Editrice, 1985.

Mackenzie, Compton. *My Life: Volume V.* London: Chatto & Windus, 1965.

Marinetti, F. T. *L'alcova d'acciaio: Romanzo vissuto.* Milan: Casa Editrice Vitagliano, 1921.

Martini, Alberto. *Alberto Martini.* Milan: S.A.D.E.L., 1944.

"Memoire della Principessa Jane di San Faustino." *Omnibus* (Rome), April–May 1938.

Meyer, Adolph de. "Paris Gossip by a Mere Man." *Harper's Bazaar* (New York), September 1922.

————. "The Substance of a Venetian Dream." *Vogue* (New York), February 15, 1916.

Milhou, Maya. *Ignacio Zuloaga (1870–1945) et la France.* Paris: Le Bouscat, 1981.

Montenegro, Roberto. *Planos en el Tiempo.* Mexico City: Arana, 1962.

Nevill, Bernard. "La Marquise Casati." *The Queen* (London), March 7, 1956.

Peyrefitte, Roger. *The Exile of Capri.* New York: Fleet Publishing Corp., 1961.

Priestley, J. B. *The Edwardians.* New York: Harper & Row, 1970.

Pringué, Gabriel-Louis. *30 ans de diners en ville.* Paris: Édition Revue Adam, 1948.

Quennell, Peter. *Customs and Characters: Contemporary Portraits.* Boston: Little, Brown, 1982.

Ray, Man. *Self Portrait.* Boston: Little, Brown, 1963.

"Remembrance of Things Proust." *Vogue* (New York), January 15, 1972.

Rose, Francis. *Saying Life: The Memoirs of Sir Francis Rose.* London: Cassell & Company, 1961.

Rubinstein, Arthur. *My Young Years.* New York: Knopf, 1973.

Ryersson, Scot D., and Michael Orlando Yaccarino. *Infinite Variety: Portrait of a Muse.* Printed privately, 2000.

————, and ————. *La Princesse de cire—Un Conte cruel.* Trans. into French by Guy Leclercq. New York: CFM Gallery, 2003.

Rzewuski, Alex Ceslas. *A travers l'invisible cristal: Confessions d'un dominicain.* Paris: Plon, 1976.

Schiaparelli, Elsa. *Shocking Life.* New York: E. P. Dutton, 1954.

Secrest, Meryle. *Between Me and Life: A Biography of Romaine Brooks.* New York: Doubleday, 1976.

Sitwell, Osbert. *Nobel Essences.* London: Macmillan, 1950.

Spencer, Charles. *Erté.* New York: Clarkson & Potter, 1970.

————. *Léon Bakst and the Ballets Russes.* London: Academy Editions, 1995.

"Splendor of Marchesa Casati's Fetes Again Brought to Memory." *San Francisco Examiner,* 1949.

"Titled Woman Visitor Scores Modern Styles." *San Francisco Chronicle,* February 20, 1926.

Toutain, Roland. *Mes 400 coups . . .* Paris: Amiot-Dumont, 1951.

"Une visiteuse nocturne." *Aux Ecoutes* (Paris), March 5, 1922.

Van Dongen, Kees. *Van Dongen: Le peintre.* Paris: Les Amies du Musée d'Art Moderne, 1990.

Werner, Françoise. *Romaine Brooks*. Paris: Plon, 1990.

Williams, Mrs. Hwfa. *It Was Such Fun!* London: Hutchinson & Company, 1935.

Wistow, David. *Augustus John: The Marchesa Casati*. Toronto: Art Gallery of Ontario, 1987.

Wyatt, Woodrow. *Confessions of an Optimist*. London: Collins, 1985.

Youssoupov, Félix. *En exil*. Paris: Plon, 1954.

The Casati Archives

The Casati Archives is the world's only data source and image bank devoted to preserving the artistic and cultural legacy of the Marchesa Luisa Casati. It was founded by Scot D. Ryersson and Michael Orlando Yaccarino in 1999 upon the original publication of *Infinite Variety* and is the result of their continuing international research and collecting. In addition to a wealth of original materials, books, and ephemera, this ever-growing library contains artwork reproductions and photographs of and inspired by the Marchesa Casati.

The Casati Archives welcomes and appreciates any comments, corrections, and additional research findings. These can be submitted to www.marchesacasati.com, the official Web site for the Marchesa Casati.

Index

Scot D. Ryersson is the author of numerous critiques and essays on film and literature. He is an award-winning illustrator and graphic artist who has lived and worked in London, Toronto, Sydney, and New York City.

Michael Orlando Yaccarino specializes in the analysis of international genre films and interviews with their creators. His writings on fashion, music, and unconventional historical figures appear in publications throughout the United States and Britain.

Quentin Crisp (1908–1999) led a long and multifaceted life. From artist's model and commentator on style and etiquette to writer and theatrical and film performer, he was a wit, a bon vivant, and a keen observer of human fancies and foibles. He is perhaps most famous for his autobiography, *The Naked Civil Servant.*